D1081503

THE DECLINE & FALL OF ROMAN BRITAIN

CONTENTS

ACKNOWLEDGEMENTS

This book has its origins in a research project concerned with late Roman towns. My inspiration, guide and mentor in this was Richard Reece (formerly Institute of Archaeology, UCL), with valuable additional advice from Ralph Jackson (British Museum). My early efforts – constructively criticised by Simon Esmonde Cleary, Alan McWhirr and Steve Roskams – were greatly improved upon when I enlisted the help of Jack Newman, a professional quantity surveyor and volunteer archaeologist, who brought his skill, enthusiasm and hard work to the task of quantifying ancient building costs. Many archaeologists with specialist knowledge of particular Romano-British urban sites shared information and ideas with me: Jane Elder (Canterbury); Neil Holbrook and John Salvatore (Cirencester); Philip Crummy (Colchester); Richard Buckley and John Lucas (Leicester); Mick Jones (Lincoln); Cathy Maloney, David Sankey, John Shepherd and Alan Thompson (London); Ernest Black, Sheppard Frere, Ros Niblett and Chris Saunders (Verulamium); John Collis, Malcolm Gomersall, Ken Qualmann and Graham Scobie (Winchester); and Peter Ellis and Roger White (Wroxeter). I must also thank most warmly those who have taken the trouble to read and comment so rigorously upon early drafts of the text: Richard Reece and Edward Biddulph, who have minutely scrutinised my use (and abuse) of archaeological evidence; Mike Tomkins and Keith Robinson, who have commented upon style, flow and general readability; and Ian Gill, who, amongst other things, has kept an eye on my renderings of ancient texts. I am also most grateful to Peter Kemmis Betty, my first commercial publishing editor, whose user-friendliness towards the uninitiated has been a pleasure to discover. Needless to say, none of the above is responsible for what follows; all would doubtless have objections to parts of it, and some, I know, disagree vehemently on many matters – and have discovered that I can be stubborn. Finally, my thanks go to my partner, Lucy Harris, for her inexhaustible tolerance of an eccentric workaholic, and to our toddler, Tiggy, for her frequent rearrangements of my papers.

St Albans
March 2000

INTRODUCTION
to the first edition

There are a lot of books on Roman Britain; perhaps too many. What is the case for another – especially one whose plagiarised title is, I am told, a trifle presumptuous? Archaeology is a young and somewhat immature discipline, and archaeological writers are often satisfied with mere catalogues of evidence, in which presentation of 'the facts' is considered an end in itself. This can sometimes make for dull reading. It is time that archaeology grew up a little, accepted its status within the humanities, and set about its real task of using material evidence to write history. There is too much anxiety about becoming 'unscientific'. There is too little of what R.G. Collingwood, the great Romano-British scholar of the inter-war years, called 'the historical imagination'. It is worth recapping what he meant by this. The past itself is irretrievably lost; we can never return to it, never reconstruct it fully. All we have are bits and pieces of it surviving as 'evidence' – whether old maps and documents, a medieval parish church, or the contents of an ancient rubbish pit. To turn this into history, we have to draw on our knowledge of what human beings in general are like, and of how they think and act in social situations. We have to invest the evidence from the past with a human significance by using our imaginations to reconstruct the past as it may have been lived, and to comprehend the motives and decisions that made it thus.

This is especially difficult for archaeologists. Historians seem to get much closer to past people because they rely for evidence on the documents they wrote. The stones and potsherds of archaeology seem mute by comparison. Perhaps this is one reason archaeology is finding it hard to develop beyond mere data collection for its own sake. But it must be done if archaeology is to be interesting and worthwhile. This study is intended as a small contribution. I have used my 'historical imagination' to try to make sense of the evidence for Roman Britain and to build from it a narrative account which both describes and explains what may have happened. I aim to 'tell the story' and to show why it happened in one way and not another. It is for the reader to judge how successful I have been – how far my 'imaginative' interpretation makes convincing sense of the evidence.

Since this book is somewhat different from others on Roman Britain, it may be helpful to explain its structure. It is not a synthetic summary of the evidence. If it were, it would not be justified, since it could not compete with such magisterial surveys as Sheppard Frere's *Britannia* (1967, 1978, 1987) or Peter Salway's *Roman Britain* (1981, 1993). Nor is it an interpretative essay, such as Richard Reece's *My Roman Britain* (1988), Simon Esmonde Cleary's *The Ending of Roman Britain* (1989), or Martin Millett's *The Romanization of Britain* (1990) – three important studies which have influenced me considerably. Instead, it is an interpretative narrative with four principal features. First, the narrative is structured by a substantially new theory of the decline and fall of the Roman Empire in the west. The evidence from Roman Britain is presented as a case study in the working out of this long-term process. There is, in other words, that most unfashionable of things, an underlying 'grand narrative' – a broad interpretative framework for making sense of the evidence. Secondly, the narrative hinges on a succession of key events. This reflects my view that history moves forwards not smoothly, but in a series of violent fits and starts, and that 'great events', in contrast to long periods when nothing much seems to happen, represent open clashes of political forces and 'turning points' in social development – moments, that is, when the surface calm of decades is broken and the inner workings of history are revealed. I see events not simply as 'one damn thing after another', but as part of the unfolding of a single, integrated, dynamic process – one which it is the job of the archaeologist-historian to describe. Thirdly, I aim to interpret events and processes as lived human experiences, and, in particular, I have tried to contribute something towards an 'archaeology from below' in which the impact of Roman imperialism on British people, and their responses to it, are central 'imaginative' concerns. Fourthly, I present only a selection of evidence to illustrate my argument, and I avoid detailed technical discussion of methodological problems and alternative interpretations. To do otherwise would be to write a different kind of book. What matters here is that I believe my interpretation does no violence to any of the evidence, including all that I have omitted; or, to put it another way, I think that my selection is representative of the evidence generally, and, moreover, that my interpretation is the most valid taking account of all the evidence known to me. It is for others to challenge that claim by making alternative use of the evidence – or by producing new evidence. The clash of competing 'historical imaginations' is the way knowledge of the past advances.

Since the rise and fall of Roman military imperialism was the working through of a single process – so that to understand the end we must understand the beginning – I have begun the book with an opening chapter on the dynamic of Roman expansion, the reasons for the attack on Britain, and the means by which imperial rule was imposed. Chapter 2 explores the limits of Roman expansion at the point where the ploughed arable of the south-east met the unploughed wilderness of the north-west. Chapter 3 analyses the social and economic order in Britain under the Romans in the second and early third centuries, and its dependence on arms expenditure and a system of military supply.

Chapter 4 examines the great crisis of the third century and the way it was rooted in the establishment of fixed frontiers, and chapter 5 looks at the attempt in the late third and early fourth centuries to resolve this crisis by a major reform of the Roman Empire. Chapter 6 returns to the discussion of Romano-British society, but the focus is now on the late empire, the impact of crisis and reform, and the decline of Romanised civilisation. Chapter 7 reviews the main events of the last fifty years of Roman rule, and interprets these as the gradual disintegration of a system already in advanced decay.

The view of the Roman Empire I present is essentially negative. Many classical scholars in the past have portrayed Rome as a model to be emulated – 'The Grandeur That Was Rome' – and have urged that it be studied for this reason. This book offers an alternative perspective, arguing that Rome was a system of robbery with violence, that it was inherently exploitative and oppressive, and that it was crisis-prone, unstable and doomed to collapse. I think there are lessons for the present in this. The Four Horsemen of the Apocalypse – Conquest, Slaughter, Famine and Death – stalk the modern world, dominated as it is by corporate capital and imperialist war, just as they did that of late antiquity. In this context, continuing discussion about the past – especially about the role of violence and exploitation in human affairs – becomes part of an urgent debate about the sort of future we want to create.

INTRODUCTION
to the second edition

The first edition of this book appeared less than four years ago, so a second edition may seem premature. But enough has happened in the interval to justify a new final chapter dealing with the fifth and sixth centuries AD. By coincidence, around the time *Decline and Fall* was first published, three other books on the end of Roman Britain also appeared, one a reissue, Simon Esmonde Cleary's *The Ending of Roman Britain*, and two that were new, Guy de la Bédoyère's *The Golden Age of Roman Britain*, and Ken Dark's *Britain and the End of the Roman Empire*. These books have fed a renewed debate among specialists about the end of Roman rule. What happened in Britain in the two centuries after AD 410 has been central to that debate. And so, while changing nothing else, and standing by everything I wrote in 1999, I have taken the opportunity afforded by the new paperback edition to extend the book and deal with the immediate post-Roman period.

Specialists will be familiar with the debate about the end. Students and general readers, on the other hand, may not be. Since this book is a contribution to that discussion – because it aims to provide not merely an account of what happened in late Roman Britain but also an explanation, which, like all historical explanations, is contested – the uninitiated may like to know something about the debate. There seem to me to be a number of related issues.

To start with, there is the old argument that Britain continued in some sense to be 'Roman' through much of the fifth and perhaps even the sixth century AD. This 'long chronology' perspective for Britain has recently been subsumed within a wider 'Late Antiquity' perspective, embracing the whole of the former Roman Empire – essentially the idea that much of Europe and the Mediterranean shared a uniform 'late Roman' culture in the entire period from *c*.AD 300 to 650.

The long chronology seems to be refuted by the archaeological evidence. For Britain this shows an almost total collapse in Roman material culture in the years *c*.AD 375-425. What I did not realise when I first wrote *Decline and Fall* was that this evidence was not conclusive for the proponents of the long chronology. Implicit in their work is a definition of *Romanitas* which does not depend on towns, villas, forts and other obvious archaeological indicators. Rather, so long as the culture of the upper classes remained essentially Graeco-Roman, then the fundamentals of classical civilisation were, for them, in place. Martin Henig is refreshingly honest about this. Believing that 'Roman civilisation was in general a "good thing" and that it neither declined nor fell, only changed,' he is equally clear that it was something for 'the educated, the more or less well-to-do and above all Romanised section of society'. This is an essentially nineteenth-century view, where Roman civilisation amounts to little more than toga-clad gentlemen reading Virgil and sipping Bordeaux in their salons. This being so, it is easy enough to understand how some scholars can convince themselves that Rome did not fall at all, merely continued in a modified form. A tombstone inscribed in scrawny Latin, a collection of Byzantine wine-*amphorae*, a British monk who writes historical commentary, a king who claims a Romano-British civitas as his realm – these scattered clues to elite culture in early Dark Age Britain are enough, for some, to make fifth- and sixth-century Britain 'Roman'.

This unashamedly elitist definition of Roman civilisation has a further, sinister implication: it amounts to an apology for imperialism. Instead of a system of exploitation and violence designed to enrich the few, the Roman Empire becomes a bizarre cross between European Union and National Trust, a beneficent mechanism for spreading peace, prosperity and high culture. These sanitised images of the Roman imperial past seem, moreover, to overlap with equally naïve images of more recent empires. As ever, discussion of the past turns out to be discussion of the present. Bush and Blair invite us to believe that economic progress and political justice come as gifts of the US army and Chevron-Texaco. The BBC inverts the meaning of language to call invasion 'peacekeeping', conquest 'liberation' and resistance 'terrorism'. The right-wing historian Niall Ferguson proclaims that an essentially progressive British Empire should serve as a model for the new American Empire. There is, in short, a live debate about the role of imperialism in history, and all of us who talk and write about ancient Rome are, like it or not, implicated in it.

This book takes a different approach from many. It is an exercise in 'archaeology from below'. It sets out to analyse Roman Britain as a system of exploitation based on violence, in which the working majority was forced to contribute but did not benefit. It argues further that, because this majority was dispossessed of wealth and power, the weakening of the Empire under military pressure exposed the ruling class to revolt from below. As the cost of empire rose, civil society decayed, resistance to the impositions of the state escalated, and the military-bureaucratic infrastructure of late antiquity collapsed. What followed – the subject of my new chapter 8 – was a period of relative freedom from the oppression of landlords, tax-collectors and soldiers for the mass of the population. This version of the story of Roman Britain – the one I think best fits the evidence – is thus very different from that offered by scholars like Martin Henig. And, if it can be believed, it contains very different lessons for the present. First, that the violence of the powerful, the forcible seizure of other people's land and the plundering of other people's resources do not constitute mechanisms for peace and progress. And second – as the New Romans begin to lose against an escalating guerrilla insurgency in Iraq, and as they confront elsewhere the biggest global protest movement in history – the further lesson that empires can be defeated.

St Albans
October 2003

1

THE MAKING
OF ROMAN BRITAIN

AD 43: THE CLAUDIAN INVASION

On the last afternoon of the Palatine Games in late January AD 41, the Roman emperor Gaius Caligula was attacked in the tunnels beneath his palace by a group of army officers and hacked to death. His assassination set in train the sequence of events which, shortly afterwards, would bring Britain into the Roman Empire for 365 years.

The assassins were not alone; they were merely the activist core of a conspiracy which had deep roots in the Roman governing class. The consuls, Rome's two senior magistrates, immediately assumed power and summoned the Senate to meet at the Temple of Jupiter on the Capitoline Hill. The conspiracy against Caligula was the culmination of the aristocracy's mounting hatred of the Julio-Claudian emperors, and the aim now was to replace dictatorship with rule by the Senate and make top magistrates accountable once more to Rome's traditional rulers. Though divided on much else, the Senate was agreed on one thing: any new emperor should be its own creature, a trusted peer from among them, a 'first among equals' – not some bloody tyrant foisted on the empire by the vagaries of bedroom-bonding and domestic squabbles on the Palatine Hill.

This, though, was not to be. As the emergency session of the Senate dragged into the night, news arrived that an emperor had already been proclaimed. The Praetorian Guard, hunting for assassins, had found the dead emperor's uncle Claudius hidden away in a remote corner of the palace. Pulled into the torch-light and instantly recognised, he had been carried off to the Praetorian Barracks, where his presence had been the occasion for a rival debate on the future of Rome. The Praetorians were the spoilt children of the emperors, enjoying easy conditions of service, high pay, generous donatives, and all the amenities and comforts of the capital city. But Praetorian privilege was inextricably mixed with Julio-Claudian power. They were the elite bodyguard troops of the emperor. No Caesar, no Guard. That night, Claudius was the best available candidate, and the barrack-square assembly broke up as 5,000 Roman soldiers roared allegiance to a new emperor.

For a short while, Rome was under a dual power. On the Capitoline Hill, an assembly of millionaires, sitting on a pile of state gold, ringed by a cordon of riot police, bickered about which of their many self-interested cliques should lord it over the rest. In the Praetorian Barracks, an embryonic court formed around Claudius, the bewildered leader's authority resting on the sword-points of several thousand cynical mercenaries. But as the decision of the Praetorians became known, and the active monarchists of the mob rallied to the Caesarian cause, the outnumbered defenders of the Capitol drifted away to safety, and power flowed through the night from Senate to court. In the light of morning, a gloomy little party of politicians and officers made its way across the city to the barracks to concede defeat. Claudius was carried in triumphal procession to the Palatine, a hastily-contrived kangaroo court dispatched the conspirators, and thus, about 24 hours after it had began, the revolution of 41 ended in Julio-Claudian victory.

The political fall-out was to be considerable. An obscure nonentity had been elevated to rule an empire of a hundred million in a sudden military coup carried out by a few thousand in one city. A fluke of history had created the Claudian principate. Another fluke could as easily destroy it. Neurotic insecurity would be the fruit of such traumatic birth.

Who was Claudius? At fifty, he was the most senior surviving male member of the ruling Julio-Claudian family – not only uncle of Caligula, but nephew of Tiberius, and great-nephew of Augustus. His immediate family included some of the greatest soldier-princes of the recent past: his brother Germanicus, his father Drusus, and his grandfather Antony. He ought to have been among the best-known Romans. In fact, he was hardly known at all. His obscurity he owed to a debilitating physical condition – probably cerebral palsy with some degree of muscle spasm – which so offended the snobbish sensibilities of his family that he had been hidden from public view as a potential embarrassment and thus denied the conventional political and military career of a Roman aristocrat. Claudius the Fool had retreated into a world of scholarship and vice, so that when he shuffled out under history's spotlight in January 41, this portly, twitching, stammering, somewhat bookish and debauched middle-aged man was hardly the popular image of a Caesar. History would demand payment for this mockery.

Claudius' accession had been an abomination. Tiberius had been Augustus' appointed heir, already, by senatorial decision, co-equal with the emperor in power and honour before the latter's death. Caligula had been carried to power on a wave of popular enthusiasm, to which the Senate, reacting against the terror of Tiberius' latter years, had willingly acquiesced. Claudius, by contrast, was a military usurper. The Senate this time had opposed a Julio-Claudian succession, and the Praetorian coup left it resentful of the army's assumed role of kingmaker and hostile to its choice. The new principate was, therefore, constitutionally naked and politically unstable. For a full month, Claudius refused to enter the Senate, fearful that he might die under a hail of republican daggers like his ancestor Julius Caesar. Naturally, the tension did ease – the

Senate soon recovered its customary opportunist balance – but it never wholly relaxed. Claudius, despite attempts at conciliation, remained the ruler whom the Senate had once denounced as political imposter and public enemy. It was Claudius the Usurper who now ruled, and against him the republican diehards waged a war of plots. In 42, the governor of Dalmatia, supported by other top officers and politicians, tried to raise the army in revolt against the government. The soldiers refused to move and the conspiracy was bloodily crushed, but other attempts would follow, and the final body-count of the 13-year Claudian regime would be 35 senators and 321 equestrians, a decimation of the top aristocracy.

Claudius, perforce, had to look elsewhere for support. His model was Julius Caesar, the archetypal populist faction-leader and real founder of the Julio-Claudian dynasty, whose alliance of decayed nobles, rising 'new men', lesser gentry, common citizens, and rank-and-file soldiers had broken the monopoly on power of the old republican oligarchy. To some extent, Claudius could protect himself by creating a government infrastructure staffed by humble and dependant loyalists, and by appeasing the city mob with cash-handouts, grain-doles, public works, and gladiatorial games. But, as the coup of 41 had demonstrated, real power grew from the point of a sword. In the network of Caesarian client-groups on which the Principate was based, the political weight of civil servants and city mob was slight compared with that of the legions. The emperor was, first and foremost, a military dictator – Commander-in-Chief of the Roman Imperial Army. The soldiers were his most important and demanding clients. And, like all serious politics, this was finally a matter of money. Power-bases had to be fixed together with the cement of material self-interest. In 41, Claudius had ensured the allegiance of the Praetorian Guard with an unprecedented donative of 15 or 20,000 sesterces per man. Later, he bought the loyalty of the rest of the army at a total cost of 750 million sesterces – over 90 per cent of a full year's tax revenue. To stay in power, Claudius Caesar needed money.

He also needed prestige. His constitutional legitimacy was non-existent, his political popularity borrowed and therefore temporary. As a Julio-Claudian, he belonged to a family of emperors and generals, but for his own part could claim neither political nor military achievement of any sort. His principate was that of a cardboard man, and its lack of substance might soon tell – perhaps fatally – in one or other of the faction fights ahead. But Rome had always accorded the right to rule to those who brought her victory in war. For the dynamic of Rome was military imperialism. Rome fed off war. The emperor, the state, the army, the aristocracy and various client-groups were all enriched by endless wars of plunder, by surplus wealth taken by force from defeated ruling classes – precious metals, military hardware, agricultural produce, looted merchandise, enslaved war-captives, levies of tribute, forced labour-services, rent and interest payments, bribes and 'gifts'. These spoils of war and fruits of empire were not incidental and secondary matters; they were as central to the dynamic of the Roman system as profit would one day be to industrial capitalism. War was an annual event, as normal to Roman governments as making a budget is to modern ones. The city was officially at peace only twice in the entire 500-year history of the Republic, so relentlessly aggressive and predatory was her foreign policy. Rome, in her very essence, was robbery with violence. No wonder, then, that her values were pre-eminently martial and imperial, her heroes warriors and generals. 'Glory in war', Cicero had said, 'exceeds all other forms of success: this is the origin of the Roman people's reputation, this is what ensures our city will have eternal fame, this has compelled the world to submit to her rule.' All the great political figures of Rome's past had been commanders of her legions in wars of empire. Now it was the turn of Claudius. The fool-usurper must assume a new guise: that of generalissimo. Only thus could Claudius demonstrate a right to rule, inspire the Caesarian faithful, and marginalise the plotters. Only thus could he win the riches with which to cement together the Julio-Claudian imperial state.

Britain was an ideal choice for Claudius' war. It was fabled as a dangerous barbarian wilderness 'beyond Ocean'. The Britons were 'the furthest nation of the world' (Horace). The Greek geographer Strabo had described the island as a heavily forested land with high rainfall and frequent fogs, where the natives' farming skills were poor and their customs often simple and barbaric. Caesar had presented a similar image of backward Britain in his Gallic War notebooks: the natives had long hair and blue-dyed bodies when they went into battle, and those of the interior wore animal skins as clothes, and lived on milk and meat instead of corn. For Graeco-Roman gentlemen, these were classic markers of the uncivilised savage. Like the Dervishes or Zulus in Victorian England, the Britons were perceived by Julio-Claudian Rome as exotic, wild, ferocious, barbarian 'others'. Moreover, the conquest of Britain was, for Rome's rulers, unfinished family business. Caesar had intended conquest, but, ground down by British guerrilla warfare in 54 BC, and then preoccupied by the Gallic revolt and the civil wars, his military foothold had been momentary. Caesar, though, had 'drawn attention to the island' (Tacitus), and recent research by John Creighton suggests that many native rulers had entered the imperial orbit, adopted a Romanising style, and come to form a strong pro-Roman faction within the island. The military challenge in AD 43 was perhaps less than the popular image of wild barbarism implied. The risks were exaggerated by the spin.

Octavian-Augustus had once aimed to complete his adoptive father's work – the court poet Horace, in 26 BC, sought divine protection for 'Caesar on his expedition against the Britons' – but nothing came of it. The British project was shelved for two generations; the legions were engaged in long hard wars on the continent, and, after the disastrous defeat of Varus and the loss of three legions in Germany in AD 9, expansionism gave way to consolidation. It was Caligula who turned the focus back on Britain in AD 40. Aspiring to emulate the military achievements of his fore-

1 *Claudian victory propaganda:
the triumphal arch. Erected in
Rome in 51, parts of the inscription
survive, the full text of which can
be reconstructed as follows:
'Dedicated to Tiberius Claudius
Caesar Augustus Germanicus, son
of Drusus, chief priest, 11 times
tribune, five times consul, 22 times
hailed 'conqueror', father of his
country; erected by the Senate and
People of Rome because he received
the submission of 11 British kings,
overcome without loss, and because
he was the first to bring barbarian
tribes beyond Ocean into the
dominion of the Roman People.'*

bears, he planned a great campaign to surpass them all: a quarter of
a million men were mobilised to cow the German tribes, stabilise
the Rhine frontier, and launch an invasion of Britain. The result,
however, was farce: Roman soldiers collected sea-shells on the
Channel beaches, the emperor declared them 'spoils of victory
over Ocean', and the absurdity of Caligula the Generalissimo was
apparent to all – the dictator was fatally diminished, murdered
within six months. But the British project was again a public talk-
ing point, a target of popular imperialism, and, with so much of the
staff work and logistics done, also an immediate practical possibility. It would, besides, be no bad thing to break up the excessive
concentration of troops in Germany – dispersing the north-western legions would make it harder for dissidents in the Roman high
command to organise a coup. Furthermore, despite the popular
stereotype of British savagery, the south-east of the island was
known to be extensively cultivated and thickly populated – rich,

therefore. Claudius was strapped for cash, and Caesarian bills were normally paid in booty; a British war would provide it.

War could easily be justified; indeed, in the circumstances, to have shirked it might have been dangerous. Caligula's fiasco had not been the end of the British crisis. The aggressively expansionist Catuvellaunian empire, based north of the lower Thames, had overrun the south-British kingdom of the Atrebates, and its king, Verica, had fled to Rome as suppliant. Caratacus and Togodumnus, the Catuvellaunian leaders, were demanding extradition of the fugitive. At the same time, there were 'disturbances' in Britain, perhaps attacks on Roman traders. The reputation of Rome and its new ruler were at stake. Reputation matters. Power is more threat than action. The imperatives of frontier security and political survival required Claudius to act – to demonstrate that he was indeed *imperator* (conquering general). The crisis exploded into violence.

General Aulus Plautius transported an army of some 40,000 men across the Channel, probably to Richborough, and shortly afterwards fought a great two-day battle on the Medway, at which the Romans destroyed the main field army of the Catuvellauni. The advance was then halted to allow time for the emperor's arrival – Claudius was to lead his army in person against the enemy capital at Camulodunum (Colchester). His subsequent return home was a slow, winding, six-month triumphal procession through the provinces and across Italy. A series of great celebrations were held in Rome: in 43 when the first news of victory arrived; in 44 when Claudius returned from campaign; in 47 when Aulus Plautius ended his term of office; in 49 when the city boundary was ceremonially extended; and in 51 when the defeated Caratacus was paraded through the streets of Rome. Claudius donned the traditional garb of a Roman conqueror, decorated his palace with tokens of victory, and named his son 'Britannicus'. The Senate decreed that a new annual festival of commemoration be added to the Roman calendar. Coins, inscriptions and sculptures – the propaganda broadcasts of antiquity – beamed the message across the empire (*1*). As Barbara Levick, Claudius' modern biographer, comments, 'his invasion of Britain was the greatest event of the reign, and one of his prime claims to rule, as his systematic exploitation of it shows'. In short, a politically motivated outburst of violence and plunder driven by weakness and fear.

'THE GREATEST AND MOST POWERFUL MEN GUARD THEIR NATIVE PLACES FOR YOU'

The Catuvellauni, dominating the whole south-east, had been the greatest military power in Britain. Their defeat on the Medway and the fall of their capital at Camulodunum were decisive events. Rome's other British enemies, however resilient, were smaller groupings, and the invasion army could now be broken up into separate battle-groups. One legion was perhaps held back as garrison and strategic reserve at Camulodunum, but the other three, brigaded with auxiliary units, were sent north and west. The details are lost, but by the end of Plautius' governorship in 47, the Romans controlled the whole south-eastern half of the island up to the line of the Fosse Way from Exeter to Lincoln (*2*). Behind this line, the Romans now set about creating a new imperial province.

The aim was simple enough: to use the wealth of Britain in land, labour and resources to enrich the Roman state and support its legions. The army was the centre of Rome's universe, accounting for more than half – perhaps much more – of state income. Vampire-like, it battened onto conquered provinces and sucked out their life-blood. Taxes levied on native peasants paid the soldiers' salaries. The tax-pay cycle used coins minted from provincial bullion. An empire-wide network of roads, ports and settlements – arteries of military supply – was maintained by peasant labour-gangs. Corn-levies in the frontier districts fed the local army-bases. There was constant demand for healthy, vigorous, young males willing to volunteer for military service. In the words Tacitus gave

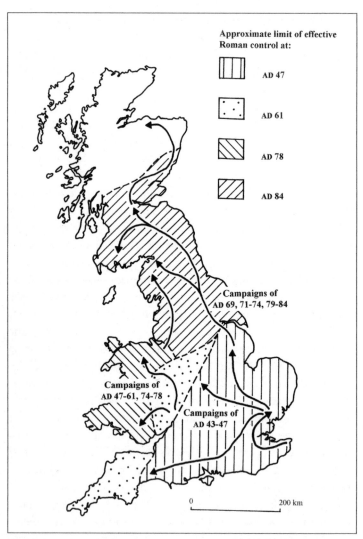

Approximate limit of effective
Roman control at:

AD 47

AD 61

AD 78

AD 84

Campaigns of
AD 69, 71-74, 79-84

Campaigns of
AD 47-61, 74-78

Campaigns of
AD 43-47

0   200 km

2 *Roman campaigns and conquests, 43-84. Whereas the south-eastern half of
Britain was overrun quickly and easily, in the north-west the Romans were bogged
down in guerrilla warfare and were soon over-extended in their efforts to garrison
and control the hill-country*

to the Caledonian war-chief Calgacus in 84: 'Our goods and money are consumed by taxation. Our land is stripped of its harvest to fill their granaries. Our hands and limbs are crippled by building roads through forests and swamps under the lash of our oppressors.' The poetic exaggeration captures the essence of Roman provincial rule, even if it obscures the need for moderation in the interests of good order and stable receipts. The emperor Tiberius was clear about the need to maintain a balance in the interests of efficient exploitation: 'A good shepherd shears his flock, he does not flay them.' The regular Roman land-tax, the *tributum*, was perhaps 10 per cent of the province's agricultural output, on top of which there was probably a military corn-requisition, and labour corvées would periodically take men away from their farms to work on state construction-projects – a substantial but tolerable, and therefore sustainable, burden. For those charged with its management, moreover, there were positive benefits, a fact that was crucial to the success of Roman provincial administration. Let us review how it was achieved in Britain.

Seventy years before, Virgil had written in *The Aeneid*: 'Your task, Roman, never to be forgotten, will be to govern the world under your domination. Your skills will be to establish civilisation when there is peace, to grant mercy when there is submission, and to crush by war when there is defiance.' They are chilling words spoken by a ghost of the Underworld, and they define the strategy of Roman military imperialism. The policy in Britain, as elsewhere, was to mix promise, threat and violence. The pro-Roman and dovish elements among the British were encouraged, isolating the militants and making it possible to concentrate massive force against them. The tribal enemies of the Catuvellauni, in particular, those near-neighbours recently conquered or under threat, sought and were granted Roman allegiance. Clues in the scanty literature of the conquest and in the distribution of early Roman forts seem to show which tribes submitted and which resisted (*3*). Especially prominent pro-Romans were three, possibly five, rulers with the status of client-kings – formal independence subject to Roman authority. Some ruler of the Cantiaci, the people of Kent, and Boduocus of the west-country Dobunni may have been clients, while Prasutagus of the East Anglian Iceni and Cartimandua of the northern Brigantes certainly were. We know most, though, about the Atrebates/Regni of south-central Britain. This tribe, repeatedly battered by Catuvellaunian aggression, had first appealed to Claudius for support, and then provided protection to Plautius' left flank in the campaign of 43. It was constituted as a client-kingdom, perhaps first ruled by the returning fugitive Verica, but later, with more certainty, by one Tiberius Claudius Togidubnus, styled 'Great King of the Britons' (4). The vast palace at Fishbourne, its highly symmetrical design and state-of-the-art luxury fittings and finish a monument to contemporary Roman style, was most likely the family residence of the king. Coupled with evidence of early urbanisation at Chichester, Winchester and Silchester, all perhaps within Togidubnus' territory, this 'Herod of the Celts' emerges as a model of precocious Romanisation. 'Togidubnus,' reported the Roman historian Tacitus, 'remained unswervingly loyal right down to recent times, and thus stands as an example of the time-honoured Roman practice of employing even kings to make others slaves.'

The picture elsewhere is more hazy, but even in areas immediately annexed and under the direct rule of Roman officers, many native notables sought an accommodation. Every tribe was split. There were always those who favoured Rome. Some sought an ally against traditional tribal enemies; others help in domestic intrigue against political opponents; yet others were seduced by the glitter of Roman trinkets or the pomp of imperial service. All, of course, feared the terrible vengeance of Rome defied. For many of the native elite there could have seemed little point in resistance. After all, the cost of empire would be borne by the peasants, not the nobles, and Rome offered a security of property, position and prestige unparalleled in former times – in place of the slippery

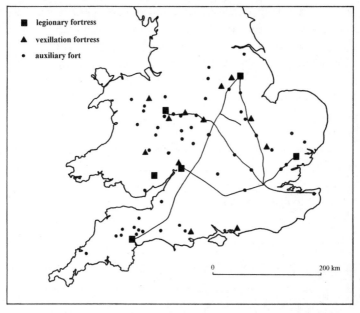

3 Known military roads, legionary fortresses and auxiliary forts of the Claudio-Neronian period (43-68). The south-east was lightly garrisoned because some tribes were pro-Roman and others were quickly defeated. Harder fighting against the Durotriges of Dorset and the Silures and Ordovices of Wales is apparent in the greater density of forts in the west. (Note that not all sites were occupied continuously.)

sands of war-band politics, there was now the monolithic solidity of the Roman Imperial Army. Even among the great Catuvellauni there was a pro-Roman faction. Prince Adminius, son of the old king Cunobelinus, brother to resistance leaders Caratacus and Togodumnus, had fled to Rome as suppliant in 40, ousted in a dynastic faction-fight. Recent excavations at Stanway, near Gosbecks, part of the Catuvellaunian capital at Camulodunum, have revealed a probable royal cemetery, where the dead, accompanied by rich grave-goods, were placed in wooden burial-chambers

inside huge ditched enclosures the size of fields. What is remarkable is that the cemetery continued to be used from the late first
century BC until *c.*AD 60 – despite the presence at nearby
Colchester of a legionary fortress after 43, and a Roman colonial
town from *c.*49 onwards. The later use of the cemetery must have
been by pro-Roman aristocrats – in contrast to their anti-Roman
peers, the 'bitter-enders' who, after defeat in 43, had followed
Caratacus west to continue the struggle.

Roman policy was to win over the bulk of the British aristocracy and to convert the warrior-chieftains of yesteryear into
Roman gentleman-landlords. These new Romans would then
form the civilian governments of their districts. The basic princi-

4 *Evidence for a Romanising client-king: the Togidubnus inscription from
Chichester. The reconstructed text reads: 'To Neptune and Minerva for the Well-
being of the Imperial House, by the authority of Tiberius Claudius Togidubnus,
Great King of the Britons, the guild of metalworkers and its members have given
this temple, paid for out of their own resources, the building-plot having been given
by [...]ens, son of Pudentinus.'*

ples were clearly explained in the mid-second century by a Greek orator Aelius Aristides in a speech addressed to the City of Rome:

> You have no need to garrison their [the native people's] citadels; the greatest and most powerful men everywhere guard their native places for you ...There is no envy at large in your empire. You have set an example in being without envy yourselves, by throwing open all doors, and offering to qualified men the opportunity to play in turn a ruler's part no less than a subject's ... Thus, towns are free from garrisons, and whole provinces are adequately guarded by mere battalions and cavalry companies ...

This goal would be achieved in Britain by reconstituting the old tribes as local government districts (*civitates*), each with its own county town (*civitas*-capital) (5), governed by an administrative council (*ordo* or *curia*) made up of the leading local landowners (*decuriones* or *curiales*) (6). A number of late-first-century town-charters have survived in Spain, and, if the pattern in Britain was the same, we can assume an annually appointed executive, chosen from among the councillors, consisting of two mayor-judges (*duoviri*), two county treasurers (*quaestores*), and two clerks of the public works (*aediles*).Thus, local government was in the hands of a property-owning oligarchy descended from the Iron Age nobility. All that was required by the provincial government – the governor, the *procurator* (or finance-minister), and the army commanders, each with their small staff of officials, clerks and soldiers – was that the town oligarchs ensure law and order in country areas, collect and forward the taxes due, and maintain the local infrastructure in a usable condition. Otherwise they could do pretty much what they liked.

The system usually worked extremely well, but it took time to set up. Crucial to its success was the wooing of Britain's erstwhile warrior-caste. Tacitus' famous account of the seduction is worth quoting:

Agricola [governor of Britain in 78-84] had to deal with men who, because they lived in the country and were culturally backward, were inveterate warmongers. He wanted to accustom them to peace and leisure by providing delightful distractions ... He gave personal encouragement and public assistance to the building of temples, piazzas and town-houses ... he gave the sons of the aristocracy a liberal education ... they became eager to speak Latin effectively ... and the toga was everywhere to be seen ... And so they were gradually led into the demoralising vices of porticoes, baths and grand dinner parties. The naïve Britons described these things as 'civilisation', when in fact they were simply part of their enslavement.

There were tangible benefits for the native aristocracy – the offer of local independence, security of property and station, and opportunities for self-advancement and enrichment within the imperial system. Tacitus throws a sidelight on this when reconstructing the speech of the Roman general Petilius Cerialis to an assembly of Gallic nobles during the revolt of 70:

You often command our legions in person, and in person govern these and other provinces. There is no question of segregation and exclusion ... if the Romans are expelled what else will result but a world-wide war ... yours will be the most dangerous situation, for you have the riches and resources which are the main causes of war. At present, victors and vanquished enjoy peace and imperial citizenship on an equal footing, and it is upon these blessings that you must lavish your affection and respect. Learn from your experience of the two alternatives not to choose insubordination and ruin in preference to obedience and security.

Whatever the attractions, however, the transition from British warlord to Romanised gentry was not entirely straightforward. To

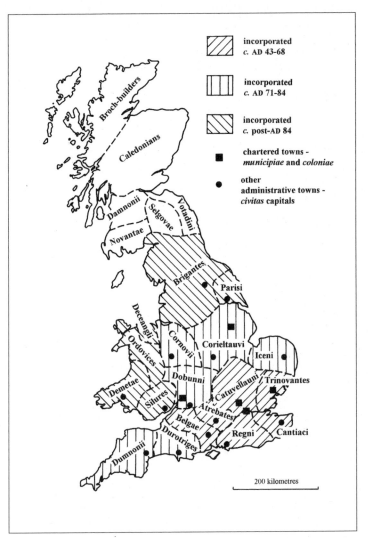

Map legend:

- ▨ incorporated *c.* AD 43-68
- ▥ incorporated *c.* AD 71-84
- ▨ incorporated *c.* post-AD 84
- ■ chartered towns – *municipiae* and *coloniae*
- ● other administrative towns – *civitas* capitals

Broch-builders

Caledonians

Damnonii

Selgovae

Votadini

Novantae

Brigantes

Parisi

Deceangli

Cornovii

Corieltauvi

Ordovices

Iceni

Demetae

Dobunni

Catuvellauni

Trinovantes

Silures

Atrebates

Belgae

Regni

Cantiaci

Durotriges

Dumnonii

200 kilometres

5 *The* civitates *(tribal communities) and major towns of Roman Britain, with
approximate dates of incorporation as self-governing entities. (Some of the original*
civitates *were probably later further sub-divided. The areas not hatched remained
beyond Roman control, and not all known tribes in this area have been named.)*

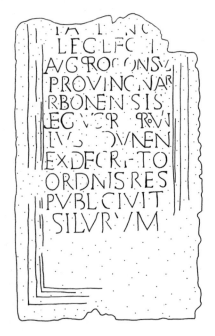

```
IA  L  NC
LEC LFC  I
AVG RO: ONSV
PROVINC NAR
RBONEN SIS
EG V:R  R=VI
IVU  )VNEN
EX DFCR.-TO
ORD NIS RES
PVBL CIVIT
SILVR`/M
```

6 *A minor British city-state: the Silurian* civitas *inscription from Caerwent. The reconstructed early-third-century text reads: 'To Tiberius Claudius Paulinus, commander of the Second* Augusta *Legion, governor of the province of Narbonensis, governor of the province of Lugdunensis, by decree of the council* (ordo), *the state* (res publica) *of the tribal community* (civitas) *of the Silures set this up.' Paulinus, whose major career postings up to this time are listed, was a powerful patron. The formal constitution of the Silures as a self-governing city-state is apparent from the legally correct Latin terminology*

some extent, Roman intervention undermined, rather than bolstered, traditional authority. Real power in the localities, at least in the brief period of direct military rule, was exercised by Roman army officers. The forts acted as magnets attracting local youth, entrepreneurs and women away from the retinues of British nobles. Many commodities, once rare luxuries conferring prestige on those who displayed and distributed them (such as coins and wine), became widely available. Above all, there was the vexed issue of the decommissioning of weapons. High-quality decorated metalwork was of three main types in late Iron Age Britain: mirrors and items of personal ornament; drinking equipment; and arms and armour, including horse-trappings and chariot-fittings. These were markers of a warrior-caste in the Homeric style – of men who decorated themselves with symbols of status, who drank and feasted in groups of their kind, and who were addicted to war and preparations for war. When the new governor Ostorius Scapula demanded disarmament in 47, the Iceni, who had been peaceful in 43, rose in revolt and were supported by others. To wear and display weaponry still mattered.

The system of display and patronage through which the traditional elite expressed power had to be Romanised. The process was already under way. A stream of Roman commodities had come into south-eastern Britain over the previous half century, mainly through trade contact with the Roman army on the Rhine and the merchants of Gaul. The Greek geographer Strabo mentions 'ivory bracelets and necklaces, amber and glassware and similar petty trifles', but archaeology suggests more substantial things: wine and oil carried over in *amphorae*, and table-services in Arretine ware from Italy or Gallo-Belgic wares from northern Gaul and the Rhineland. So, in the business of status competition, a new Roman currency was in use before 43, and if some of this was now devalued by inflation, other coin in which to express prestige and power was soon available: Latin literacy, wearing the toga, membership of the local council, rebuilding in the classical style, mosaic and fresco, sculpture in bronze and stone, commemorative inscriptions, and much more. The principal arenas of the new *Romanitas* were, of course, the towns, and to these we shall shortly turn. But first, I conclude here with a comment on that cataclysmic failure of Romanisation which came so close to scotching the whole project: the Boudican revolt of 61.

The government took the death of the client-king Prasutagus as the occasion to annex the territory of the Iceni. Soldiers and officials moved in like a conquering army. Title to landed property in Norfolk suddenly looked unsafe. The brutal treatment of the royal widow Boudica and her daughters symbolised the threat to the nobility, and they raised revolt to protect their estates and their rank. The East Anglian peasantry (not just the Iceni) was ready to explode – primed by Roman taxation, labour-corvées, land seizures, and arbitrary pillage. But, dispersed across the countryside on isolated farmsteads, the peasants had lacked the organisation to concert action. No doubt they had resisted as best they could, as their kind always do, invisibly, beneath the gaze of history, hiding grain in the ground, pigs in the woods, and sturdy sons on cousins' farms. But now came the call to arms from the Icenian nobles, and it was decisive: summoned by their traditional leaders, they formed for battle as in the old days, armed with the rusty weapons of their fathers. A fast-growing army of tribal revolution swept south, and the new towns of Colchester, London and *Verulamium* (St Albans), parasitic growths on native soil, were burnt to the ground. The survival of *Britannia* was momentarily in the balance. But Fortune favoured Rome. Governor Suetonius Paulinus confronted the rebels somewhere in the Midlands and engineered a battle in which their vastly superior numbers could not be brought to bear. The revolution broke itself against the iron front of Paulinus' legions. But it had been a close-run thing – a measure of the dangers of predatory imperialism. If the greed of the conquerors plundered the native nobility, Roman power would wobble precipitously on a tiny base of foreign bullies and robbers. Romanisation – defined here as the politico-cultural assimilation of the local landowning class – was the key to the stability and longevity of Roman rule in Britain.

THE RISE OF THE MUNICIPAL GENTRY

Roman civilisation was quintessentially urban. Its public life was played out on an urban stage. All the principal acts of civilisation's pageant – political meetings, religious ceremonies, popular entertainments, rituals of exercise, cleansing and refreshment – were performed in a standardised *ensemble* of monumental urban buildings. For Tacitus, men who lived in the country were uncultured and warlike, and the key to their 'civilisation' and 'enslavement' was to introduce them to 'the demoralising vices of porticoes, baths and grand dinner parties' – that is, to the social round of the municipal gentry. However Romanised a country-house, the facilities affordable on even the grandest estate could not compete with those of a town. The villa was a sleepy retreat, socially isolating and culturally limited. The town was the place to be. Here, where the resources of an entire *civitas* could be concentrated at a single central focus, an urban infrastructure could be built and a full range of Romanised facilities offered within a few decades of the conquest. This, clearly, was a Roman priority, the early towns providing 'the delightful distractions' which Tacitus believed would 'accustom [the natives] to peace and leisure' and 'familiarise [them] with a government of law and order'.

Towns, anyway, were the essential nodes of an administrative network spread across the empire to manage and exploit the imperial domain. Viewed from the top, Rome's rural hinterland – from which its life-blood of tribute and labour was drawn – was an uncharted ocean of a hundred million peasants. Because there was no great machine of internal surveillance and security – no bureaucracy of officials, clerks, police and spies – the native aristocracy was the locus of imperial power in the *civitates*. Their reward was a share in wealth, prestige and honour. But local power could easily degenerate into feudal autonomy, and the river of gold flowing to Rome might then be drained away to feed ten thousand rural manors. The decentralisation of power was an ever-present threat to the surplus-accumulating capacity of the imperial state, and mechanisms that guaranteed the emperor his share had to be carefully tended. In this, the towns were crucial: not just centres of Romanisation where new allegiances could be forged, but central places which could stamp Roman order on their hinterlands, organise tax-collection and labour-corvées, and give proper account to the emperor's men in London. Rome was a military engine fuelled by agricultural surplus, and towns were the bolts that held imperial state and native countryside together.

Tacitus records that when the Germanic Frisians submitted to Roman authority in 47, 'Corbulo [the Roman general] settled them on lands which he had marked out, gave them a senate, magistrates and laws, and constructed a fort to ensure their obedience.' The example is instructive, since much debate has focused on the degree of state intervention in early urbanisation in Roman Britain. Were sites chosen because there was already a Roman fort and associated civilian settlement? Were the early towns laid out by military engineers, their first structures raised by military builders? Were there perhaps direct government subsidies – or at least generous loans – made available to local authorities for their urbanisation programmes? The archaeological evidence is inconclusive, probably because the relationship between Roman officers and British nobles was in fact quite subtle. Both the Roman authorities and the Romanising aristocracy favoured urbanisation and fostered it in different ways; only the relative contributions are uncertain. In the long run, the vitality of Romano-British urbanism certainly depended on local wealth and *Romanitas*. But in the short term, the lack of any pre-Roman urban tradition may have meant the British needed help getting started – from Roman officers, bankers, surveyors, architects and interior-designers. It is certain that many Romano-British towns were founded on Roman fort sites, and the few exceptions may simply lack evidence at present.

The presence of conquest-period garrisons in south-east Britain must have been very disruptive of the established social order. High expenditures by the army and its soldiery – the latter, one might say, 'over-paid, over-sexed and over here' – meant that forts acted as powerful magnets to craftworkers, traders, innkeepers, carters, boatmen, prostitutes, mistresses, and many others, who formed themselves into *vicus* (or village) settlements around the military bases. These settlements probably grew up spontaneously as entrepreneurial responses by native people to opportunities for self-advancement provided by military spending-power, but they were doubtless subject to regulation by Roman officers. They formed clusters of small, rectangular, timber-framed buildings, with walls of wattle-and-daub and thatched roofs, which lined the roads leading into the forts and the muddy backstreets in between. Here were the shops and workshops, the taverns and brothels, the cottages and backyards of new frontier towns-in-the-making. But fulfilment of urban potential depended upon much else. When the army moved on – as it soon did from its early bases in the south-east – many civilian *vici* disappeared. Their prime function had been to provide goods and services to the soldiers; they had been parasitic upon state arms-expenditure; and they dissolved back into the countryside when the army bases shut down. The transition from military settlement to civilian town was conditional on two other factors.

First was the continuity of the imperial tribute-cycle. The fort-*vicus* settlements had been places not only of tribute distribution (in the form of army contracts and soldiers' purchases), but also of tribute collection. Under direct military rule, peasants would have paid their tribute at local forts. They must have exchanged part of their agricultural surplus for coin in a civilian market, presumably the *vicus* around the fort. When the army moved out, some fort-*vicus* sites must have been selected as centres for new civilian tribute-collecting authorities, and this would have guaranteed continued business in the *vicus* markets and a livelihood for their communities of traders. But which sites? Those which developed into towns were usually within or close to major Iron Age strong-holds (or *oppida*). Forts were first built at these sites as a check on warlord power, but they also brought the Roman military into direct contact with the traditional elite: the process of Romanisation could thus begin, and embryonic civilian govern-ments form. The second key determinant of urban potential was, then, the presence nearby of a large body of sympathetic notables. The transition from military to civilian rule would in this case be straightforward: when the military pulled out, power would pass from Roman army officers to a new council of Romanised local landowners headed by their own elected magistrates – this, henceforward, would be the all-important tribute-collecting authority.

Though some towns in the south-east acquired their first grand buildings before the Boudican revolt, the main period of public building was *c.*75-150. Civic centres, temples, baths, theatres, amphitheatres and market-halls were constructed to provide an urban infrastructure for the administration of empire, the display of oligarchic status, the enjoyment of *Romanitas*, and the exchange of agricultural surpluses for coin. This type of urbanism – where legal incorporation as a *civitas*-capital was followed by large-scale construction work to provide a full set of essential public buildings – spread out from the south-eastern heartland of the province as the Roman army moved further west and north. Together with the abandonment of early forts, it is our clearest archaeological measure of the advance and limits of civilian rule within the province. Figure 5 shows the major towns of Roman Britain and the approximate dates of their incorporation, figure 7 the growth in their population, and figure 8 the major periods of urban construction work. It is notable that, though the amount of private-house building rose steadily from the pre-Boudican period until the mid-second century, with a growing proportion of this devoted to the construction of elite town-houses, the dominant element was public construction-work. There were great

Opposite page:

7 Above: *The number of rooms occupied in private houses in Romano-British towns by period. These figures probably give an approximate indication of changing urban population levels. Sample: 1361 buildings. Source: Faulkner 1998*

8 Below: *The value of construction work in Romano-British towns by period. These figures show sharp changes not only in overall levels of activity, but also in the types of buildings constructed in different periods. Sample: 1497 buildings. Source: Faulkner 1998*

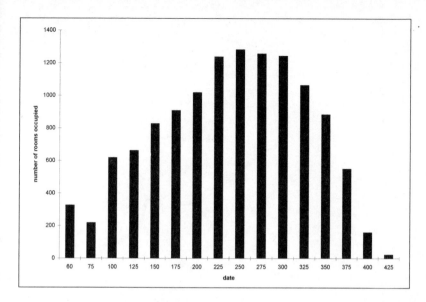

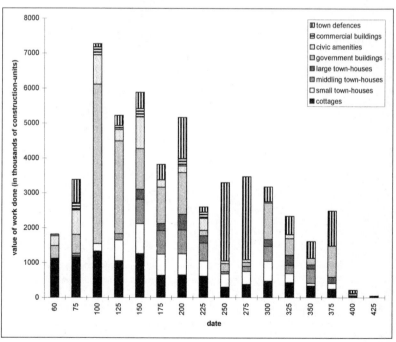

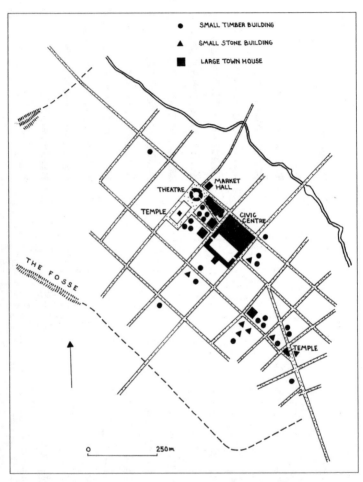

SMALL TIMBER BUILDING

SMALL STONE BUILDING

LARGE TOWN HOUSE

THEATRE

MARKET HALL

TEMPLE

CIVIC CENTRE

THE FOSSE

TEMPLE

0   250m

9 Verulamium *(St Albans) in c.150. The town had a full* ensemble *of civic buildings, but otherwise the streets were still lined by small structures with timber frames, wattle-and-daub infill, and mainly thatched or shingle roofs. This, though, was a fully functioning local centre for Roman imperial administration and Romanised public life.* After Wheeler, Frere and Niblett town-hall complexes to accommodate the council offices, the law-courts and the central market, and temples for the worship of Rome's patron gods and the spirits of her emperors (classed as 'government buildings'); there were baths, theatres and amphitheatres for Roman-style recreation and culture ('civic amenities'); and there were market-halls, warehouses and waterfront facilities ('commercial buildings'). Let us consider one example of this process in more detail.

Verulamium, Roman St Albans, was an early developer. Though nothing can be proved – the evidence so far is limited to a stretch of turf-rampart and some first-century military equipment – it would be most surprising had there not been a conquest-period fort at *Verulamium*. The site is also likely to have been a major Iron Age *oppidum*, with stretches of outer rampart-defences, internal enclosure-ditches, and scattered occupation debris, including the clay coin-moulds of a royal mint, extending for some 3km along the south-western side of the Ver valley and up onto the crest at Prae Wood. Early evidence for Roman-style urbanism comes from a centrally-placed city-block (*insula* XIV) excavated by Professor Frere in 1955-61, where he found a range of timber-framed shops along Watling Street, one of them used by bronzesmiths, dating from *c*.49. The *insula* XIV shops were probably typical of the pre-Boudican settlement as a whole, and the evidence for more substantial public buildings at this time is slight. But from *c*.75, and for the next 75 years, there was a rolling public-works programme which gradually endowed *Verulamium* with a full set of large, stone-built, lavishly-decorated civic buildings. We can best picture this by imagining the town as it might have looked in *c*.150 (*9*).

Facing Watling Street on the approach from London there must have been a timber gateway, for an earth rampart with timber palisade, fronted by a ditch, had been built around the town. Watling Street continued through the town and formed its central axis, exiting at another gateway on the opposite side and heading on towards Chester – it was one of the principal highways of Roman

Britain. The major public buildings were ranged on this central axis. Just inside the London Gate was an exotic triangular-shaped temple built in the early second century, but this part of town was mostly occupied by street-front shops and private residences. Most were still modest timber-framed structures, with floors of earth or wood, though many had painted plaster on the walls, and some had tiled roofs. The *insula* XIV shops in the town centre best represent this typical vernacular architecture of early second-century *Verulamium*: after the Boudican destruction of 61, they had been rebuilt on a broadly similar plan, first in *c*.75, and then again in *c*.105, 130 and 150. By contrast, there were, as yet, very few of the large, stone-built, highly-decorated houses that would characterise *Verulamium* later in the century – only one example is known, for instance, of a mosaic floor in a private house before *c*.155. A ten-minute walk from the London Gate would have brought one to the town centre. Here there was a huge civic centre, its assembly hall, municipal offices, state temple and enclosed market-square filling an entire city-block; a fragmentary inscription tells us it was dedicated in 79 or 81. Nearby stood a large temple-sanctuary built around 100, a pedestrianised shopping-mall or market-hall dating from *c*.100-25, and, still under construction or only recently opened, a sizeable municipal theatre designed to accommodate both stage and arena entertainments. (The main baths at *Verulamium* have not yet been located, but, on the evidence of other Romano-British towns, we can be sure that they existed, and from an early date.)

Mid-century *Verulamium*, then, wore a very mixed aspect: the grandeur of its public buildings contrasted sharply with the tattiness of its backstreets. It was an uneven, unbalanced, disconcerting sort of place. The public buildings were overblown, their cost disproportionate, the waste prodigious. The townscape was pathological. The scale is difficult to exaggerate. Ten million pounds is a modern cost-estimate for erecting the *Verulamium* civic centre; for a traditional agricultural society, that would be like a billion today. The ancient sources record the dangers inherent in monumental building on this scale. The letters of Pliny the Younger, extraordinary governor of Bithynia and Pontus in Asia Minor in the early second century, tell us, for instance, that Nicomedia blew 3.5 million sesterces on two failed attempts to build an aqueduct, while Nicaea wasted 10 million on an unfinished theatre which sank and cracked, and yet more on a gymnasium which the experts said would fall down. (For comparison, a million sesterces was the minimum property-rating of a senator, one of Rome's 600-odd super-rich, or the annual pay of over 800 soldiers.) The archaeology of Romano-British towns occasionally hints at similar problems. Work on London's civic centre appears to have been more or less continuous from shortly after the Boudican revolt to *c.*130-40. The first *forum*, built between *c.*75 and ?90, had only just been completed when work began on a new and much larger complex. This second *forum*, however, was never actually completed, or at least never fully used, and parts appear to have been in decay within little more than a century. It was waste expenditure on a colossal scale: a duplication of facilities which strained resources to breaking point.

Ill-conceived, over-ambitious, badly planned, excessively costly, inadequately funded, jerry-built, never finished, under-used, or just plain useless – all are features of Roman urban building. This bloated and wasteful urbanism had deep roots. Municipal elites were divided by intense rivalries as different families and communities strove for self-advancement within the imperial system. There were tensions, too, in the relationships between elites, their client-groups, and the mass of rural producers. The municipal gentry competed with one another in architectural displays of munificence, grandeur and *Romanitas*, and by the same means expressed their social status, ideological legitimacy and actual dominance in relation to subordinate social groups. Powerful competitive pressures drove the monument-builders to the limits of what was possible – financially, technically and aesthetically. What we see, then, in the early imperial towns of Roman Britain, is not a rational direction of scarce resources into the provision of utilitarian buildings, but their consumption in spectacular displays of art and power, Roman-style. The public-town architecture of the second century symbolised, on the one hand, Rome's reconstruction of the native warrior aristocracy as a Romanised gentry of tax-collectors and justices-of-the-peace, and on the other, the subordination of the peasantry to the new regime of officers and nobles. But the tensions which found distorted expression in Romano-British urban building were fluid and changeable. Should the balance of advantage shift a little, such that public service turned from honour to burden, the gentry might retreat back into the primeval countryside, leaving Britain's thin veneer of classical urbanism to be washed away. That countryside, moreover, was a dark continent harbouring danger. The imperial town was a parasite, a concentration of expropriated agricultural surplus, its monuments built by the muscle-power and food-renders of the peasantry. In the towns of Roman Britain, the common people, through their sweated labour, had erected 'a citadel of servitude' (Tacitus) in every district. In this respect, too, things might one day change.

2

THE NORTH-WEST FRONTIER

THE WAR IN THE WEST, AD 44-78:
'THE ENEMY MUST BE TOTALLY EXTERMINATED'

The Catuvellaunian empire had collapsed quickly under the first onslaught of Claudius' legions in the summer of 43. Only in part was this a Roman feat of arms. As Claudius' marshals doubtless calculated, the prize was easily taken. Top-heavy with its imperial warrior caste, the structure of the Catuvellaunian empire, once shaken by defeat on the Medway, had been crushed beneath its own weight. It had grown rapidly in the previous two generations, absorbing the Kentish tribes, the Trinovantes of Essex, and most recently the Atrebates of south-central England; these were all subject-peoples likely to resent their imperial masters. Even in Hertfordshire, the Catuvellaunian homeland, there would have been tensions. Caesar claimed that the south-eastern tribes were descended from recent Belgic invaders and were in most respects similar to the Gauls, and he described Gallic society, which he knew well, as highly stratified: only the warrior-nobles (*equites*) and the druids were 'of any account or consideration', whereas 'the common people were treated almost as slaves ... crushed by debt or heavy taxation or the oppression of the powerful'.

The archaeological record for south-eastern Britain in the late Iron Age confirms that social divisions were acute. The earthworks of an *oppidum* like Camulodunum stand as a monument to wealth and power: a great expanse of pasture was enclosed, presumably for the maintenance of royal herds brought inside the fortress in an emergency; and the massive defensive dykes must attest the mobilisation by royal decree of thousands of forced labourers from the countryside. The grave-goods found in high-class cemeteries at the site, like the imported wine *amphorae*, fine tablewares and bronze knick-knacks in the Lexden Tumulus, were the prestige goods of a privileged few. The coins minted here could not have been used in everyday transactions – the bullion issues were too high in value, the bronze too few in number – but they would have allowed the elite to hoard wealth for status-enhancing distributions of largesse and payment when appropriate. These are all archaeological markers of a gulf separating lord and peasant in south-eastern Britain before the Romans. The Catuvellaunian nobility was a small military caste ruling a sullen empire; defeated on the Medway and driven out of Camulodunum, in all their vast territory they had few reserves of support they could call on.

Pushing north and west in the years following, the Romans encountered somewhat stronger-rooted opposition. We know best about events in the south-west, where the future emperor Vespasian led the II *Augusta* Legion against the Durotriges tribe based in Dorset. Suetonius, the emperor's biographer, tells us, '... he fought thirty battles, crushed two warlike tribes, and captured more than twenty fortresses ...' This simple sentence is the only written reference we have to what archaeology shows to have been a vicious little war. Several West Country hillforts have yielded evidence of violent assault and destruction. The interior at Hod Hill was found to contain considerable numbers of iron bolt-heads shot from Roman field-catapults. At Maiden Castle, part of a sizeable late Iron Age cemetery appeared to contain British warriors slain by Roman weapons, one with a bolt-head still lodged in his spine. This is grim testimony to contemporary Roman siege techniques: fast and furious, enemy strongholds were stormed by Rome's first-rate infantry attacking under cover of lethal long-range shooting. Even so, here, against the

Durotriges, the Romans found themselves fighting a more difficult kind of war than in the south-east. The great army of the Catuvellaunian empire had massed in one place and been destroyed in pitched battle. This was the ideal, for Roman commanders expected always to win such battles, and they offered the chance to achieve war's central aim in a single day: the destruction of the fighting forces of the enemy. But the Durotriges did not fight in this way. Vespasian's 'thirty battles' must have been small, most little more than guerrilla skirmishes, or there would never have been so many. Too weak to confront the Roman army in the open, the Britons probably massed for their main effort in defence of the hillforts; but there were 'more than twenty' of these, so here too the enemy's military power was organised in small packets on the 'hedgehog' principle. Military organisation always mirrors the social order. Dorset fought differently from Essex. If we turn to the Iron Age archaeology, we can see why. Broad zones with distinct cultures have long been recognised by specialists: the pottery assemblages, the coin types, and the patterns of settlement change as we look outside the 'Belgic' south-east (*10*). The countryside north of the lower Thames, dotted with small undefended villages and farmsteads, was dominated by a handful of huge fortress-enclosures or *oppida*. The territory of the Durotriges, on the other hand, lay in a belt of landscape with large numbers of hillforts. The largest Catuvellaunian *oppidum* (Camulodunum) covered 12 sq miles (31 sq km), the largest Durotrigan hillfort (Maiden Castle) only 47 acres (19ha) – the latter an area just 0.6 per cent the size of the former. Here is the difference between a centralised royal state and a confederation of clan-chiefs – that is, between a polity where military power was wielded by a single authority and concentrated in one or a few places, and one where there were many with the power of command, each with his own baronial stronghold. The distribution of Roman forts tells a similar story (*3*). In Essex, much of the garrison was concentrated in a 5000-man legionary fortress at Camulodunum; in Dorset, the occupation-forces were distributed across the countryside, usually in single-battalion forts of 500 or 1000 men, like that at Hod Hill.

By 47, the West Country had been conquered, and the Roman advance had reached the Severn Valley. Beyond this, in south-east Wales, was the land of the Silures. Here were many small hillforts and other defended enclosures – the settlement pattern, as in Dorset, of a confederation of local chieftains. But whereas the Durotriges were principally cereal-farmers, ancient Siluria was a land of boggy uplands, wooded slopes and narrow valleys and plains, where arable was limited and most land was pasture or wilderness. It was a rougher, harder, more impoverished land, and its people, skilled in war, were doubtless accustomed, like the borderers of later ages, to supplement their meagre incomes by rustling their neighbours' cattle, carting off their corn-stocks, and abducting their children as farm-hands. Siluria lay on the edge of the pale, straddling two worlds: eastwards stretched the rich farmlands of proto-civilisation; northwards were the mountain wastelands of barbarism. In this shadow-land, war was normal, but it was the war of raid, ambush and feud, not of organised battle. Siluria was bandit country, and when the Romans reached its borders, they were soon embroiled:

> Battle followed battle. Mostly they were guerrilla fights in bogs and woods. Some were planned with boldness, others were chance encounters. The motives were plunder or vengeance. Sometimes the clashes were directed by commanders, sometimes not. The Silures were exceptionally stubborn. (Tacitus)

Here, among the Silures, and in the further wildernesses of central and northern Wales, the fugitive Catuvellaunian prince Caratacus found the reserves of British resistance with which to continue his struggle. With him were the 'bitter-enders' from the conquered tribes of the south-east, those nobles and retainers who preferred exile and 'the good old cause' to the baubles and trinkets of Roman service. In the hills and mountains, they recruited bands of guerrilla-raiders, and the Roman army was soon sunk in a military morass. No quick victory here. Even after Caratacus himself had been crushed – defeated in pitched battle and shortly after handed over to the Romans (AD 51)

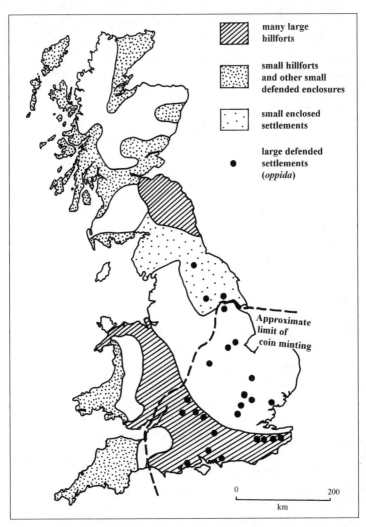

many large hillforts

small hillforts and other small defended enclosures

small enclosed settlements

● **large defended settlements (*oppida*)**

Approximate limit of coin minting

0   200
km

10 A summary of the late Iron Age settlement pattern in Britain. Broadly, zones with a few large oppida, *the practice of coin minting, and unenclosed villages and farmsteads are more socially stratified and politically centralised than zones dominated by many small and medium-sized defended settlements. This is, to a large extent, a south-east:north-west divide.* After Cunliffe

– his spirit lived on in the Silurian war. Roman detachments sent out to construct new forts were attacked and almost destroyed before relief could arrive. A foraging party was routed, and when auxiliary reinforcements were sent, a full-scale battle developed; only when the legions were committed did the Britons break off. Two auxiliary regiments, out plundering native territory, were ambushed and destroyed. The war was relentless and savage, the protagonists implacable. Governor Scapula threatened to exterminate the Silures, and when the gods struck him dead – 'worn out by worry' – the Silures celebrated by mauling a legion and plundering the province (AD 52).

Guerrilla war wins by attrition. It is a dilute acid burning slowly at bone and sinew. It also attacks the nerves. It produces irritable tension, flashing sometimes into violent anger, relapsing otherwise into exasperated despair. Roman policy in Wales veered from punitive aggression to retreat and retrenchment. There was uncertainty, indecision, vacillation. The cross-border raiding was an affront to Roman prestige and an incitement to provincial revolt. But a forward policy – aimed at securing the frontier by spreading a network of roads, forts and patrols across the wilderness beyond – looked like costing years of inglorious 'dirty war'. Rome had to fight three major campaigns against the Welsh tribes – under Scapula in 47-52, under Veranius and Paulinus in 57-61, and under Frontinus and Agricola in 74-8. The end was as vicious as the beginning. The Ordovices of north Wales wiped out a cavalry garrison. It was late in the campaigning season and the governor was new. But Agricola mobilised a punitive column, led it into the hills to destroy the Ordovices' main force, and then crossed the straits to Anglesey to capture the tribal bread-basket. The Welsh wars had been long and hard, and the hill-post garrisons would remain for good. Romanisation would be restricted to the southern fringe: the *civitas*-capitals of the Silures at Caerwent and the Demetae at Carmarthen were tiny townlets, mere villages by our standards, and there was nothing but a handful of villas, none on the grand scale. This was a different world from south-east Britain. Why so?

The Welsh wilderness had good mineral resources – gold, silver, lead and copper – but little else to attract the invader. Agriculture was restricted and settlements were scattered and small. Slave-hauls were low, the plunder poor, and the cost of war here excessively high. Even if conquered, the yield of tribute and labour-service could never pay for the numerous hillpost-garrisons needed. The aristocracy was third rank, its potential for evolution into a class of Romanised country-gentry and part-time officials limited. Here in the Welsh mountains, Rome strained at the limits of what ancient military imperialism and classical civilisation could achieve. Hers was a dynamic system of imperial expansion through military force – of robbery with violence – but its success depended on the profits of war outweighing the costs. War was an investment. It was expected to return a reward in plundered wealth which, in the long run at least, not only paid for the war, but made the warmongers richer and stronger. Indeed, it was imperative that it should, for the Roman ruling class was locked into a competitive battle with its neighbours for control of land, labour and wealth. The accumulation of means for making war was the heart of this competition, and upon Rome's continuing success in this depended the size and power of her army and the survival of her empire. The competitive struggle was an end in itself. Rome's conquests were her storehouses. Provinces paid tribute and labour to provide the bullion, corn, other foodstuffs, stone, brick and tile, timber, cloth, leather, metals, pottery and everything else needed for the military infrastructure. Fresh wars could supplement this greatly with extraordinary levies imposed on defeated enemies. But the accounts had to balance, and returns exceed outlays. The system operated best in regions of intensive agriculture, high population, and large accumulations of surplus wealth. Generally speaking, the lower the level of economic and social development, the more marginal the gains, and the more problematic the military effort. In regions with little or no agriculture, with sparse populations of widely scattered farmers and pastoralists, where settlements were few, small and impoverished, there was little return to be had. On the other hand, great tracts of empty wilderness were easy to defend and difficult to

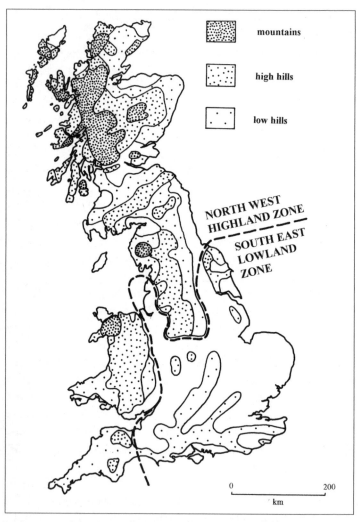

mountains

high hills

low hills

NORTH WEST
HIGHLAND ZONE

SOUTH EAST
LOWLAND
ZONE

0   200
km

*11 Physical relief in Britain. The island is divided sharply between a south-eastern
lowland zone of low hills and plains composed of newer, softer rocks, and a north-
western highland zone of high hills and mountains formed of older, harder rocks. In
ancient times, this geographical division had a decisive impact on economy, society,
culture and history.* After Fox

control: the natural habitat of the rural guerrilla, against whom large investments of men and hardware might count for little. Everywhere, the Roman Empire reached its natural limits where the ploughed met the unploughed, where modern agriculture bordered primitive waste-land, where civilisation confronted barbarism – in the mountain ranges of north-west Africa, at the desert fringes in Libya, Egypt, Palestine and Syria, and along the Danube and in the Rhineland of continental Europe. Classical civilisation stopped along the plough-line. Rome could not conquer the wastelands.

The north and west of ancient Britain was such a wasteland (*11*). Roman nerves frayed here: wars were long, booty meagre, glory hard-won, and the accounts did not balance. The boundary between two worlds ran through the middle of Britain. Physical geography was decisive – ancient Britain was shaped by relief and rocks before all else. The island is divided into two broad zones. Lowland Britain com-prises most of the south-eastern half, and includes the Vale of York, Humberside, Lincolnshire, East Anglia, the Midlands, the Home Counties, south-central England, and the Cheshire Plain. Here are newer, softer rocks forming limestone uplands, chalk downland, sand-stone hills, gravelly river valleys, and rich, heavy clay-lands. Some wilderness remained – the Weald of Kent and Sussex was probably still thickly wooded, and much of the Fenland remained a bog – but most of the lowlands had been cleared for farming in prehistoric times and could now support the rich agriculture and dense settlement of ancient civilisation. Not so the highland zone of north and west. This included the whole of Scotland, the Pennines, Cumbria, the North Yorkshire Moors, the Peak District of Derbyshire, the whole of Wales, and Devon and Cornwall. These highlands are made of older, harder rocks – granites, slates, red sandstones, and ancient limestones. In many areas, relief and altitude precluded arable farming, and in others, thin, poor, badly-draining soils made it a hard life. The good arable of the highland zone was limited to pockets, like the valleys of Wales, Yorkshire and Scotland, or occasional larger tracts, as in big river estu-aries or coastal plains like Anglesey, the Vale of Eden, or the Central

Lowlands of Scotland. Pastoralism on rough upland grazing was a dominant feature. The settlement pattern was dispersed, population low, material culture impoverished. Not just in Wales, then, but in the highland zone generally, the cost of empire could be expected to exceed the fruits of victory. The symmetry – lowland:highland, ploughed:unploughed, civilised:barbaric, viable:non-viable – was no coincidence. These were different aspects of a division so basic that it sealed the fate of Rome. British geography dictated that Rome's frontier should run through the middle of the island, and the whole story was written here of Rome's high-tide, the limits of her empire, and the point beyond which her system did not allow her to grow.

THE WAR IN THE NORTH, AD 69-142: 'THEY CREATE A DESOLATION AND CALL IT PEACE'

If the conquest of Wales strained the engine of Roman imperialism in Britain to the limit, the war in the north burnt it out. The client kingdom of the Brigantes in northern England had fallen apart in 69-71. The pro-Roman queen Cartimandua was overthrown by an anti-Roman faction led by her former consort Venutius. The new Flavian governor Petilius Cerialis invaded Brigantia, crushed the opposition, and annexed the territory (AD 71-4) (*2*). But the outbreak of the third Welsh war prevented the conquest from being consolidated under governor Frontinus (AD 74-8), and the great northern war of his successor Agricola therefore opened with a renewed assault on Brigantia (AD 79). This was followed by an invasion of Scotland as far as the Tay (AD 80), and culminated, after two years consolidating these gains, in a final big push to destroy the Caledonian confederation of the north and conquer the Highlands (AD 83-4). The Caledonians risked pitched battle at a place called *Mons Graupius* (now unknown), and they were routed with the loss of a third of their 30,000-strong army. It looked decisive. Victories like this were supposed to be. Tacitus claimed that 'Britain had been completely conquered'. But no Caledonian delegation arrived to offer submission, and Agricola fell back on his winter bases with the war incomplete. The following year, he was replaced by a new governor with orders to remain on the defensive. A few years later, the Romans withdrew from the far north. The unfinished earth-and-timber legionary fortress at Inchtuthil on the Tay, lynchpin of the defences on the south-east fringe of the Highlands, was dismantled and abandoned in the late 80s. Soon, all forts north of the Forth-Clyde isthmus had been evacuated, and the Romans held a new line across the Southern Uplands, anchored on Newstead, where excavation has shown an earlier, middle-Flavian fort overlain by a larger, stronger, late-Flavian complex. Around this time, certainly before 92, the II *Adiutrix* Legion, accompanied no doubt by many auxiliary units, was withdrawn from Britain. Finally, even the Newstead line had to be given up, and the Romans fell back in *c*.105 to a position along the 'Stanegate' between modern Newcastle and Carlisle. It seemed to Tacitus that Britain had been no sooner conquered than 'immediately lost again'. What had gone wrong?

After the battle of *Mons Graupius*, fought late in the campaigning season with the Scottish winter approaching, the defeated Caledonians had retreated down the glens into the depths of the Highlands, and 'an awful silence reigned on every hand, with the hills deserted, houses smoking in the distance, the scouts finding not a soul' (Tacitus). Agricola had got his great battle and won it, but the Caledonians, like the Silures after the defeat of Caratacus in 51, refused to surrender. The war – a difficult guerrilla war in the mountains – would continue next year. The Romans were already terribly stretched (*12*). Wales was relatively small, and in their three big Welsh wars the Romans had available for front-line use most of the 40,000 men they had in Britain. From the Peaks of Derbyshire to the north coast of Scotland, from North Sea to Atlantic Ocean, the northern wilderness was five times the size. When the Roman spearheads pushed forwards into it, the weight behind them weakened, as a network of hill-posts was constructed to control hundreds of miles of newly conquered uplands. The field-army in front shrank as the garrison-detachments behind increased. In 79, when

Agricola marched north, he left around 20 forts and (in theory) 10,000 men to garrison Wales. By 80, when he moved into Scotland, there may have been as many as 30 forts guarding northern England, whose full garrison would have been 15,000. In the next five years, perhaps another 30 forts were built in Scotland, with the Southern Uplands requiring 10,000 men, and the northern frontier beyond the same number again. Garrison work would not normally be done by the 20,000 men of the four legions. They were usually massed in a few huge fortresses – not dispersed in numerous hill-posts – forming a strategic reserve at all times, and the core of the governor's field-army in summer campaigns. Thus, if all the Flavian-period forts throughout the newly conquered highland zone had been occupied at once, 45,000 auxiliaries would have been needed. But Agricola also had nearly 15,000 auxiliaries (in addition to his legionaries) at *Mons Graupius*, so ideally he would have needed some 60,000 in all. In short, the Roman army in Britain was doing the work of 80,000 men with probably half that number. Agricola's army, quite simply, was nowhere near big enough to control that half of the highland zone already taken in (essentially Wales and north Britain as far as the Tay), let alone to attempt the conquest of the rest (the whole Highland massif). The campaign of 83-4 had been risky. The defensive cover over the hill-country to the south had been stretched perilously thin. This could only be done as a short-term measure – but the Caledonians refused to surrender in the short term. Instead, they threatened full-scale guerrilla war in the Highlands. For this, Agricola would have needed far more than the 25,000 or so he had massed at *Mons Graupius* by stripping his garrisons further south. To invade the Highlands, he needed heavy reinforcement. Now and for a generation, none was available.

Far away, north of the middle Danube, a much greater enemy than the Caledonian confederation had arisen: the kingdom of the Dacians. Close to the imperial heartlands, militarily formidable, and dazzlingly rich, Dacia was both a terrible threat and a glorious prize. Three great wars were fought, in 85-9, 101-2 and 105-6, culminating in the annexation of the whole kingdom. Rome may have mobilised as many as

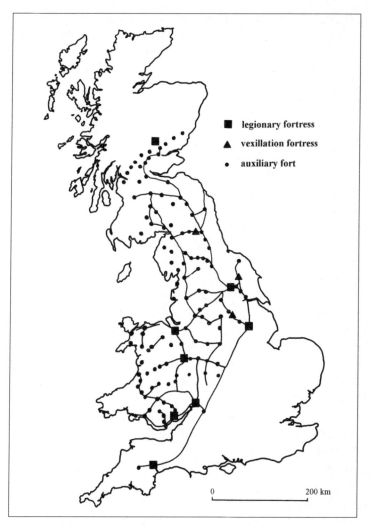

legionary fortress
▲ vexillation fortress
• auxiliary fort

0   200 km

12 Known military roads, legionary fortresses and auxiliary forts in the Flavian period (69-96). Though not all sites were occupied at the same time, the map indicates the density of Roman military occupation in the highland zone (in contrast to the earlier occupation of the south-east shown on figure 3), and the danger of over-stretch confronting an army of only about 40,000 men

100,000 men for these campaigns, and, with no strategic reserve to call on, this was only possible if other fronts were retrenched. Nor was this all. The cautious Flavian regime had ended at the assassination of Domitian in 96. Two years later, Rome was ruled by Trajan, a veteran general who aspired to be a great warrior-prince in the mould of Alexander. His Dacian wars brought him immense glory and booty with which to buy adulation and allegiance, but, since the time of Xerxes, the Graeco-Roman elite had regarded war against the East as the greatest test of arms and the surest promise of riches – the ultimate challenge and prize. So Trajan-Alexander, Conqueror of Dacia, planned a great eastern crusade. It was a delusion of grandeur. Repeatedly, Rome's top warlords had been seduced by the dream of eastern conquest, but each time the Parthian Empire had found deep within itself, in the fabulous wealth and city-walls of Mesopotamia, and in the rich military recruiting-grounds of Persia, the reserves of strength needed to throw back the invaders. So, too, with Trajan. He reached the Persian Gulf in 115, but the Parthian army remained undefeated, his forces were stretched paper-thin across the East, and the frontiers elsewhere had been stripped of defenders. The following year, the East struck back. Parthian cavalry armies counter-attacked from the Iranian plateau, there were uprisings in the captive cities of Mesopotamia, and a popular Jewish revolt erupted in Egypt, Cyprus and Palestine. By 117, when the old emperor died, his eastern empire had unravelled as fast as it had formed. He had called a halt on every other front and trawled the Empire to build his crusader army, yet the old-fashioned military imperialism that was his programme had still crashed to defeat. The war in north Britain had been dissolved in an oriental fantasy.

Rome's expansionist dynamic was exhausted. She had first conquered the Mediterranean heartland of classical civilisation and then pushed deep into the continental hinterland, but now she could proceed no further. Rome was blocked in the East by a still-mighty Parthian empire, and elsewhere – in Africa, on the Danube and the Rhine, and in Britain – the frontier lay on the edge of a barbarian wilderness of unploughed desert, forest and mountain. On all fronts, Rome faced impenetrable barriers; the Empire had reached its outer limits. For a century, the pace of advance had been slowing. In AD 9, the greatest phase of imperial expansion in Rome's history had ended when two great revolts in newly conquered territories, one in Pannonia (roughly western Hungary and northern Yugoslavia), the other in Germany, culminated in the defeat and loss of three legions in the battle of the Teutoburg Forest. Subsequently, with the exception of the conquest of Britain, the strategy of the Julio-Claudian emperors (30 BC-AD 68) had been defensive and reactive. Their successors, the Flavians (AD 69-96), fought a series of small-scale wars designed to pacify the frontier districts and rationalise the Empire's borders. This was the context for the great drive west and north in Britain, where the security of the lowlands demanded a push into the uplands to create a buffer zone and a shorter, simpler, stronger frontier-line. The emphasis of military deployment changed in accordance with the new perspective of strategic defence. Instead of an army concentrated in a few large bases, as the offensive army of Caesar and Augustus had been in the first century BC, the troops were now dispersed in many small posts along the frontier. In the 80s AD, east of the middle Rhine in the Taunus region of Germany, Domitian had driven the hostile Chatti clear of the border, and then established a line of watchtowers and auxiliary forts along his new frontier. It was typical of the limited, localised, frontier-fixing wars of the period. Thus, the engine of Roman imperialism had already spluttered almost to a halt under the Julio-Claudians and Flavians – before it suddenly kangarooed forwards and crashed under Trajan.

Hadrian (AD 117-38) inherited the wreckage. Unpopular with the governing class – four of Trajan's top marshals were executed for plotting at the beginning of the new reign – Hadrian's inauguration was tainted by military disaster. Traditionally, a weak Caesar had sought legitimation through imperialist war, but the Empire had been prostrated by Trajan's campaigns, and for Hadrian the usual resort was therefore shut off. Indeed, his policy represented the definitive end of

Rome's whole tradition of victory, conquest and plunder, now seven centuries' old and irremovably rooted in the city's institutions and values. Hadrian personified the exhaustion of Roman military imperialism. But this terrible betrayal could not be squarely faced, and the new perspective of strategic defence was dressed in monumental style. The frontiers were reconstructed in stone, the Empire re-invented as a commonwealth of peoples, and the emperor repackaged as divine incarnation of the Roman spirit. To achieve it, Hadrian embarked on a series of grand tours, visiting cities, frontiers and army bases, and initiating a massive programme of military building-work, monumental town architecture, and cultural 'improvement'. His first tour was of the western provinces, and he came to Britain in 121-2.

Scotland had by now been altogether abandoned. As we noted, Agricola had been severely over-extended in the north in 83-4, so subsequent troop withdrawals associated with the Dacian and Parthian wars had made a pull-back from the Highlands unavoidable, and by c.105 even the Southern Uplands had been evacuated and a new Trajanic frontier established on the Stanegate line along the Tyne and Solway between Newcastle and Carlisle. Old forts had been renovated and new ones built, the gap from one to the next being about half a day's march. There may have been smaller posts in between, and perhaps a line of watchtowers on the high ground to the north. This was now the Roman front-line in Britain, and it was here that Hadrian inaugurated the 20-year construction programme which would give us the greatest surviving monument to his new frontier policy. The emperor's biographer tells us, 'the Britons could not be kept under Roman control ... [and in Britain] he put right many abuses, and was the first to build a wall, 80 miles long, to separate the barbarians and the Romans'. It comprised a ditch, a berm, and a 4.5m-high curtain wall with a protected walkway on top. There were milecastles at regular intervals along the whole length, each with accommodation for a small detachment (perhaps 20 or 30 men). There were also two lookout turrets between each milecastle. It was a recasting in more solid form of the linear border defences which had been evolving now for two generations. Tacitus tells us something about earlier frontier regulations on the Rhine and Danube: to enter Roman territory, you had to disarm, pay a toll, and move under escort. We may assume something similar in northern Britain. The new wall would, it was hoped, facilitate the enforcement of border controls, and allow a higher degree of surveillance and policing in general, making small-scale cross-border raiding more difficult, and giving better warning if large-scale hostilities were planned.

The Wall was a failure. The original scheme was impractical and was not carried through. It was perhaps too expensive, for the wall thickness was reduced from ten to eight or even six Roman feet, and a long stretch was at first built in turf, not stone. It appears also that the line was insecure: it had to be extended four extra miles eastwards, protected in the rear by a giant earthwork known as the 'Vallum', and defended by 12 (later 16) forts newly constructed astride or just behind the Wall (a replacement for the old forts on the Stanegate a mile or two back). It still did not work. The frontier remained turbulent, the hostility of the north British perhaps increased because the construction of the Wall and tighter Roman control were disrupting traditional patterns of transhumant pastoralism, commercial exchange and social intercourse in the border region. Full-scale war seems to have erupted again in c. 139-42, at the beginning of Antoninus Pius' reign. The new emperor's biographer tells us that 'Lollius Urbicus, a legate, conquered the Britons for him, and when he had driven the barbarians off, built another wall, of turf'. There is much corroboration from building inscriptions in northern Britain, and perhaps some from commemorative coins issued at the time. Hadrian's Wall was abandoned, the Southern Uplands were overrun, and a new wall of turf and timber was constructed on the Forth-Clyde line. History was repeating itself. Rome's north-west frontier was still out of control. Smuggling, arms-dealing and cattle-rustling were endemic. Ambushes and raids were frequent. All-out war exploded every generation. The northern hills remained an alien continent. The Roman army had gone north again in a renewed search for a permanent solution to the now century-old British Question.

THE WAR IN THE NORTH, AD 142-211: 'LET NO-ONE ESCAPE UTTER DESTRUCTION AT OUR HANDS'

The Antonine Wall ran for 37 miles from a point on the Firth of Forth west of modern Edinburgh to the Firth of Clyde just north of modern Glasgow. It comprised a 4m-wide base of cobbles on which rested a rampart of turf or clay blocks with a timber palisade on top, the whole structure something over 4m high. To the north was a huge defensive ditch, some 12m wide and 3.5m deep. The original plan had been to have a fort approximately every seven miles along the length of the wall (i.e. half a day's march apart), but this was later modified by the addition of smaller 'secondary forts' which reduced the spacing to only about two miles. Though the forts varied greatly in size (Mumrills was about 7.5 acres (3ha), Duntocher 0.6 acres (0.25ha)), the garrison overall was much denser than it had been on Hadrian's Wall – some 175 men per mile compared with 115. The Antonine Wall might have been out-flanked on the east by raiders crossing the Firth of Forth from the north, so a line of strong outpost forts was constructed up as far as the Tay to cut off and guard the Fife peninsula. Also, in the recently recon-quered hill-country to the south, many new forts were built, including the third one at Newstead, the key site where Dere Street, the main north-south road, passed through the Tweed valley on its way from Northumberland to the Central Lowlands. A huge redeployment of the Roman occupation forces in Britain was therefore entailed in the Antonine advance. There may have been 4,500 men in the north-eastern outpost forts, 6,500 on the new wall itself, and 13,000 in the Southern Uplands – a total of 24,000 men moved into new posts north of Hadrian's Wall. The garrison of Brigantia was cut to a fraction. Most of the forts on Hadrian's Wall, on the Cumberland coast, and in the Pennines were abandoned, and this huge area was guarded by perhaps 7,000 men in a dozen posts.

Northern England had never been pacified and civilised as the south-east had been. The foundations of Romanisation were missing here. A striking feature of ancient Brigantia was its lack of a settlement hierarchy. The population lived in isolated farmsteads or small hamlets widely dispersed across the landscape. Hillforts were rare. Only one *oppidum*-like centre is known: the great enclosure at Stanwick in north Yorkshire, dating to the mid-first century AD. Defended by colossal dykes enclosing an area of 730 acres (295ha), yielding high-status finds of Celtic-style metalwork, imported tablewares and Roman building materials, its anomalous character and brief period of occupation make it unrepresentative of any well-rooted feature of Brigantian society. Most likely it was Cartimandua's capital, a client-queen whose power was artificially inflated by Roman subsidies and soldiers, and the fragility of whose support at home is well attested in the pages of Tacitus. Her nebulous authority floated briefly above the realities of life in the dales, where simple cultivators and pastoralists operated an independent subsistence economy still largely beyond the reach of landlords and tax-collectors. The client kingdom was a brittle carapace beneath which lay a loose federation of clansmen who were geographically dispersed, socially undifferentiated, and politically decentralised. The Roman annexation after the fall of Cartimandua could not change these fundamentals. Brigantia under the Romans remained *barbaria*. Whereas the southern plains were ruled by a Romanised municipal gentry and dotted with townships and villas, the northern hills had changed hardly at all and were kept under direct military rule. Long before the Romans, the southern peasants had grown used to paying tribute and performing labour-service to British masters, and little of substance changed when these same masters reinvented themselves as Roman gentlemen. But in Brigantia, Roman tax-collectors, press-gangs and requisition squads battened directly onto a population of free hill-farmers. The clash of class and culture was unmediated. The people were proud and independent. That so much of the fruit of their hard labour should be stolen from them was a new idea. It had to be taken by force – by gangs of soldiers – and over the years the abyss of hatred no doubt widened as native farmer and Roman centurion confronted one another in a thousand little encounters up and down the dales.

In the mid-150s, with a Roman garrison of just 20,000 holding some 200 miles of hill-country behind the new Forth-Clyde frontier, northern Britain exploded. We have three uncertain fragments of literary and epigraphic evidence: an obscure passage in a mid-second-century Roman travel guide may refer to a Brigantian revolt around this time; an issue of coins depicting *Britannia* and dated 154-5 probably celebrates a recent military victory in Britain; and an inscription dredged out of the Tyne at Newcastle could indicate the arrival of reinforcements from the Rhine in *c.*158. If this was the limit of our knowledge, no conclusions could be drawn. But the corroborative archaeological evidence is spectacular. Newstead and other northern forts were burnt and evacuated. The Antonine Wall was abandoned, and Hadrian's Wall and the Pennine forts were reoccupied. A few years later, the pattern was reversed: the forts of the Antonine Wall and the Southern Uplands were rebuilt and occupied again for several years. The conclusion seems unavoidable: a great revolt in the hill-country south of the Antonine Wall had forced the wholesale redeployment of the Roman army to Brigantia for several years. Why the Romans afterwards reoccupied the Antonine Wall, we do not know. Perhaps it was a matter of prestige. Perhaps they needed to reassert control over the Southern Uplands. But the revolt had demonstrated that the Roman army in the north was stretched too thin for safety, and early in the reign of Marcus Aurelius (AD 161-80) the decision was taken to pull back again to Hadrian's Wall. On this occasion, though, events elsewhere in the empire, bearing more closely on its vital interests, again, as in the 80s, had undermined the defence of the north-west frontier.

The Romans had been able to prosecute the British wars of Antoninus Pius' reign so vigorously because elsewhere the frontiers had been relatively untroubled. In the new reign, the frontiers burst apart, first in a Parthian invasion of the East, then in a German descent on Italy. War in the East and on the upper Danube dominated Marcus Aurelius' reign. Britain faded from the picture. The Roman grip on the Forth-Clyde line and the Southern Uplands could not be maintained.

Even the Tyne-Solway line was vulnerable. The emperor's biographer reports that war looked imminent in Britain both in 161 and again in 169, and Dio Cassius records the dispatch of 5,500 barbarian Sarmatian cavalry as reinforcements in 175. The crisis finally broke in 180-4. Local Roman forces were defeated and Hadrian's Wall overrun by a sizeable body of northern invaders. Ulpius Marcellus was sent to assume command: he 'inflicted a major defeat on the barbarians', British victory coins were issued, the emperor assumed the title 'Britannicus', and building inscriptions attest restoration work at frontier forts. The punitive columns that Marcellus had no doubt sent into the hills – destroying grain-stores, burning homesteads, slaying any living thing in their paths – did their work well. The frontier was quiet for another generation. The military terror of their youth weighed on the minds of the older men into the 190s. Not so their sons. A Roman civil war broke out in 193, and in 196 Clodius Albinus, formerly governor of Britain, now usurper-emperor in the West, took his army to the continent in an abortive attempt to assert his power against Septimius Severus. The north British forts were stripped of troops, a new generation of young barbarian warriors was ready for a 'washing of the spears in blood', and the frontier defences again collapsed in a chaos of ambushes and raids. Severus' new governor Virius Lupus was compelled 'to buy peace from the Maeatae for a considerable sum of money' while he reconstructed the Pennine forts, and his successor Alfenius Senecio, also under pressure, continued the rebuilding programme with work on the Hadrian's Wall forts. Still there was no peace: Senecio informed Severus in 207 that rebellion, pillage and destruction were widespread, and that more troops were needed if the frontier was to be secured.

Two near-contemporary historians, Dio Cassius and Herodian, have left descriptions of the north British barbarians and the emperor Severus' campaigns against them. They were organised as two great confederations. Probably in the Highlands beyond the Forth-Clyde isthmus were the Caledonians, Agricola's enemies in 83-4, while the Maeatae 'lived by the wall which divides the country into two halves', which presumably puts them in the Southern Uplands. This great expanse of hill-country, some 120 miles across and 70 from north to south, was the epicentre of Rome's strategic problem. Twice before, under the Flavians in the 80s, and under Antoninus in the 140s and 150s, the Southern Uplands had been occupied and a new frontier established on the Forth-Clyde line – and on each occasion the Roman position had quickly collapsed. In Agricola's time, there had been four tribal confederations in the Lowlands – the Votadini in the east, the Selgovae in the centre, the Novantae in the south-west, and the Damnonii in the north-west (5). None of these had controlled a great *oppidum* like Stanwick, but each perhaps had a single large hillfort centre. Eildon Hill North, for instance, which covered 42 acres (17ha) and contained at least 300 hut-platforms, had been the capital of the Selgovae. Some political centralisation is thus indicated, but otherwise the settlement pattern implies a high degree of local autonomy: there were large numbers of smaller hillforts (usually less than an acre (0.4ha)), grading down into individual farmsteads defended by a ditch and palisaded rampart, or a thick drystone wall (the so-called 'duns') (*10*). The degree of agricultural development, social differentiation and political organisation was probably higher than that among the Brigantes, but these Lowland tribes would still have had deep reserves of local strength on which to base a protracted struggle for independence. Like the Silures of south-east Wales, whatever the outcome of the first big clashes, in the security of a hundred forested glens they might long continue a stubborn resistance to the invader. Little had changed in the period since Agricola, except that the four tribal groupings of the late first century seem to have merged themselves into a single great confederation by the late second. This was a common pattern on the barbarian frontiers. The Roman imperial army was a concentrated military force controlled by a highly centralised state. No small tribe could resist alone. Confrontation with an enemy of terrible power forced the frontier tribes to confederate to survive. War in the borderlands was forging new polities. The Maeatae retained all the military strengths of their past: the power of attrition that lay in the dispersed, slow-motion offensive of the guerrilla fighter, and the defensive resilience of a hundred independent clans, each guarding its own hills, forests and bogs. But to these advantages the enlarged confederation added new ones: the ability to generalise the struggle across huge tracts of upland, and the capacity to mobilise the concentrated force needed for a decisive blow at moments of enemy weakness. In this way, the balance of military power on the barbarian frontiers was shifting against the Empire.

In 208, the great soldier-emperor Severus arrived in Britain with his entire court entourage, set on a final solution to the British Question: the liquidation of the Maeatian and Caledonian confederations. A vast new stores-base was built at South Shields on the east coast, its granaries sufficient to hold three months' rations for 40,000 men. A large fleet must have been assembled to supply the advancing army and harry the enemy ahead from the sea. The army mobilised – the emperor's continental field-army plus the British legions – must have been huge. The invasion penetrated deeply into Scotland: a line of Severan marching camps has been traced running up the south-eastern edge of the Highlands beyond the Forth-Clyde isthmus. The fighting raged for two or three years, but Severus could not bring it to a decision, for 'he fought no battle and saw no enemy drawn up for battle'. Though he could win immediate success and temporary submission by unleashing 'Mars in full fury' on his line of march, he could not smash the enemy's military power and will to resist permanently. The war was a military quagmire. The spade predominated over the sword. Forests were cut, hills levelled, bogs infilled and rivers bridged to establish roadways through the wilderness. Roman scouts, foragers and punitive columns were often ambushed, but the attackers would vanish into woods and marshes when help came up. In the pages of Dio and Herodian, ethnography is distorted by the bragging of soldiers, the sensationalism of travellers' tales, the racial stereotypes of imperial masters, and by the Chinese whispers which translated authentic tit-bit into pure fantasy. Even so, we can sometimes just make out some shadowy images of the barbarian enemy. Their government was 'democratic', their rulers were 'the bravest men', and their warriors fought 'both in chariots and on foot'. They 'decorated their waists and necks with iron', their bodies were tattooed 'with various patterns and with pictures of all kinds of animals', and in action they were 'fearsome and dangerous fighters, defended only by a small shield and a spear, with a sword slung from their naked bodies'. When the war flared up again in 211, the emperor – litter-borne, pain-wracked, close to death – raged in temper that his soldiers should invade again and kill everyone they met: 'Let no-one escape utter destruction at our hands; let not the infant still carried in its mother's womb, if it be male, escape from its fate.'

But it was Severus who was taken by fate, in York before the start of the new campaigning season, and his great British war, Rome's last attempt to conquer Scotland and bring her north-western frontier to rest on the sea, dissolved. Caracalla, Severus' elder son, a most reluctant frontier soldier, made peace with the barbarians, withdrew his forces from the north, and raced back to Rome to murder his brother and secure sole power. Rome never tried again. The northern barbarians had won.

3

BRITAIN UNDER THE PAX ROMANA

THE MILITARY-SUPPLY ECONOMY

Romano-British urban civilisation was at its peak in the years *c*.150-225. This was the period Edward Gibbon, the great eighteenth-century historian, described as Rome's 'golden age'. Even in so marginal a province as Britain, archaeology testifies to an abundant material culture, and the people of the island appear rich and successful. We see a landscape of towns, villas and stone-built settlements, networked together by well-maintained roads and waterways, and filled with mosaics, frescoes, classical statuary, fine tableware and delicately crafted knick-knacks. The contrast with the modest material culture of the Iron Age – and yet more with the grim austerity of the early Dark Age to come – seems to show Antonine and Severan Britain to be part of a great civilisation. The Grandeur That Was Rome appears, briefly, as an end in itself: civilisation for civilisation's sake. But Rome's rulers were not, of course, waging a Crusade for Europe to spread enlightenment and prosperity; like all history's rulers, they contended not for high ideals, but for their own wealth and power. Rome's mission was not to civilise, but to conquer. She was driven by military competition with foreign enemies and political tensions at home to seek control over the land and labour needed to support her war machine. Provincial and local government were simply gearwheels in an empire-wide system of military supply. The imperial economy was a mechanism for converting state levies on agriculture into state spending on the army. This was the dynamic core of the Roman world; it is here that we must seek the power sources of provincial life. The cycle of official levies and payments was a giant economic turbine: its action turned numerous lesser wheels and cogs deep inside civil society. For a time, this 'multiplier effect' spread wealth to the municipal gentry and petty-traders of the larger settlements. The mechanism, however, was highly delicate. It depended on fine balance. A small shift could tip the scales, and, as a mere by-product of the imperial order, this trickle-down of wealth could easily be turned off. Because of this, the golden age of peace and plenty was to be a fleeting moment in history's passage – a flash in the pan, not a new world order. But for the municipal gentry of the time, it was a splendid moment. Let us try to understand it.

The multiplier worked in various ways. Iron Age society must have been tribute-paying, but its renders of produce and labour-service had been moderate, direct and local: payments from peasant to chieftain without the use of money. The Iron Age state had been unsophisticated, and even the great lords of the Catuvellauni had been essentially warband-leaders, still living in round-houses surrounded by their cattle – like the Zulu kings of the nineteenth century. The knock-on impact of economic exchanges would have been limited. Rome, on the other hand, operated on a different scale. An entire Roman state infrastructure was implanted in the British economic landscape in the middle of the first century AD. At the top, based in London, was the governor, whose command (*imperium*) covered military affairs, provincial government and the administration of justice. His London staff included a personal retinue of friends and advisors (*amici*), a central civil service organisation grouped in six departments and headed by army officers, a corps of orderlies and police agents (*beneficiarii* and *speculatores*), and a unit of guard-troops (*singulares*) who were stationed in the Cripplegate fort on the north-west side of the city (*13*). Also based in the capital was the *procurator*, or finance minister, who ran a separate department directly accountable to the emperor. Governors, *procuratores* and their staff are attested on several inscriptions recovered from Roman London – such as that on the tombstone of Gaius Iulius Alpinus Classicianus, who is titled '*procurator* of the province of Britain', and who, as it happens, is known from a reference in the work of the historian Tacitus to have held this office in *c*.61-4. These great departments of state were represented in the localities by officials on detached duties or permanently outstationed. In 191, for instance, a guardsman (*singularis*) and a policeman (*beneficiarius*), both of the governor's staff (they describe themselves as *consularis*), recorded on a stone inscription that they had restored an altar 'to the god who devised roads and paths' at a place near Catterick in Yorkshire. Presumably their duties included the supervision of road repairs. If so, it would be no surprise.

The state of the roads was a major worry for the London administration. The Empire was knit together by a system known as the public post (*cursus publicus*), comprising the road network itself and, at regular intervals along it, a series of horse changing-stations (*mutationes*) and wayside travel-lodges (*mansiones*). It was for official use only – permits were required – and its main purpose was to move information fast: the normal rate was about 50 miles a day. Such rapid transmission of news and orders was, of course, a key feature of imperial power – good communications mean effective command and control. It also enabled high-ranking imperial officials to travel in the comfort and style to which they were accustomed: the *mansiones* were the four-star hotels of their day, cocooning their privileged clients against the inconveniences of provincial travel. Arrival at the *mansio* after a day on the road would have been welcome relief. Flunkies would be on hand to take away the horses and escort the VIPs to the baths, where they could relax and freshen up while their meal was prepared. Afterwards they would dine together in the *triclinium* (formal dining-room), enjoy whatever entertainment the establishment could offer, and then retire to one of the little suites of rooms ranged around the courtyard garden. These *mansiones* were spread along the major roads of Roman Britain like beads on a string.

Then there were the imperial estates. The greatest landowner in Roman Britain was the emperor himself. Much of East Anglia, for instance, was probably confiscated after the Boudican Revolt, and, in particular, a huge imperial estate seems to have been formed when the Fenland was drained in the early second century and the reclaimed land filled up with hundreds of villages and farms. The settlement pattern we can see is anomalous: it bears the impress of the state. The Fenland farmers lived in wooden cottages with thatched roofs, set in rectangular enclosures formed by drainage ditches, and here they made a modest living rearing sheep for wool and meat, staying close to subsistence level, owning little above bare necessity. There were no private villas, no evidence for a class of yeomanry raising themselves up or gentry established in control of large estates. But large-scale enterprise is apparent in some of the drainage canals and well-made roads, and at Stonea one very grand and most unusual building has been excavated. Stone-built, finely-decorated and centrally-heated, this huge high-rise structure towered over the native cottages huddled close by. Soldiers were stationed here, and salted meat was probably exported. Was it the centre of an imperial estate supplying the army in the north, administered for the emperor by a man appointed by the London *procurator*'s office? A man like Gaius Severius Emeritus, perhaps, who described himself as a 'district officer' (*centurio regionarius*) on an altar dedication found at Bath, and who has sometimes been supposed to have had charge of an imperial estate in the West Country.

Mining was also a state activity. Gold was extracted at Dolaucothi in south Wales, and silver from lead deposits in the

13 A London civil servant of the first century. This high-relief tombstone sculpture was found reused in a bastion of the late Roman town-wall. Though a soldier is depicted – he is wearing military cloak, tunic and sword – his lack of armour and the scroll and writing-tablets in his left hand indicate that he was a bureaucrat on the governor's staff, probably a beneficiarius consularis. *He represents the peak of an administrative pyramid which reached down to the most remote rural farmstead*

Somerset Mendips. Lead was mined elsewhere for its own sake – in the Peak District of Derbyshire, in the northern and central Welsh Marches, and in the Yorkshire Dales. There were iron-workings in the Weald, in the Forest of Dean, and at a string of sites along the Jurassic Ridge between Lincoln and Somerset. Ancient writers often referred to gold, silver and other metals as prizes awaiting the victor in war – Cicero was disappointed that Caesar had found not 'a scrap of silver on the island', Strabo listed gold, silver and iron among the exports of Britain in the late Iron Age, and Tacitus felt that it was these and other metals which made Britain 'worth conquering' for the Romans. It is difficult to exaggerate the importance of metals as strategic commodities in the ancient world. Gold and silver were minted into the coins on which the entire tax-pay cycle depended: without bullion, the

Roman imperial order would have seized up and ceased to function. Other metals – copper, lead, and above all iron – were forged into the arms and armour, the military tackle, the base-camps and fortresses of the Roman war-machine. Metals, quite simply, meant economic and military power; whoever controlled them ruled the world. So mining in Roman Britain was both state monopoly and political priority. We have an ingot of Mendip lead stamped with the emperor's name and titles which dates from as early as 49, and there is another, dated to 60, which bears the name of one Gaius Nipius Ascanius, a concessionaire (*conductor*) who had landed the government contract to run one of the mine-workings. Official exploitation of British iron deposits also began early; the island was supplying all its own needs by the end of the first century. In the Weald, four eastern sites have produced tile-stamps of the British fleet (*classis Britannica*), implying that these were under direct state control; the western workings may have been operated by concessionaires.

Government offices, roads and highway services, the imperial estates, mining and metals: these were major state enterprises. But they pale beside the economic significance of the army. In place of the tribal militias of the Iron Age, there was now a permanent standing army in Britain of 40,000 men. This generated a heavy additional demand for grain, fodder, meat, dairy products, fruit and vegetables, beer and wine, hides, cloth, wood for fuel, timber for building, stone, tile, iron, lead, bronze, pottery, and much else. The *Vindolanda* tablets have taught us something about this. Some 200 slivers of wood inscribed in ink have been recovered from water-logged deposits just beyond the fort wall: they turn out to be a mass of discarded Roman army 'paperwork' of *c*.95-120. We learn of a wide variety of consumables supplied to the army; many tablets, for instance, were food-supply lists, and items range from staples like wheat (for bread), barley (for fodder or porridge) and Celtic beer, to luxuries (for the officers' table or a festal occasion?) like venison, suckling-pig and imported Italian vintages. Some things, of course, the soldiers supplied themselves. The XX Legion stationed at Chester operated an industrial plant making pottery and roof-tiles about eight miles away at Holt on the river Dee. There are quarries near Hadrian's Wall which bear inscriptions carved by the Roman soldiers who worked to hack out the build-ing-stone. The land around Roman forts was reserved for the use of the garrisons, and we can assume that, amongst other things, animals were grazed on such 'meadows of the legion' (*prata legio-nis*). The mines and the imperial estates, as noted above, were state enterprises managed by soldiers and probably used to supply the army direct. But not all needs could be met in this way – by the state's direct-works department, as it were – and the army attracted to it a swarm of civilian petty-traders.

The exchange mechanisms involved are obscure. It is probable that each link in the chain was forged in face-to-face encounter, and that bribes and favours counted as much as price and quality. The middlemen, the dealers and fixers, those the Romans called *negotiatores*, would have been key players connecting the mass of petty-producers in the provincial hinterlands with the soldiers on the frontiers. These hundreds of arms-dealers and military-suppli-ers battening onto the army in its northern cantonments were the people of the *vici*, the 'markets' that grew up outside the forts in the third century. One such was Barates the Palmyrene, who described himself on his third-century tombstone at Corbridge as 'a trader in military standards' (*vexillarius*). But the scale of opera-tion was usually small; there is little evidence for big commercial capital at work. Most of the army's needs were supplied by 'the lit-tle man' nearby; the *Vindolanda* tablets repeatedly record supplies arriving in very small quantities. We must imagine a farmer turn-ing up with his cartload – a barrel of beer, two bushels of wheat, and half a dozen hides, perhaps – rather than a big merchant bringing in a wagon-train of grain and a herd on the hoof. Most large-scale, long-distance movements of goods are likely to have been state enterprise. Roman *amphorae*, the large pottery storage-vessels used to transport wine, oil, condiments and other food-stuffs, show a markedly skewed distribution-pattern: coming from southern Spain, southern Gaul and Italy, they are found concentrated along the river valleys of the Rhone, Saone, Moselle and Rhine, apparently following the obvious routeways to the frontier armies of the north-west in Germany and Britain. Many petty-traders probably 'hitched a lift' on the military transport system, where, for a small premium perhaps, they could buy unused space on wagons and barges, thus carrying luxury items long distances to high-income customers on the edges of the Empire. Marcus Secund(inius?) Silvanus may have operated in this way: he was 'a trader in pottery with Britain' (*negotiator cretarius Britannicianus*), and we know of him because he raised two altars to the goddess Nehalennia at the mouth of the Scheldt in Holland in the later second or third century, one of many of his kind to do this (over 150 dedications are known).

The argument here is that the Romano-British economy was pump-primed by government defence spending, and that one result was the emergence of a class of petty-traders at the interface between the military and civil society. These petty-traders included a variety of people able to sell on the market for a profit – not just the dealers, artisans and shopkeepers in the larger settlements, but also the better-off farmers nearby who were able to produce a surplus for sale. We can detect archaeological traces of these activities in the frontier *vici*. Few civilians had been able to settle close to forts in the second century, presumably due to official regulation of activity within the military zone. Such regulation was now relaxed – the Vallum ceased to function as a barrier – and vibrant communities of retired veterans, soldiers' families, artisans and retailers grew up around the forts. These *vici* had a distinctly military flavour. The settlement might contain an army bathhouse, a public-post travel-lodge, temples built by officers from the base, the family homes of married men, craft-workshops geared towards military supply, and bars and brothels where single men could pass time off-duty. Several examples – like Chesterholm, Corbridge and Housesteads in the well-preserved central sector of Hadrian's Wall – have been part-excavated. Housesteads *vicus* has yielded an inscription with the letters '*D(ecreto) VICA(norum)*', meaning 'by decree of the villagers', clear evidence that the civilian community had both corporate identity and political structure. A total of 26 buildings are known, mainly small one-room cottages, or strip-buildings fronting the main street leading up to the south gate of the fort; only two or three buildings were larger than this. Foundations were often of stone, but timber superstructures infilled with wattle-and-daub panels can be assumed, and perhaps thatched or shingle roofs. Sometimes there are clues to former use: an oven large enough for industrial activity, a furnace for metal-working, a slot for shop-front shuttering. In the village itself, also on nearby Chapel Hill, and elsewhere in the vicinity, dedications to many different pagan cults have been found – to Jupiter, the patron god of Rome, to the mixed Romano-Celtic Mars-Thincsus, to the strange eastern saviour-god Mithras, and to the native spirits known as *Matres* (Mother-goddesses) and *Genii Cucullati* (Hooded Spirits). Housesteads *vicus* was a meeting-place of two worlds, one Roman, imperial and urban, the other Celtic, local and rural. As such, it was a place where the rules were relaxed and one could 'get on', a place of opportunity and social mobility.

Like the army bases of the north, the roadside travel-lodges of the public post constituted another interface between state and society, attracting similar communities of petty-traders and street-hawkers. Such commercial flotsam might easily crystallise into a new Roman small town providing highway services for travellers and a market centre for local farmers. Godmanchester in Cambridgeshire was such a place. It lay on Ermine Street, the main Roman road north, at the point where it crossed the river Ouse, and also at the junction with two secondary roads leading to other Roman small-towns. A *vicus*-settlement had grown up around two successive conquest-period forts, and many of the houses – traditional round-huts and small square or rectangular cottages built in timber, clay and thatch – had continued in use after the army had pulled out. Godmanchester around 100 must have been a scruffy roadside hamlet. But in the early second century, a large area by the central crossroads was cleared for the construction of a stone courtyard-building of thirty rooms with associated bathhouse – a travel-lodge of the public post. It is thought to have comprised stables and tack-rooms in the northern range where the main entrance was located, rows of bedrooms on the eastern and western sides of the courtyard, and reception-room, dining-room and kitchen to the south (with rubbish-pits just outside the latter). The bathhouse immediately to the south consisted of two full suites of rooms, each with changing-room and the usual hot, warm and cold facilities. Further development at the central crossroads followed in the early third century, when a large, stone, rectangular hall with a small enclosed courtyard in front was constructed, and an extensive, gravelled market-square was laid out beside it with timber porticoes on three sides. The only other public buildings known in the town are two small temples in the native 'Romano-Celtic' architectural style. Private houses remained much as before. Third-century Godmanchester seems, then, to have been a small roadside settlement of perhaps 200 people grouped around an imperial travel-lodge and an administered market. We know of bakers, blacksmiths, coppersmiths, potters and bone-workers, as well as many who were simply farmers, but nothing of grand town-houses and the idle rich. There were a hundred or so such places in Roman Britain: small towns distinguished by the unplanned irregularity of their street plan, the restricted character of their public architecture, the near-complete absence of high-status residences, and the blurring of the boundary between the settlement itself and the agricultural hinterland beyond.

Still, though, we have not explored every aspect of the military-supply economy. Behind these visible interfaces around the forts and travel-lodges of the Roman state, long nerve-lines of imperial power stretched deep into the Romano-British countryside. Indeed, the significance of booming garrison and roadside towns can easily be misunderstood. They may appear to represent the belated Romanisation of the frontier zone and the rural hinterland – a process of 'civilisation' like that already well established in the major towns of the south-east. In fact, these outposts were islands of privilege which, in the larger scheme of things, were parasitic on the native countryside, whose resources were plundered to support the soldiers and officials of the imperial state. The military *vici* and the small towns were points of mediation between state and society – not places where, as has sometimes been supposed, the British countryside was dissolved in *Romanitas* – and the civilian camp-followers of the state, those who travelled life in Rome's baggage-train, shared a little in its riches. For sure, wheels of activity turned and wealth trickled down. But as always, while some gained, others lost. Roman power shored up established wealth and offered new opportunities for wealth acquisition. Those who had wealth could now produce for the market and grow richer. This, as we have seen, included the burgeoning class of petty-traders, among whom were the better-off farmers (those who in the Middle Ages would have been called 'yeomen'). The mass of small and medium peasants, on the other hand, those who lived close to subsistence and could produce little for the market, knew only the disadvantages of the Roman system: they were the losers.

Most Romano-British peasants faced heavy burdens. Direct imperial taxes took perhaps 10 per cent of agricultural output. Much if not all of this was paid in money, so producers had to bring a surplus to market and exchange it for coin before their taxes could be paid. The necessary coin had previously entered the economy in the form of state spending on military contracts and soldiers' pay. This circulation of coin was regulated and enforced by the state – and without the state would have collapsed – but its effect must have been to generate countless subsidiary transactions throughout Rome's 'Common Market'. The bronze coinage illustrates this. The state collected taxes and made disbursements in gold and silver, yet it still issued many low-denomination bronze coins. The purpose was to facilitate everyday transactions in money, a circulation of coin through the economy, and the acquisition by taxpayers of the bullion they needed to pay the state. A special category of petty-trader emerged to mediate the exchange of bullion and base coin: these were the 'money-changers' (*nummularii*). From them, in exchange for the gold and silver received in an army pay-packet, you could obtain base coins for everyday use in the market place, or you could trade in the bronze accumulated in everyday transactions for the bullion needed to pay state taxes; naturally, the money-changers took their cut. Indirectly, then, the state's fiscal and monetary cycle generated a vast number of transactions in the towns, roadside settlements, local market-places and villa courtyards of Roman Britain, as several million peasants came to market to find the means to pay the tax-collector. Another burden was the military corn-requisition, probably in the form of forced sales at fixed prices, an imposition likely to have fallen mainly on those living close to the army bases. More widespread was the corvée: forced labour-service on public projects. The upkeep of roads, bridges and public-post buildings, for instance, was the responsibility of local authorities, and we can assume much heavy labouring on highway maintenance and repair by local peasants. In addition to these regular levies of tribute and labour, there might also have been occasional demands for goods and services to support soldiers, officials and supplies passing through – traction-animals and vehicles for transport, billets for temporary stopovers, food and drink if the commissariat ran low. Rome was a great pyramid of power and wealth built on a foundation of peasant labour – at bottom, a primitive, tribute-levying, agricultural state.

The municipal gentry were the cement that fastened these foundations together: they were the locally rooted agents of efficient exploitation. Because of this, Rome's power sheltered and succoured them: the security of property and privilege was the gentry's reward. Or, to view the matter from the peasant angle, tribute and labour were due not just to the Roman emperor, but also to the local lord, and the debt-collectors and press-gangs were the same in either case. Thus did the military-supply economy reach down into every native farmstead. Furthermore, if the enlarged markets of this system benefited the petty-traders, the municipal gentry benefited much more, for big property-owners have more surplus to sell. Power and property: the Romano-British gentry had it made – at least for now, in the sunshine years of *c.*150-225.

THE GOLDEN AGE OF THE MUNICIPAL GENTRY

Traditionally, in the Graeco-Roman world, public life and status display were urban activities. Of necessity, therefore, it was in the early towns that the British elite had forged their new identity as Romanised gentry in the period *c.*75-150. Civic construction-work had boomed and the towns had acquired full *ensembles* of public architecture: a centrally placed *forum* with a paved open space and covered porticoes all around; a grand assembly-hall of basilical design (i.e. a large rectangular hall with nave and two aisles) with associated council-offices; elaborately decorated baths for public exercise, hygiene and relaxation; maybe a theatre near the town centre, and certainly an amphitheatre on the edge of town for popular entertainment; various temples, shrines and cult statues to honour approved deities; probably a spacious and luxurious travel-lodge for the use of official parties and imperial messengers; perhaps a purpose-built market-hall, a cattle-market, waterfront facilities, or other commercial premises; maybe an aqueduct and water-and-sewage system; and around the town, properly ordered and well-maintained cemeteries. The government did not pay for such urban infrastructures. The custom, in the Roman world, was that monumental buildings were bestowed on urban communities by municipal authorities, other corporate bodies, or wealthy private benefactors. The circumstances varied. Sometimes the city-fathers, assembled in council, decided that local toll payments, excise duties and municipal rents were to fund a desirable capital project. Sometimes it was a legally enforceable obligation on a prominent citizen, as when customary 'liturgies' (financial burdens on wealthy citizens) were performed on the assumption of magisterial office. Sometimes there was sponta-neous generosity, whether by members of a town guild paying through joint subscription, or a private sponsor eager to enhance his standing and popularity (what Romans of the old school might have called *fama*).

The evidence from Roman Britain is sparse indeed, but what little there is suggests such a pattern. A commemorative inscrip-tion of 129-30 records that the Wroxeter forum was erected by 'the *civitas* of the Cornovii' – which means by decision of the town-council – and another of 79 or 81, though more fragmen-tary, probably records a similar venture at *Verulamium*. Tacitus tells us that in the mid-first century the Temple of Claudius at Colchester was paid for by 'those chosen to serve as priests [who] found their whole wealth drained away in the name of religion', while a Chichester inscription of similar date speaks of a guild of metalworkers (*collegium fabrorum*) building a temple to 'Neptune and Minerva for the Well-being of the Imperial House' (4). Another inscription records that Brough-on-Humber's officer of public works (*aedilis*) paid for a new stage-building at the theatre in 139-44. Others tell of benefactions by provincial governors, probably in the third century: the repair of London's Temple of Isis 'collapsed from old age', and the restoration of Cirencester's Column of Jupiter 'erected under the ancient religion'. The need to fund large-scale urban building soon after the conquest may, incidentally, be the reason that leading Romano-Britons received hefty loans from the emperor Claudius and the multi-millionaire Seneca; the historian Dio Cassius cites sudden demands for repayment as a principal cause of the Boudican revolt in 61.

After about 150, the pace of public building in towns decreased (*8*). The major towns had now acquired all the culturally correct amenities expected of a fully Roman community. The various stages on which the dramas of civilised public life were acted out had been constructed. A gentleman of standing could show off his oratory in a council-chamber debate or a town-hall court case, he could display political reliability by visits to the emperor's temple and cultural orthodoxy by attending the games, and otherwise, man of property and leisure that he was, he could lounge around with his peers at the baths or pose elegantly for the plebeians in the porticoes of the *forum*. The would-be Romano-British gentleman had his architectural props. Home comforts were another matter. Early-second-century towns had few private houses of any refinement; typically, the residential areas were still made up of timber-and-clay strip-buildings like the *insula* XIV shops at *Verulamium*. Only in *c.*125 were the first Romanised town-houses constructed, and it was still not really until the second half of the century that these became the fashion (*14*). Many such have been excavated at *Verulamium*. Building XXI.2 is an example.

This house comprised at least 14 rooms and corridors, some with tessellated floors and painted-plaster, organised as three wings around a central courtyard (*15*). The design had many virtues. Shutting out the public world of the streets beyond, the house achieved privacy by looking in on itself: the courtyard would have been laid out as a formal garden, there were covered corridors running on three sides of this, and all the rooms in the ranges behind opened into these corridors. There was the additional advantage of interior privacy: not only were separate rooms partitioned off, but they were not needed as walk-throughs, so these compartments offered seclusion from household to-ing and fro-ing. The change from the noisy intimacy of the one-room

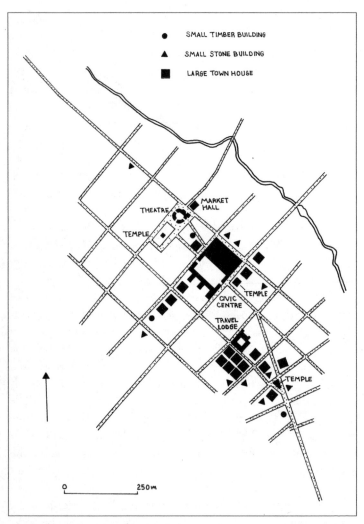

Legend:
- ● SMALL TIMBER BUILDING
- ▲ SMALL STONE BUILDING
- ■ LARGE TOWN HOUSE

THEATRE

MARKET HALL

TEMPLE

CIVIC CENTRE

TEMPLE

TRAVEL LODGE

TEMPLE

0   250m

14 Verulamium *(St Albans)* in c.225. *On most sites, as comparison with figure 9 shows, the small timber buildings of the early town had been replaced by large stone-founded houses belonging to the local gentry, the result of a private-housing boom which affected all the Romano-British towns in the late second and early third centuries.* After Wheeler, Frere and Niblett round-hut implies a transformed conception of the relationship between self and others – a revolution, among the elite at any rate, in domestic manners. Of particular importance was the opportunity afforded to maintain privacy while still allowing public access: we know next to nothing about the use of domestic space in Romano-British town-houses, but, in this vertically stratified patron-client society, where lesser men routinely sought the protection and patronage of greater, we can assume that some rooms were reserved for receiving dependants and conducting business. The design was classical, of course: it was an architecture of straight lines and right-angles, arranged in a way that was symmetrical, orderly and balanced. This was complemented by conventionally classical decoration on the floors and walls (about which more below). Important, too, was the overall setting: Roman town-houses were often surrounded by ample grounds laid out as market-gardens, orchards and paddocks: part of the classical taste for bringing nature into the urban environment – a controlled, sanitised, made-to-order nature, that is. This consistent style, modelled so closely on that of the Graeco-Roman Mediterranean, was an effective signifier of the new identity sought by the Romano-British landowner: no longer the beery chieftain carousing with his retainers, but a Roman gentleman 'of dignified leisure' (*otium cum dignitate*).

There was gentrification in the countryside, too. Some 600-odd villas are known in Britain, and there must have been at least a thousand all told, perhaps many more. They were distributed unevenly across the province, and the patterning apparent in the archaeological record seems highly significant (*16*). Let us pursue this by conjuring up an image of the typical villa-estate: an 'ideal-type' for the Romano-British country seat of the late second century onwards. It would lie in the more Romanised south-eastern half of the island – there were hardly any villas in Devon and Cornwall, Wales, the west Midlands, or the north-west. It would be part of a developed *civitas* community where there was strong,

local, civilian self-government. Some areas of the south-east seem
to have lacked this – the Fenland, the north-eastern part of East
Anglia, southern Essex, the Weald of Kent and Sussex, Salisbury
Plain in Wiltshire – perhaps because they were imperial estates
worked by tenant-farmers under the direct authority of army officers, bailiffs or concessionaires. Our villa would be close to a major
town or one of the principal highways – not out in the sticks –
and it would be located in a river valley, where the soils would be
deep and heavy: harder to work, yet more fertile. Take the villas
around *Verulamium*. There were some 50 close to the town, the
highest concentration in the Catuvellaunian *civitas*, and they were
concentrated especially in the numerous little river valleys of the
Chilterns to the west, where the average estate was perhaps around

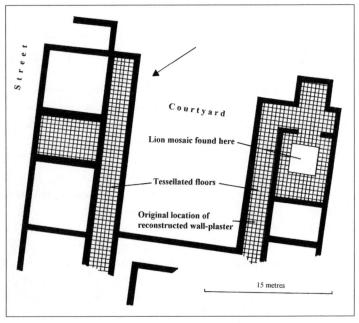

15 The excavated remains of Building XXI.2, Verulamium. After Frere

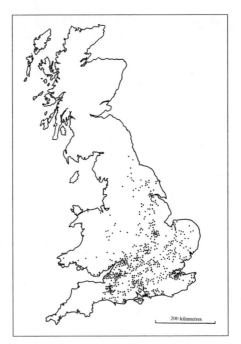

16 The distribution of known Roman villas across Britain. The pattern of villa distribution corresponds very closely with the south-east:north-west divide which is so central to Romano-British history. Within the south-east, various factors are likely to have affected villa distribution, including the presence of forest and marsh, the existence of imperial estates, and the wealth and outlook of the local gentry

500 acres (200ha) in extent. These, surely, were the country seats of the Catuvellaunian gentry, who were, at the same time, building town houses for themselves in *Verulamium*. The typical villa-estate seems geared, on the one hand, to efficient farm management and production for the market, and, on the other, to facilitating the owner's full participation in the public duties and social rounds of his class.

In some cases, the metamorphosis from Iron Age lord to Roman gentleman is archaeologically apparent. At least three sites near *Verulamium* – Gorhambury, Lockleys and Park Street – have revealed evidence for pre-Roman occupation in the Iron Age round-house tradition underlying later Roman villas. At Lockleys and Park Street, two separate Iron Age phases were recognised in excavation, and at Gorhambury no fewer than five, which suggests these were well-established family farms at the time of the conquest. In the mid-first century AD, new timber structures with some Roman features were erected at two of these sites, but both were burnt down in the Boudican revolt. Subsequently, when rebuilding was carried out in the Flavian period (69-96), replacement structures at all three sites took the form of small Romanised residences – a range of four or five rooms fronted by a corridor or veranda – and in one case there was also a small, free-standing bath-house of two rooms. During the second century, these villas became somewhat grander, principally with the addition of either one or two wings at the ends of the main ranges, and with more elaborate interior finish, notably the provision of mosaic floors in the more important reception-rooms of two of the villas. Let us picture Gorhambury in the late second century (*17*). There was a small projecting wing at either end of the principal range of rooms, along the front of which ran the main access-corridor. Decoration included mosaic, painted wall-plaster, and figured stucco-work, and the building also contained its own bath-house. Outside, in the grounds of the house, there were various outbuildings and enclosures, including, in an outer farmyard compound and an aisled hall and bath-house for the estate workers. Beyond stretched the arable fields of the farm, and beyond them pasture and woodland. The farming regime was mixed and market-oriented. Sheep, cattle and pigs are represented in the assemblage of animal-bones; the discovery of a grain-store, a corn-drier and quernstones indicate cereal production; and the presence of steel-yards, weights, coins and *styli* (wax-tablet writing implements) imply the accumulation of marketable surpluses.

Such Romanised sophistication depended upon access to a wide range of luxury trades. These were based in the towns and the industrial areas (many of which were rural), where numerous members of the petty-trading class found a living as a miniature Romano-British version of the Roman plebs, delivering the goods and services intrinsic to *otium cum dignitate*. These trades were almost certainly organised as guilds operating in regulated markets under the authority and protection of powerful patrons. The famous Togidubnus inscription referred to above is relevant here, since it records that the guild of metalworkers in Chichester had erected their temple 'by authority' (*ex auctoritate*) of the client king – his permission was needed, it seems, even though the construction site had been donated and the guild-members were to pay for the work themselves (*4*). The urban economy, in other words, was not driven by the 'hidden hand' of the free market, but by the open manipulation of the local governing class.

Two luxury trades stand out in the archaeological record at *Verulamium*: wall-painting and mosaic-laying. The first wall-painting in the town was done in the 50s, because fallen fragments of decorated plaster have been found below the Boudican destruction-level of 61. A strong school of fresco-painters must have been at work in the area from then on, as public buildings, town houses and country residences continued to be decorated throughout the Roman period. Up to the mid-second century, decorative schemes were limited to two-dimensional imitations of wall-pan-

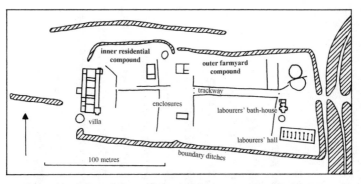

17 Gorhambury villa and farmyard, Hertfordshire, in c.175-250. An Iron Age estate centre has now been Romanised, with a medium-sized, stone-founded villa in the inner compound, and a timber aisled-hall and stone bath-house for the farm labourers in the outer one. After Neal et al.

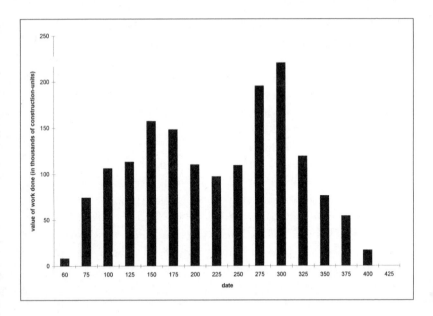

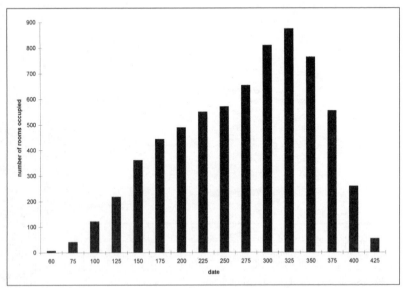

elling, but thereafter, more elaborate architectural schemes with an impression of depth and space were also produced. Mosaic art was a little slower to develop – the earliest workshops were established around 125 – but this too became highly accomplished in the later second century. The *Verulamium* school specialised in angular geometric schemes with much use of thick borders of 'guilloche' (a linear pattern like twisted multicoloured rope), decorated with such standard motifs as floral scrolls and rosettes, dolphins and other wild beasts, *canthari* (Bacchic wine-cups), and occasionally a central figured scene depicting a pagan deity or the hunt. If we retrace our steps a moment to Building XXI.2 (*15*), the well-preserved south-west wing contained some splendid examples of later-second-century frescoes and mosaic (now superbly displayed in the Verulamium Museum). The corridor walls included red panels decorated with yellow candelabra, blue and yellow swags, and green doves on perches. Reconstruction of fallen ceiling-plaster has revealed a coffer-design, like an overhead garden-trellis, decorated with birds and feline heads. Floors were tessellated, and in the main living-room there was also a very fine mosaic-panel, comprising guilloche borders, flower and *cantharus* decoration, and a vivid image of a lion holding in its jaws a stag's head dripping blood. The contrast with Iron Age art is extreme: in place of abstract designs of intertwining curves and loops (perhaps now

Opposite page:

18 Above: *The value of construction work on Romano-British villas by period. Based on a random sample of 78 sites, the graph shows two pronounced peaks in villa construction, a moderate one in c.150-75, and a stronger one in c.275-300. Periods of recession correspond with the third-century crisis and the fourth-century decline in Roman Britain as a whole. Source: Newman*

19 Below: *The number of rooms occupied in Romano-British villas by period. The 'golden age' of villa culture in Roman Britain in c.275-350 is apparent. Sample: 78 sites. Source: Newman*

seen as *barbaricus* and *sine dignitate*), there was a naturalistic tradition, one which, as it were, 'held up a mirror to nature', and the designs were replete with such signifiers of the new *Romanitas* as the wild-beast hunt, the wine-drinking party, and the cults of Graeco-Roman myth.

If the first three generations after the conquest had built Roman-style public monuments, the next three built Roman-style town-houses. The rise of the urban private house is apparent in figure **8**. In the sample represented here, fewer than ten excavated examples can be dated to *c.*125, compared with about 35 in *c.*175, and as many as 65 in *c.*225. The private-housing boom was, then, a special feature of the years *c.*150-225, at the end of which time the Romano-British towns were at a peak of development and population (*7*). There were still many strip-buildings used as shops, workshops and domestic residences by artisans, traders and labourers. The great public buildings were still generally well maintained and in regular use. But the rest of the intramural area had now filled up with grand residences, often set in ample grounds, giving the Romano-British towns of around 225 a distinctive character as quiet, genteel, residential garden-cities of a cultured landed-gentry. This urban development was complemented by changes in the countryside. Figure *18* shows construction work on villas reaching its first peak in the mid-late second century, and figure **19** shows this reflected in a steady rise in the number of villas extant and under occupation. In a sample of 78 villas, nine were occupied in *c.*100, 22 in *c.*150, and 31 in *c.*200 (compared with an eventual maximum of 53 in *c.*325). We are witness, then, to a construction boom at the upper end of the housing market, starting in the countryside in the later first century, reaching the towns in the mid-second, and at a sustained peak from *c.*150-225. This boom supported the growth of the luxury trades, the development of numerous production-centres, and the fortunes of the petty-trading class. All are archaeological markers of the Romano-British gentry's golden age.

What manner of life is represented here? Archaeology cannot give direct testimony to the thought-world and social round of this elite. This is the stuff of literature. But they were mimicking their Italian peers so closely in the design of their buildings and their taste in art that we can assume the relevance of some contemporary Latin writing. The letters of Pliny the Younger (AD 61-113), that quintessential Roman aristocrat-of-office, are a case in point. He was immensely rich, owned estates in various parts of Italy, and paid close attention to the administration of his property. This involved him in regular visits to his various villas, which he appears to have greatly enjoyed, and he often expressed the longing for escape from the city to a rural idyll, which was a conventional literary motif among the Roman upper class at the time:

> Are you reading, fishing or hunting, or doing all three? You can do all together on the shores of Como, for there is plenty of fish in the lake, game to hunt in the woods around, and every opportunity to study in the depths of your retreat. Whether it is everything or only one thing, I cannot say I begrudge you your pleasures; I am only vexed at being denied them myself, for I hanker after them as a sick man does wine, baths and cool springs. I wonder if I shall ever be able to shake off these constricting fetters ... New business piles up on the old before the old is done, and, as more and more links are added to the chain, I see my work stretching out further and further each day.

But this was only half the story. For Roman gentlemen, the tension between Arcadia and The City was insoluble; the latter, whatever its stresses, was the essential arena for public service, status display and popular acclaim. Pliny pursued a traditional and highly successful senatorial career at Rome: he pleaded cases at the bar, held a series of junior magistracies, became a treasury official, attained the consulship, had responsibility for flood-control and sewer-maintenance, and was finally appointed extraordinary governor to the disorderly province of Bithynia-Pontus in Asia Minor. Such self-imposed 'constricting fetters' were intrinsic to aristocratic status. Consider his delight in the accumulation of honour:

> I am well aware, Sir, that no higher tribute can be paid to my reputation than some mark of favour from so excellent a ruler as yourself [the emperor Trajan]. I pray you, therefore, to add to the honours to which I have been raised by your kindness by granting me a priesthood, either that of augur or member of the septemvirate, as there is a vacancy in both orders. By virtue of my priesthood I could then add official prayers on your behalf to those I already offer in private as a loyal citizen.

Velvet fetters, then – especially since his wealth and offices allowed Pliny to play the essential role of great patron. He was ever writing letters to secure favour and advancement for relatives, friends and dependants – members of his *clientela* – and he was the principal benefactor of his home town of Como. His provision of a public library there led to an angst-ridden discussion of whether it was proper to advertise his generosity by publishing the speech he had made on the occasion of its opening:

> It was delivered not as a public speech in the open, but before the council in their senate house, so that I am afraid that it is hardly consistent at this point to court by publication the popular favour and applause which I avoided when I was speaking. I put the doors and walls of the senate house between myself and the populace whom I was trying to benefit, so as not to appear to court their favour; but now I feel that I am going out of my way to display my powers and thus win over those whose sole concern with my benefaction rests in the example it presents.

Thus the delicate dilemmas of *noblesse oblige*. The aristocratic culture of Pliny the Younger is probably that to which the

Romano-British gentry aspired. Writ small, his attitudes represent a possible model for provincial gentility, one where a gentleman had his country seat, a Romanised villa-estate within the *civitas*, but lived in his Romanised town house when attending to his public duties of service, patronage and self-advertisement. Golden, indeed, was this moment. But in the passage of historic time, it was to be no more than a moment. The mole of history was at work undermining the foundations of second-century tranquillity: the balance of military power on the frontiers was shifting, slowly but surely, in favour of Rome's enemies, and the imperial state was lurching towards a sharp political crisis with profound implications for all.

THE RISE OF THE MILITARY MONARCHY, AD 167-235

'I set upon the Romans boundaries of neither space nor time; I have bestowed upon them empire without limit.' Thus spoke Virgil's Jupiter, patron god of ancient Rome. For so it had seemed at the time of Augustus (30 BC-AD 14). Rome then had been an expanding imperialist system: driven to aggressive war by the twin pressures of military competition abroad and political competition at home, mountains of plundered wealth had been accumulated to support the state, the army, the imperial grandees, and 'the bread and circuses' of the Roman mob. All that Rome was depended on expansion. What had seemed to Virgil the will of God had in fact been an historical imperative. Two centuries later, however, it appeared there were, after all, boundaries of space and time. The unploughed barbarian wilderness on the frontiers was beyond the reach of Roman power. Classical civilisation could not grow there. In these great tracts of untamed nature, stretching endlessly north and south from the Mediterranean, Rome faced inglorious guerrilla warfare able to drain away her lifeblood. There were no more rich corn-lands filled with treasure left. The age of conquest and plunder had passed. The inflow of booty had slowed to a dribble. Rome was no longer subsidised by war.

Yet the cost of empire had changed little. Between half and two-thirds of state revenue still went on the army. Augustus had had 28 legions in 25 BC; Severus had 33 in AD 210. The soldiers of Augustus had been paid out of the spoils of war. The emperor tells us, in a party political broadcast known as the *Res Gestae* ('Achievements'), that he spent 1,430 million sesterces on land and pensions for the soldiers – a sum equivalent to the wealth of two Roman senates. Private patronage on this vast scale was possible only because Augustus was heir to the war-booty of a dozen conquests from Gaul to Egypt. His was the age of Rome's greatest imperial expansion. Between 133 and 9 BC, Rome gained all or most of Spain, Gaul, the Balkans, Asia Minor, Syria, the Levant, Egypt, Libya, and Numidia (modern Algeria). Between AD 6 and 138, by contrast, the only notable permanent additions to Roman territory were Britain, the upper Rhine-Danube region, Dacia (modern Romania), and Nabataean (or north-western) Arabia. Thereafter, in general, territory was lost, not gained. Latterly, Rome's wars were mainly reactive and defensive, fought as often on home ground as abroad; struggles to protect imperial territory and Roman property from barbarian raiders. These wars made work enough for Severus' 33 legions – a Roman army as big as that 200 years before – but now payment had to come from within the Empire itself. To survive and support a military budget no longer subsidised by plunder, the Roman state increased the wealth it extorted from civil society. Unable to rob barbarians abroad, the emperors robbed civilians at home. Like the mythical Erisychthon, whose hunger was so insatiable that he finally devoured himself, Imperial Rome, a predator-state in relentless search for prey, was transformed into a cannibal-state feeding off itself. And here – in the eating away of the economic and social infrastructures on which the military state rested – we find the deepest cause of the decline and fall of Rome.

The reign of Antoninus Pius (138-61) – for Gibbon the golden age *par excellence* – was a promise of peace and plenty which could not be fulfilled. For, as Roman military imperialism faltered, stalled and retreated, the scales tipped in favour of its enemies. In 167, with the western empire weakened by famine and plague, a powerful barbarian confederation broke through the upper Rhine-Danube frontier and invaded Italy. For the first time in 250 years, the Germans laid waste the Po valley. The emperor Marcus Aurelius (161-80) fought throughout the rest of his reign to eject the barbarians and stabilise the frontier. In the fierce fires of this struggle were forged the instruments of a new order. The desperate *ad hoc* measures of the later Antonine emperors (161-92) became, under their successors, the Severans (193-235), the solid substance of a political system. The frontier battles of the late second century spawned the military monarchy of the early third. Septimius Severus (193-211), founder of the new dynasty, was explicit about his regime's war on civil society: 'Make the soldiers rich and spurn everyone else,' he told his sons. Caracalla (211-17), the son who succeeded, agreed: 'Nobody in the world should have money but I, so that I may bestow it upon the soldiers.' Legionary pay, raised to 300 *denarii* a year by Domitian at the end of the first century, had remained unchanged for well over a century. Now Severus raised it to perhaps 450 *denarii*, and almost immediately Caracalla raised it again to perhaps 675 – a rise of 125 per cent in a generation. The aim was to increase recruitment, morale and loyalty. But who was to pay?

Various money-raising schemes were devised – all involving direct transfers of wealth from civil society to central state. Repressive inquisitions collected *bona damnatorum* ('the goods of the condemned') and filled the imperial treasury with the wealth of defeated civil-war opponents. The emperor made everyone legally 'Roman', so that all had to pay the citizen taxes on inheritance and manumission, and these, for good measure, were raised from 5 to 10 per cent. Payment of *aurum coronarium* ('coronation gold'), traditionally due only on the accession of a new emperor, was demanded every year. The coinage was debased: the government melted down old *denarii* and issued new double-*denarii* with a lower *pro rata* silver content – and pocketed the proceeds. This was not all. The army on campaign – increasingly inside imperial territory to check enemy penetrations – generated relentless demands for transports, billets and supplies. Deficiencies in general tax-receipts and the military commissariat were made up by extraordinary levies on the goods and services of communities in the army's line of march. Much the same was true of the court and other official parties as they moved about the Empire with their huge retinues of guards, orderlies, clerks, servants and flunkies. Countless opportunities for corrupt self-enrichment arose. State officials charged 'fees' to grant access to a magistrate or bring a case to court. Tax-assessors could be bribed to reduce obligations, or requisition-officers to pass by one farm and levy more heavily on the next. Bullying soldiery might extort with force (and impunity) whatever took their fancy. Each agent of the military monarchy, accountable only to those above, never those below, wielded his precious fragment of imperial power to personal advantage. The state became a junket.

From the emperor's estates in Lydia came four peasant petitions claiming ruin through arbitrary impositions, the cost of entertaining imperial officials, and bribes extorted under threat of imprisonment or death. In Egypt, many peasants, crushed by taxation, forced-labour services and extraordinary levies, abandoned their villages and fled to the city slums of Alexandria or to remote areas of the countryside beyond the law's reach. In the heart of Italy close to Rome itself, Bulla the bandit-chief, at large for two years at the head of 600 men, taunted his upper-class enemies: 'Feed your slaves if you would put a stop to brigandage.' But the war on civil society was unrelenting, and the ruthlessness of the military monarchy only increased. Herodian, a contemporary commentator, describes the situation in Africa under the rule of Maximinus Thrax (235-8):

[The emperor] expropriated whatever public funds there were – those collected for the grain supply or for distribution to the people, or earmarked for shows and festivals. Dedications in temples, statues of gods, honours to heroes, and whatever embellishment there was of a public nature, or adornment of a city, or material out of which money could be made – he melted down the lot ... In the cities and provinces the hearts of the masses were inflamed. Now that exactions were being made upon themselves, they resented the soldiers ... Maximinus was doing these things on behalf of the soldiers.

In the front-line of the class war between imperial officers and working masses were the *decuriones*, the landowning gentry of each locality organised as municipal councillors and magistrates. Until now, membership of the decurionate had, for most, been an honour. Roman society, as we have seen, awarded recognition and status not so much to those who amassed wealth as to those who dispensed it in lavish public service. A gentleman's power was secured by a thousand ties of patronage binding lesser men to him in debts of gratitude and obligation. The measure of a man was not wealth as such, but the weight of his influence (*auctoritas*) in public affairs (*negotium*), and this depended largely on his network of contacts and dependants. Service as town-councillors, municipal magistrates and high priests had, at least in the early empire, provided an opportunity for the exercise and enhancement of elite status. But there had always been a pay-off. The decurionate was collectively responsible for enforcing tax-payments and labour-services, for maintaining local infrastructure, and for upholding law and order. The councillors were personally liable in the event of failure: any shortfall could be made good by direct levies on their private estates. The balance of advantage offered by decurial service was, in consequence, always a modest one. Now, as state demands increased, the advantage began to be lost.

Regular taxes were increasing. Supplementary requisitions were more frequent. The new mobile army needed billets, supplies and transport services. Peasant labour was being drafted onto massive military construction-projects. Everywhere, among the dark masses, there was resentment and obstruction. It is a reasonable guess that across the Empire, in a thousand towns and a hundred thousand villages, largely hidden from history, a low-intensity class war was fought to frustrate the tax-collector and evade the press-gang. The decurionate was in the middle – squeezed between the mounting demands of the military monarchy and growing resistance from below. If enforcement was ruthless, the councillors' prestige was befouled by popular contempt; if enforcement was lax, their property was forfeit to the state. Under pressure, the gentry tried to withdraw from public life and the burdens of office. The decurionate began to disintegrate. The state, trying to stitch together the rotting fabric of local government, turned to the law: decurial service was declared compulsory, its delivery legally enforceable, and there were dire penalties for deserters.

The condition of the town councillor became a compound of compulsory and expensive duties, a standing threat of fines and confiscations, and the smouldering hostility of social inferiors. The trauma destroyed the cohesion and solidarity of the gentry as a class, and, pulled in opposing directions by the pressures from above and below, it shattered into antagonistic fragments. Boards of Ten (*decem primi* or *principales*), comprising the richest local decurions, now assumed responsibility for local government. One of their number would act as 'Guardian of the Community' (*curator civitatis*), an imperial agent directly accountable to central government and charged with overseeing local administration and financial management. A minority of rich grandees, owners of the largest local estates, thus became differentiated from the lesser gentry. Perhaps sometimes elevated to senatorial, equestrian or other honorific rank, and certainly networked into the power structures of the military monarchy, these grandees found in state power a valuable protection for their property and privilege. The majority of ordinary gentry, in contrast, those with only modest estates and little social weight, found that their lack of contacts and influence exposed them to the full vigours of state service. Power, privilege and property were re-crystallising around the state apparatus.

What evidence does Romano-British archaeology provide for this change? Can we detect the beginnings of a shift from a commonwealth of self-governing communities to a more centralised and militaristic empire in the Severan era? I have already discussed the relative decline of monumental building in Romano-British towns after *c*.150: the boom slowed down in the later second century and fizzled out almost completely in the early third. The need for further work was, of course, less now that the towns had acquired all the main amenities. But that is to oversimplify matters. Monumental architecture was only partly a matter of utility. It was also a highly prestigious activity, winning recognition, status and power for the benefactors; it expressed the competition to accumulate 'political capital' inherent in classical civilisation. It is for this reason that towns were often provided with buildings that strained resources to breaking point and exceeded any actual need; superfluity and waste were central features of antique urbanism. We considered earlier the case of Roman London's civic centre: an original *forum-basilica* complex built between *c*.75 and ?90 was abandoned in favour of an enormous replacement built around it in the years *c*.?95-130, but this new complex may never have been completed, parts were almost certainly never used, and before the end of the second century there seem to have been serious problems of subsidence, fire damage, building decay, and the prohibitive cost of repair and maintenance. It was too big and too expensive. It was not rational. It was an architectural display of grandeur, power and *Romanitas*. The decline of such public building therefore indicates not the logical end of a more-or-less rational process – the completion of an urban development plan – but the exhaustion of a certain type of essentially ideological energy. The Romano-British gentry's enthusiasm for urbanism waned as the burden of decurial service weighed more heavily. The resources to spare shrank. The military monarchy was leeching out from the provinces the material and moral reserves which had sustained the urban project. The fragile flower of Romano-British urban civilisation had no sooner opened than it began to wilt.

There were other priorities for town councils in late-second-century Britain. The German wars of 167-80 demanded heavy concentrations of Roman troops in defence of the imperial heartlands, and the security of marginal provinces like Britain was compromised. The Antonine Wall had to be abandoned, raiding and border-wars became endemic in the north, and reinforcements were needed from the continent. Then, in 180-4, Hadrian's Wall was overrun and successive governors were left struggling to restore control and rebuild the frontier defences. The Romano-British towns further south were prime targets for barbarian raiders. Most were open sites – the *Pax Romana* had made defences and garrisons unnecessary in the early empire – and inside them were the greatest concentrations of movable wealth in the province: gold and silver coin, rich jewellery and ornaments, exotic textiles and clothing, fine ceramic and glass tablewares, imported wine and other foreign delicacies, numerous animals and carts used for transportation, storehouses full of grain and other foodstuffs, and, not least, a large supply of potential slaves in the resident civilian populations. With the frontier defences down, the towns were perilously exposed, and their rulers rapidly set about constructing defensive circuits in earth and timber.

An order from above, rather than independent initiative, is strongly implied: the fortification of a town had to be authorised by the emperor, and the defences appear similar in character and date across the province. Deep ditches were dug to break the force of an enemy assault and expose it to a close-range hail of missiles. Upcast from the ditches was used to construct a high, wide, earth bank, revetted with timber-shuttering, and supporting a timber palisade along the top to form a protected fighting-platform for the defenders. Gateways were also built in timber, and of these there were commonly four, one on each side of the town. The earth-and-timber construction method, and the speed with which most previously open sites were enclosed, implies, if not panic, then concern and urgency. Such defences, nonetheless, would probably have deterred all but the largest and most determined of barbarian raiding-forces.

Towns are never static; they are constantly modified by the changing needs, aspirations and resources of those who live and work in them. But they have inertia: an infrastructure of material fabric, established institutions, networks of social relations, and the custom and practice of everyday life inherited from the past. No town can change all at once; some of the past is always carried forward into the present. For this reason, it is not enough simply to record the fullness of the ground-plans and the richness of the remains from Romano-British towns in this period. The archaeological record may, at the same time, contain clues that new forces were arising, forces which might threaten long-term prosperity. Three features of urban development in the late Antonine and Severan periods stand out in this respect: the boom in monumental architecture was coming to an end; the gentry were constructing grand town-houses in the residential areas; and public resources were being diverted into the hasty construction of defensive circuits (8). What was the meaning of these developments? Perhaps, when the government had insisted that labour gangs be mobilised to dig ditches and throw up banks and palisades around the towns, this had been one among many burdensome duties sapping the enthusiasm of the gentry for public life. And perhaps that, because of this, the grand municipal buildings of the early second century began to look tatty a few decades later, as the idealism and resources necessary for their maintenance and replacement failed. Instead, maybe, the gentry retreated a distance from the public arena into the privatised luxury of their new town-houses, where, one assumes, they were less accessible to the powers above, yet could still give adequate expression to their noble status in the efficient management of their property and estates, in the patronage of their private dependants, and in surrounding themselves with the trappings of classical culture. The tensions accumulating within the new military monarchy may, then, already have been apparent in the towns of Roman Britain. We might expect as much, for, in the early third century, the Roman Empire stood on the brink of its greatest crisis since the war against Hannibal. The age of gold was about to turn into an age of iron.

4

THE END OF THE ANCIENT WORLD

THE THIRD-CENTURY CRISIS, AD 235-84:
'ALL IS EVERYWHERE IN CONFUSION'

Some old-fashioned history books describe Rome's rulers between 96 and 180 as the 'Five Good Emperors'. The rule of Antoninus Pius (138-61) was, as noted above, especially praised as a 'golden age'. Such phrases are, of course, naïve. They were coined by gentlemen-classicists who viewed the Roman world from above – like the ancient historians whose work they cited. But any reappraisal – to encompass the full range of past experience and produce a more comprehensive picture – must still include the view from the top. For about a century, the Roman Empire was indeed remarkably united and stable. There had been a great civil war in 69, a palace assassination in 96, and an ugly military demonstration in Rome in 97. Thereafter, no civil war, revolution, coup or assassination disturbed the orderly succession of Trajan, Hadrian, Antoninus Pius, Marcus Aurelius, and Commodus. The Roman ruling class presented to its enemies at home and abroad a confident and solid front. Then things began to change. The reign of Commodus (180-92) was punctuated by a series of internal coups against successive chief-ministers, culminating in the assassination of the emperor himself. This sudden collapse of the Antonine dynasty detonated first a military revolt in Rome, and then a full-scale, three-sided civil war involving the frontier legions (192-7). The victor, Septimius Severus (193-211), consolidated his regime with ruthless persecution of defeated opponents. Caracalla (211-7), the dynastic successor, first killed his own brother to secure sole power, and was then assassinated himself by his Praetorian Guard commander. The Severans were restored after a brief civil war, but Elagabalus (218-22) proved to be a dangerous religious fanatic, and he was promptly murdered by members of his own family and replaced by Severus Alexander (222-35). Under the later Severan emperors, then, the Roman state lost much of its cohesion and splintered into warring factions. These splits at the top reflected long-fermenting and deep-cutting divisions within the Roman ruling class as a whole. After 235, the crisis worsened sharply and the military monarchy was torn apart.

The men of the Rhine army mutinied, murdered Severus Alexander, and elevated Maximinus Thrax, a rough Balkan soldier risen from the ranks. The Severan court was perceived as pro-eastern, short on martial spirit, and dominated by women; the soldiers of the German front had wanted one of their own to lead them. Maximinus plundered the Empire to support his German war, provoked a revolt of the propertied classes in Africa and Italy, and was then murdered by his own defeated and starving soldiers during the resultant civil war in 238. All the main elements of the 'third-century crisis' were present here in its opening moments. A regionally based rebellion by the Rhineland officer-corps had been directed against a court controlled by eastern favourites, officials and generals. The rebels were motivated in part by careerism: their belief that opportunities for advancement and enrichment in the imperial service were being monopolised by easterners. But officers embittered by poor promotion prospects cannot overthrow governments unless they tap into wider pools of discontent and opposition. The military monarchy lacked the resources to make all frontiers secure, forcing it to prioritise the defence of the more vulnerable sectors, where available men, military hardware, supplies and financial reserves were concentrated. This draining of resources to the main battlefronts left officers defending other frontiers dangerously weak. Forts, towns and villas were open to attack, plunder and devastation. A century of stable frontiers, fixed garrisons and local recruitment had forged strong bonds between soldiers and the districts where they served. Many men were defending families, homes and farms nearby. The centralism of the embattled Roman state was therefore challenged by strong regionalist allegiances within the army. Any state which cannot protect the territory and property of its citizens loses legitimacy. The Roman state of the mid-third century, lacking resources sufficient to the tasks imposed upon it, could give protection to some only by denying it to others. The Rhineland officers who destroyed the pro-eastern Severan regime were acting in the interests of the Romanised Celtic and Germanic elite of the north-western provinces as a whole. Such regionally based revolts were a central feature of the third-century crisis, and they would culminate in the formation of rival secessionist empires in different parts of the Roman world.

Cutting across the regional fracture-lines were other divisions: between soldiers and civilians. Emperors were under pressure to increase the exploitation of civil society in order to support a burgeoning arms-bill. Military expenditures – to keep frontier-defences up to scratch, to repel barbarian incursions, and, not least, to appease the soldiers' demands for pay, perks and pensions – were heavy and rising. But exploitation could provoke rebellion. Maximinus was assassinated by his own soldiers when a revolt of civilian property-owners in Africa spread to Italy and turned into full-scale civil war. The emperors were trapped in a 'scissors crisis': the *ad hoc* measures of the early military monarchy had not proved sufficient for the demands of the army, the frontiers and the wars; but further impositions yielded fast-diminishing returns as they faced evasion, obstruction and revolt. This conflict between a centralised, authoritarian, military state and the civilian communities within its territory operated at different levels. Central-government officials exploited their position within the power network to demand a pay-off for every 'favour'; and what began as informal corruption became, in time, a fixed tariff of charges based on the rank of the recipient and the value of the service. The urban *principales*, the ten state-backed grandees on each town council, dumped demands for payment of tax-arrears on fellow decurions who lacked the wealth and connections to secure protection. Regiments of rough, foreign, overbearing soldiers were billeted on hinterland towns and villages, where goods and services were extracted by force without payment. In the countryside, the peasants met the tax-squads and press-gangs sent out from the towns with lies, concealment and subterfuge, while in some more distant parts passive resistance turned active, and inaccessible hills, forests and marshes became the haunts of outlaws, bandits and rebels. A complex, drawn-out, multi-faceted class struggle pitted soldier against civilian, grandee against provincial, state against society. The war was coming home, and this resistance from below provoked, through the mid-third century, a series of revolts by officers alienated by regimes considered effete and incompetent.

The internal crisis was fuelled, and repeatedly brought to explosive condition, by a series of catastrophic military collapses on the frontiers. New peoples were pushing west and south through continental Europe, forcing a new militancy upon the German tribes of the Rhine and upper Danube, and bringing the scourge of the Goths to the middle and lower Danube. The barbarians were forging new polities in these fires of war. Small tribes were vulnerable both to Rome's centralised army and the barbarian hordes from the East. The pressure of military competition gradually dissolved the petty squabbles of local chieftains in great confederations able to engage in the battle of peoples now unfolding in continental Europe. There was new danger, too, on Rome's eastern front. In 224, the decadent and unstable Parthian Empire, shattered by military defeat and internal revolt, finally disintegrated. It was swept away by the Sassanids of Persia, who now seized control of the East, declared the old empire of Darius restored, and launched a war of *revanche* against the Graeco-Roman successors of Alexander. Henceforward, Rome would face an Orient strong, implacable and aggressive. The Sassanids would turn the great warrior tradition of the East – feudal armoured cavalry and clouds of light horse-archers – into a disciplined instrument of imperial power. On both the northern and eastern fronts, then, as on lesser fronts like the hills of northern Britain or the mountains of central Morocco, Rome's military advantage was crumbling.

We need not review the highly complicated course of events in detail. It is sufficient that the immense internal and external pressures on Roman imperial society produced a period of chronic political instability in which some forty official and rebel emperors rose and fell in a fifty-year succession of coups, revolutions and civil wars. The crisis reached its climax in the 260s under the emperor Gallienus (253-68). In the West, in both 258 and 260, the Alamanni crossed the Rhine, broke through the Roman defences, and poured across an open land of unwalled cities. The traumatised Roman elite abandoned allegiance to Gallienus, raised their own 'Gallic' emperor, and set about organising an independent defence of the north-west. In the East, in 260, Gallienus' co-emperor Valerian (253-60) was defeated and captured by the Sassanids, and here too, as in the West, responsibility for imperial defence passed into local hands. When Gallienus was killed in 268, the Empire seemed fatally stricken. The West was run by secessionist 'Gallic' emperors. The East was ruled by the independent queen of Palmyra. The North was threatened by German and Gothic invasions. Italy was controlled by a rebel Roman general. Earthquake, plague and famine had devastated the Empire. Taxation, requisitioning and compulsory services were crushing. The treasury was empty and the currency valueless. The hundred years between the German invasion of Italy in 167 and the assassination of Gallienus in 268 had so shifted the balance of world military power that the Roman state now seemed close to extinction.

But the forces ranged against Rome were still highly disparate and localised. They lacked the sense of purpose, organisational coherence and continental reach necessary to replace the Roman military monarchy. The Roman ruling class retained such resources of centralised political control and military power that the greatest of disasters could still be set right. The barbarians could invade and raid when the emperor's war-machine was elsewhere, but they could not hold when it returned for the counter-attack. Three great Illyrian soldier-emperors, risen from the ranks in the chaos of war, organised Rome's recovery and reform. Claudius Gothicus (268-70) destroyed armies of Germans and Goths to restore the northern frontier. Aurelian (270-5) liquidated the Palmyrene and Gallic empires to reunite the Roman state. Probus (276-82) consolidated these victories with further triumphs over German invaders, Asian bandits, and Gallic usurpers. No force had existed capable of destroying the Roman state at its moment of supreme crisis in the 260s – neither a coalition of invaders from without, nor a revolutionary class rising against it from within – so, having fought for its life and won, it came forth purged and reformed, its military machine leaner, fitter and stronger. The third-century crisis was to produce a late Roman counter-revolution orchestrated by the great reformer-emperors Diocletian (284-305) and Constantine (306-37). But this is to jump ahead. Let us first review the impact of the third-century crisis on Roman Britain.

The history and archaeology of the north-west frontier in Britain bear testimony to the power of the army under the military monarchy. In the early 180s, the soldiers of the British army mutinied against their disciplinarian governor Ulpius Marcellus, attempted unsuccessfully to make a legion commander called Priscus emperor, and then sent a delegation to Rome to participate in the overthrow and murder of Perennis, the leading minister in Commodus' government. A new governor, Pertinax, was sent to replace Ulpius Marcellus, but he fared little better than his predecessor: the troops mutinied again, events culminated in bloody repression, and Pertinax was recalled in 187. When Commodus was assassinated in 192, the British legions backed the then governor of the province, Clodius Albinus, in his challenge for supreme power, joining the civil war against Septimius Severus. The British army was one of the biggest in the Empire, and its mutinous temper in the 180s and 190s was a warning to the new Severan regime that emerged from the civil wars. While Severus and his elder son

Caracalla were campaigning in northern Britain in 208-11, his younger son Geta was charged with reforming provincial administration. Although information for Britain is lacking, we hear elsewhere of bloody assizes and property seizures to destroy the parties of Severus' defeated civil-war opponents. The emperor's agents must have been active in Britain after 197 rooting out former supporters of Clodius Albinus – everyone from the hopelessly implicated to the vaguely suspect. Now, or at least around this time, the Severan grip on Britain was tightened by its division into two provinces. The south – populous, prosperous and Romanised – was reorganised as Upper Britain (*Britannia Superior*); it probably retained London as its political capital and included the two legionary bases at Chester and Caerleon. The north – still largely a wild *barbaria* – became Lower Britain (*Britannia Inferior*); the capital was probably at York, where there was a legionary fortress, and the province included most of the auxiliary garrisons on the island. There is little doubting the purpose: Britain held a tenth of the Roman army, and such concentration of force in a single province – as the army mutinies of the recent past had shown – threatened internal security. The over-mighty subject was to be weakened permanently by a division of power.

Such purges and reforms were sufficient in the short run, but long-term stability meant regaining the soldiers' allegiance. Fear could impose obedience, but only favour would win back loyalty. The ancient world was very much a face-to-face society, and the presence of the emperor, his family and the court in Britain during 208-11 will have created countless ties of personal allegiance and obligation. The new regime offered many solid benefits: big pay rises, the right to marry and have families during service, and a promotion ladder open to talented officers risen from the ranks. In the garrison-forts, the austerity of second-century frontier life gave way to a new regime of comfort and ease. Many military building-inscriptions refer to improved amenities – ducted water for South Shields, an aqueduct repaired at Caernarvon, and bath-houses built or restored at Bowes, Lancaster and Lanchester. Other work was more strictly utilitarian, but the new or reconstructed barrack-blocks, drill-halls and granaries recorded on inscriptions no doubt added further to the general comfort and convenience of the rank and file. This was also the period, as we have seen, when military *vici* or markets were permitted to develop outside the northern forts, their communities of petty-traders and camp-followers doing much to ease the rigours of military life. The military-civilian distinction became blurred: many civilians probably had easy access to the forts, perhaps to undertake dirty jobs the soldiers did not fancy, or to negotiate the terms of military contracts; some soldiers probably lived in family accommodation in the *vici*, while others must have spent much of their off-duty time lounging about in its bars and brothels. Bath-houses, occasionally inside forts, usually outside, may have been particular levellers, places where soldiers and civilians mingled freely and easily. The *vici* were, after all, among the principal recruiting-grounds of the late Roman army, where the sons of soldiers were expected to follow their fathers into 'the regiment'. But if life was easy in these northern army settlements in the third century, much of this was due to the *Pax Romana* won by the Severan emperors in the campaigns of 208-11.

The Romans had pulled back from Scotland after the death of Severus in 211, and Caracalla had anchored the northern frontier again on Hadrian's Wall. Rebuilding had been more or less continuous under the Severan governors, with much work on the Pennine forts in 197-208, intensive work on both Wall and outpost forts in 205-25, and some further work thereafter until as late as the 260s. This restored third-century frontier, in contrast to the vicissitudes of the second century, would endure. The curtain-wall itself was run down – many turrets were filled in and some milecastle gateways were narrowed or even blocked – but the forts were maintained with improved defences and stronger garrisons. Four outpost forts north of the Wall in particular – Netherby and Bewcastle in the west, Risingham and High Rochester in the east – received enlarged and more mobile garrisons. The proportion of cavalry on the frontier as a whole was increased from a quarter to a third. Special units of rangers (*exploratores*) were formed, and there is cartographic evidence (in a late seventh-century geographical compendium known as the 'Ravenna Cosmography') for Roman supervision over places of meeting and exchange across the Southern Uplands. Traprain Law hillfort, probable capital of the traditionally pro-Roman Votadini tribe, peaked in size in the third century, and many high-status Roman trade-objects have been found there. A new strategic system is implied. The war of 208-11 must have shifted the balance of power against the anti-Roman elements north of the Wall. The tribes of the Southern Uplands may not have participated in the war at all, in which case they perhaps welcomed fuller Roman intervention to protect them against powerful neighbours further north, or, if they were protagonists (the 'Maeatae' of the ancient sources), they must have been effectively cowed by fire and sword, and their old war-leaders replaced by moderates prepared to accept the formal status of client rulers under loose Roman sovereignty. In return for Roman backing and subsidy they would suppress the border-raiders and 'bitter-enders' within their own territory, and provide a buffer between the Wall and any still-hostile barbarians in the Central Lowlands and Highlands. Roman soldiers, especially from the outpost forts, patrolled and policed the region. Probably, as on the Danube at this time, there were bans on inter-tribal warfare, cross-border raiding, and unauthorised assemblies, and there may have been tribute and conscript levies. The fragile *Pax Romana* in the Southern Uplands meant that Hadrian's Wall no longer 'separated the barbarians from the Romans' and its maintenance mattered less. But strong garrisons in the Wall forts remained essential as a strategic reserve to support Rome's insecure and unreliable friends. We hear little of trouble in the north for the rest of the century. Perhaps the ancient sources, so scrappy for the third century generally, were too preoccupied with bigger events elsewhere to notice low-intensity fighting in northern Britain; or perhaps the Severan frontier system really worked. We cannot be sure – but the stability of the new Roman frontier dispositions is beyond doubt, and that alone constitutes a sharp contrast with the preceding century.

Further south, though, the anguish of the third-century crisis is more apparent. We noted above the reduced rate of public-building construction in the later second century, and a shift towards the provision of large private town-houses for the municipal gentry. Many towns probably had a score or more of these by the early third century, but then, abruptly, the private-housing boom collapsed. For the fifty or so years of the crisis, civic construction-work in Romano-British towns was severely depressed. In the years *c*.250-75, work on public buildings was only about a quarter of that in *c*.200, work on private buildings about a third (*8*). There was some decline in the countryside, too, where construction-work on villas in *c*.225 was down to less than two-thirds of the peak 75 years before (*18*). The luxury trades were also in recession: long-distance trading of fineware pottery was much reduced, and hardly any mosaics can be dated to this period. The evidence is in sharp contrast to the oft-repeated claim that Roman Britain was unaffected by the third-century crisis, an island haven of peace and prosperity while the continent was ravaged by war, revolution and slump. In fact, third-century Britain, whatever its peculiar features, was part of a world system in crisis, and its archaeology bears the scars of trauma. The municipal gentry, dumped on from above by the officers of the imperial state and obstructed from below by an intractable peasantry, were a decaying class with neither the will nor the resources to undertake further Romanisation.

Power and priorities had changed. In the later second century, the previously undefended towns had been surrounded by circuits comprising ditches, earth ramparts and timber palisades. Probably there had been urgency and haste: it would have to do for now. But earth slumps and timber rots, whereas stone endures. Anyway, a bank and a fence are much less serious obstacles than a solid wall. The emergency of the 180s may have been the context for the first defences, but insecurity must have remained acute, for in the following century the Romano-British towns acquired stone-built *enceintes*. The stone defences of *Verulamium*, probably built in *c*.220-70, ran for 2 miles

(3.5km) around the town, had an average thickness of 2.5m, a height of perhaps 4m, and comprised a core of mortared rubble, walls of roughly cut flint, and tile bonding-courses (*20*). There were two large gateways, probably three small ones, and a number of projecting towers. In addition, the wall was supported by a 15m-wide earth rampart, and, except on the north-east side where it was fronted by the river, a massive ditch was dug in front, 6m deep and 25m across. It was a colossal undertaking for a traditional agricultural community – about 10 million pounds' worth costed in modern money. The earlier earth-and-timber defences had cost only a fraction as much: the post-Boudican '1955 Ditch' perhaps one-twentieth, the mid-second-century 'Fosse' perhaps one-tenth. Heavy drafts of local peasant labour must have worked on the third-century walls for decades. It is hardly a surprise that civil construction-work all but collapsed at this time. In *Verulamium*'s wall, much of it still standing impressively, we see the policy and power of the military monarchy to direct local resources into imperial defence. But if there was peace on the northern frontier, why was the defence of Upper Britain, the Romanised heart of the island, such a priority? It seems that a new enemy had arisen.

THE SCOURGE OF THE NORTHERN SEAS

Hygelac's thane ... was the greatest in might among men at that time, noble and powerful. He bade a good ship to be built for him ... The valiant man had chosen warriors of the men of the Geats, the boldest he could find; with fourteen others he sought the ship. A man cunning in knowledge of the sea led them to the shore. Time passed on; the ship was on the waves, the boat beneath the cliff. The warriors eagerly embarked. The currents turned the sea against the sand. Men wore bright ornaments, splendid war-trappings, to the bosom of the ship. The men, the heroes on their willing venture, shoved out the well-timbered ship. The foamy-necked floater like a bird went then over the wave-filled sea, sped by the wind, till after due time on the next day the boat with twisted prow had gone so far that the voyagers saw land, sea-cliffs shining, the steep headlands, the broad sea-capes. Then the sea was traversed, the journey at an end. The men of the Weders mounted thence quickly to the land; they made fast the ship. The armour rattled, the garments of battle. They thanked God that the sea voyage had been easy for them. (*Beowulf*)

The area of modern Denmark and north-west Germany had always remained outside the Roman Empire. It was occupied by three large groups of Germanic people: the Jutes of north Denmark, the Angles of south Denmark, and the Saxons of north-west Germany. These groups are recorded in later historical sources, such as the work of the Venerable Bede in the early eighth century, and they can be detected archaeologically by subtle differences in material remains, like different pottery styles. Broadly, though, they shared a similar Iron Age culture, and, since they also came to play a similar historical role, the ancient writers referred to them all simply as 'Saxons'. This term does no harm and remains convenient: the eruption of Jutes, Angles and Saxons in the third to fifth centuries was a uniform phenomenon. Our knowledge of them is still modest. Many lived in villages near the coast, often very low-lying, and long accumulations of occupation-debris on these sites have left mounds known as 'terps' which define the extent of settlement areas. These villages comprised a number of rectangular timber 'long-houses', each partitioned inside for domestic accommodation at one end and animal-stalling and storage at the other. There were often also small sunken-floored huts, probably used as ancillary buildings for domestic crafts like weaving and pottery, or as additional storage-space. These were small agricultural communities, with little social differentiation, and a lack of larger, higher-status sites in the Saxon homeland implies that political power was decentralised, kinship-based and paternalistic. But it was also a warrior culture. Caches of rich weaponry have been found, ritually buried in the bogs as offerings to unknown pagan deities, and sometimes among these are

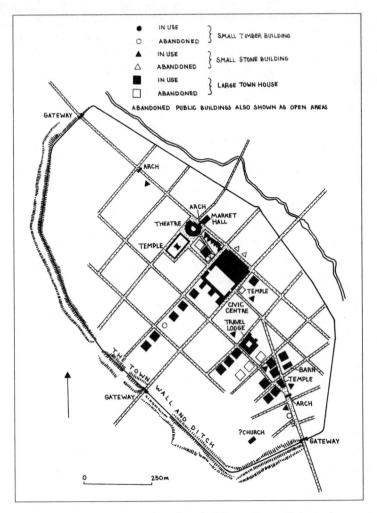

20 Verulamium *in c.325. Benefiting from the 'Constantian renaissance', when many Romano-British towns experienced significant rebuilding and renovation, Verulamium was still vibrant. But the town was changing: massive mid-third-century investment in a stone wall circuit had turned the place into a fortress, and some town-house plots had already been abandoned for good.* After Wheeler, Frere and Niblett hoards of captured Roman gear, including brooches, shields, swords, spear-heads, military breast-decorations, and even cavalry parade-helmets. This, then, was a society organised and equipped for war, where the highest value was given to arms and armour, and the greatest prestige to men who won glory and booty in battle. The long-house, we might surmise, was home to a farmer-warrior, master over family and dependants in his own household. The village comprised a group of such farmer-warriors, fellow-clansmen maybe who owed allegiance to a clan-chief in their own village or another nearby. Saxon warfare was endemic but small-scale, the organised raid a frequent event but involving only a small band numbered in tens away from home for a week or two. The glory won would nonetheless be recorded in epic poems recited for evermore round the winter hearth. The booty seized would be conspicuously consumed – displayed on long-house walls, distributed as gifts to worthy retainers, or deposited as offerings to the bog-god. Warrior status would be affirmed and enlarged. The social order would be secured.

By the third century, this society was under stress. In the following century, some of the coastal settlements of Denmark and north-west Germany contracted, and in the fifth most were abandoned. Rises in sea level were general in this period, and many Saxon settlements were perhaps lost to inundation. Ecological crisis was a central feature of long-term change in the ancient world, and much Saxon land was viable by only the smallest of margins. But where could displaced Saxons go? To the south-west lay the formidable frontier-defences of the Roman Empire, and to the south and east were powerful Germanic and Gothic confederations, themselves driven west under the pressure of migrations started deep in Central Asia. The small war-bands of Saxon clan-chiefs counted for little in the titanic folk-movements and peoples' wars now beginning. Failed by their gods and displaced by nature, yet barricaded into the continent's far north-west by more powerful neighbours, the Saxons were land-starved, impoverished and desperate. Marginalised by history, the choice was extinction or war. When they appear in the works of ancient writers at the end of the third century, they inspire a terrible fear: tall, strong, heavily-armed barbarian warriors, emerging from the sea as from nowhere, suddenly, without warning, to strike with merciless cruelty, to deal death and devastation on the innocent and defenceless. Only much later do they speak to us with their own voices: the surviving literature of the Anglo-Saxons, such as *Beowulf*, belongs to a period long after the Heroic Age of the third to fifth centuries. Even then, the passage above describes an event that was peaceful and ceremonial, not hostile. Perhaps the closest we get in medieval literature to finding a window into the mind of the sea-raider is this extract from *Egil's Saga*, a much later Norse poem (suggested to me and translated by John Frankis):

> ... there must be brought for me
> a ship and fine oars
> to travel away with Vikings
> to stand up in the prow
> to steer the beloved vessel
> to keep course then to harbour
> to hew down a man or two.

As with the Vikings of the ninth, the Saxons of the third century had evolved into a culture which placed a premium on seafaring, slaughter and spoil. The pressures on Saxon society must have enhanced the role and status of the warrior: success in war can win wealth, land and power, and warfare will intensify when these are scarce and contested. All competitive struggle favours the strong, and war, the ultimate struggle, favours them most of all. Big war-bands defeat small war-bands; great lords subordinate village-chiefs; military power becomes more centralised, lethal, terrible. There was, above all, the matter of ships. For long, probably, the Saxons had used ships, and some no doubt had used them in war. But a seaborne raid is no light matter. A number of Saxon long-ships have been found (though all of later date). They were usually constructed of overlapping planks ('clinker-built') with high bows and sterns, ranging from 15 to 30m in length, and from 3 to 5m in the beam. Some, those with tightly curved end-posts and deeper keels, seem especially adapted for the heavy waves of long sea-voyages. The ships had no masts or sails but were powered by between 14 and 40 oarsmen. For Saxon society, the vessel, the equipment and the supplies necessary for a long-distance raid must have represented a huge investment of resources. The number of warriors needed as complement for such an expedition must imply a similar investment of prestige. A Channel raid was the work of a great warrior-chief. Economic crisis, military intensification, political centralisation: these were the features of Saxon society which, during the third century, gave birth to the Germanic pirates of the northern seas.

Ancient writers first refer to seaborne attacks on Britain in the late third century, but this proves nothing, since surviving contemporary accounts are meagre for the period 235-84, and such as there are remain preoccupied with great events on the continent. We have no reason to expect a written record of the earliest Saxon raids – such episodic, low-scale threats to one of Rome's most marginal territories were hardly likely to have attracted much notice at this time. Archaeology is more informative: there is a pattern of third-century sites in the south-east best explained as a military response to attacks from the sea (*21*). One feature of this was the walling of the towns noted above. Many were close to the sea or on navigable rivers. Their improved third-century defences would certainly have made them secure against small Germanic war-bands, and, if provided with flotillas and garrisons, they would have guarded access routes into the hinterland. There is no reason to assume the deployment of regular Roman troops. The municipalities were certainly authorised – and most probably ordered – to construct town-walls. It would be rather surprising if they were not at the same time expected to make some provision for local self-defence, perhaps by creating a militia, perhaps by hiring mercenaries; town-walls mean little without men on the parapets. But this would still have left gaps in the line through which raiders could pass. These were filled by other, purely military, installations. The old naval bases of the British Fleet (*classis Britannica*) were remodelled to play an enlarged role – Dover definitely, Richborough probably, and Lympne possibly. Elsewhere new forts were constructed on virgin sites. Three are likely to have been built in the first half of the century. Brancaster, near the Wash on the north-west Norfolk coast, covered the approaches to the Witham, Welland, Nene and Ouse river-systems, which offered raiders deeply penetrating access routes into the Fenland, East Anglia, the Midlands and Lincolnshire. Caister-on-Sea on East Anglia's east coast covered the large tidal inlet into which the Yare and Bure river-systems emptied. And Reculver on the north Kent coast complemented Richborough and Rochester in covering the approaches to the Lower Thames estuary. Each of these forts was built in the old style: they had traditional 'playing-card' shapes – rectangles with rounded corners – and they lacked the heavily-defensive features characteristic of later Roman military architecture. By mid-century, then, a defensive screen was emerging in the south-east to guard coastal landing-points and the major river-systems. It comprised a line of walled towns and military bases, presumably networked together by signal-stations, offshore patrols and the excellent road-system, with armed flotillas, detachments of regulars and a local militia available to meet an attack.

It was not enough. The military pressure on Britain and the north-west provinces increased in the later third century, and the political tension soon exploded in revolt and secession.

THE REVOLT OF CARAUSIUS, AD 286-296

The north-west was under threat from Saxon and Frankish sea-raiders and from Germanic armies massed across the lower Rhine. Yet this was not the central government's prime concern in the mid-third century. More immediate dangers were posed by the Sassanids, who threatened the rich provinces of the East, and by the Germans

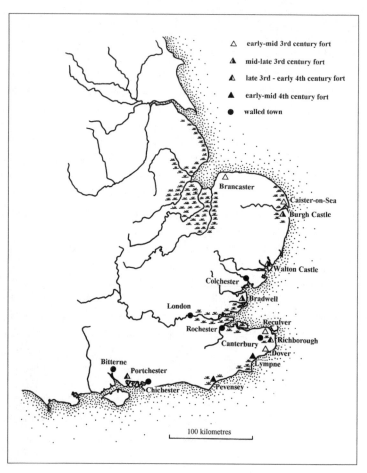

21 Late Roman defences on the 'Saxon Shore'. A line of forts and walled towns developed between the early third and mid-fourth centuries along the south-east coast of Britain. Probably there were also signal-stations, naval patrols, home-defence flotillas, and strong garrisons. The term 'Saxon Shore' occurs only in a late-fourth-century source, but circumstantial evidence strongly suggests that this defensive screen was anti-Saxon in intent from its inception

and Goths ranged along the Danube within striking distance of Italy and Greece. On these battlefronts were to be found the soldier-emperors, the top generals, the best regiments, and the lion's share of military hardware and supplies. The property and position of the Celtic and German grandees of the north-west were thus left exposed and insecure. In self-defence, they came to espouse a politics of north-western nationalism, regionalist revolt and secessionist imperialism. They found ready support among the army rank-and-file, the local gentry, and the urban petty-traders, all of whom felt abandoned and endangered by a distant government preoccupied elsewhere. In the years 258-9, the Rhine-Danube line was assailed simultaneously at several points, the emperor Gallienus' defences collapsed, and the barbarians broke into the Empire. Postumus (259-69) broke with Gallienus (253-68), declared himself emperor, and was soon recognised by all Germany, Gaul, Spain and Britain. Succeeded in due course by Victorinus (269-71) and Tetricus (271-3), his secessionist 'Gallic Empire' endured as a wholly independent Roman state for almost fifteen years; only in 273 did military victories on other fronts leave the legitimate emperor Aurelian (270-5) free to use his main field-army to crush the rebels. But secessionism remained latent. Although the last of the Gallic emperors had been discredited by military failures against the barbarians, the restored central empire fared no better, and in 276 a massive German attack broke down the Rhine defences again and captured fifty Gallic towns. The frontier districts never fully recovered from the massacre, devastation and plunder, and in the bitter aftermath of defeat the secessionist banner was raised again. In 281, the Roman general Bonosus, with Gaulish and perhaps British and Spanish support, led an abortive revolt against the legitimate emperor Probus (276-82). The following year, Probus dispatched Victorinus to Britain to suppress rebellion there – presumably a continuation of the Bonosus revolt or a reaction to its defeat by die-hard opponents of the legitimist regime. Secessionist sentiment was then in abeyance for a few years, perhaps because the senior emperor Carus (282-3) made his son Carinus (282-5) junior emperor in charge of the West, where he defeated the barbarians and assumed the titles 'Conqueror of the Germans' (*Germanicus Maximus*) and 'Conqueror of the Britons' (*Britannicus Maximus*). Well protected by a legitimate emperor with an effective field-army, the north-west provinces had no reason to revolt. A moment of loyalty in the presence of the emperor, it soon passed, and the north-west again looked to its own defence. For the third time in a generation, Britain was to be removed from central control by a rebel emperor.

Carausius was a local man made good in the imperial service. We know that he had been born on the Belgian coast, had served with distinction in the Roman army, and was then appointed in 285 to the command of a fleet based at Boulogne and charged with clearing the Channel of Frankish and Saxon pirates. The sources for his career are hostile panegyrists – court poets of the legitimist emperors who composed works of fawning praise for their masters – so we are obliged to read between the lines. By 286, Carausius' campaign against the pirates had achieved some success, but he was accused of keeping the booty he recovered rather than returning it to the provincials or handing it over to the imperial treasury. The emperor Maximian decided to arrest him as a traitor, and in self-defence Carausius revolted, seized northern Gaul and Britain, and declared himself joint ruler with the two legitimist emperors. The rebel empire was, for a time, successful. Carausius clearly had the allegiance of the troops in the north-west, and when Maximian sailed down the Rhine with a new fleet in 289 to confront the rebels, something went badly wrong, for the panegyrists, while recording the expedition, are strangely silent about its fate. The strength of the rebel regime gives the lie to the court poets' claim that Carausius was nothing more than a criminal.

More likely, the story of the booty was a garbled and distorted version of some dispute about resources and priorities – and this, no doubt, was the heart of the matter. In contrast to a distant legitimist emperor preoccupied with events on the Euphrates or the Danube, Carausius was a successful military commander with a strong local base committed to the defence of the north-west. He used his control of the British mines to stop the export of bullion from the region and to create a reformed high-standard coinage (in contrast to the debased and inflationary issues of the central empire). The resources of the territory he controlled were deployed to improve local defences rather than being siphoned off to Central Europe. We learn from the court poet Eumenius, for instance, that Carausius diverted regular troops to his own service in the north-west, hired Frankish mercenaries to augment his forces, and built many new warships to enlarge his existing fleet. Archaeology indicates that a number of new 'Saxon Shore' forts were built in the late third century, and it seems likely that some, if not all, of this work was due to Carausius (*21*). The rebel emperor's political appeal was probably considerable, both to the soldiers stuck in the remote, isolated, rundown army-bases of the north-west, and to the grandees and gentry of Britain and northern Gaul, who wanted effective protection for their property, which, in the circumstances, seemed more likely from the independent regime than the legitimist one.

Much of our understanding of the regime depends upon its own 'sound-bite' propaganda: the images and legends on Carausian coins. Guy de la Bédoyère's research has recently added greatly to our knowledge of this much-studied subject. The very fact that good-quality silver coins were circulating again – at 90 per cent purity, they were the best for over two hundred years – was itself a powerful argument for the legitimacy of the issuing authority; the contrast with the shabby, base-metal coins of the recent past was especially stark. But the Carausian 'director of communications', whoever he was, identified some key themes for the regime, and these were hammered onto some of the coins produced by the London mint in the years of independence. Virgil was plundered for ideas about a second coming, a new beginning, and an imminent golden age, and Carausius was presented as a saviour-ruler arriving to deliver his people from bondage. One coin depicts him on horseback with the legend 'the coming of the emperor' (*adventus augusti*); another has him in messianic posture with the appeal 'come, expected one' (*expectate veni*) addressed to him; many silver and some gold coins bear the letters *RSR*, thought to stand for *redeunt Saturnia regna*, 'the reign of Saturn is back' – in other words, 'the golden age has returned'. These paraphrases of Virgil are cunning. They combine the promise of a new start after a period of crisis and failure with the reassurance that order, property and tradition remain secure. The respectable classes need have no fear: weak central government has been replaced by strong local government, one equally firm in the suppression of barbarian piracy and civil disturbances. Further reassurance was provided by issues which harped on familiar Roman themes: Carausius delivered 'imperial victory' (*victoriae augustorum*) and 'imperial peace' (*pax augustorum*), and thus he was 'the restorer of Britain' *(restitutor Britanniae)* and 'the spirit of Britain' (*genius Britanniae*). Moreover, he was a reliably 'normal' sort of emperor: he claimed descent not only from the Olympian gods (as did the legitimist emperors Diocletian and Maximian at this time), but also from the great Marcus Aurelius, the philosopher-king, whose names he adopted as his own; and, to add political to divine and genealogical legitimacy, he awarded himself two consulships, thus becoming holder of Rome's highest magistracy and honour. All quite unexceptional; all reassuringly normal. So the character of the regime seems clear: it was thoroughly conservative, elitist and Roman, but it represented a concentration of resources for the defence of the north-west. It was, then, a government of Romanised officers and landowners in Britain and northern Gaul. This, though, was both its strength and its weakness.

The Carausian government existed as a reaction against the movement of troops, hardware and supplies out of the region. It concentrated military power in the north-west and this won it strong local support. Carausius could not, therefore, challenge the legitimist government of Diocletian and Maximian for supreme power, because to try to move his army against them would be to destroy his own power-base. The rebel regime was rooted to the spot. The best to be hoped for was recognition as a co-equal emperor. Carausian coins honoured Diocletian and Maximian and implied a tripartite division of the Roman world; one most explicit coin-issue depicted busts of all three emperors surrounded by the legend 'Carausius and his brothers' (*Carausius et fratres sui*). Such compliments were not reciprocated by the legitimist mints. Britain, as the court poet explained, 'was a land that the state could ill afford to lose, so plentiful are its harvests, so numerous are the pasturelands in which it rejoices, so many are the metals whose seams run through it, so much wealth comes from its taxes, so many ports encircle it, to such an immense area does it extend'. So the central government wanted it back. It was, in short, too valuable a source of bullion, revenues, supplies and recruits to lose. Prestige was also at stake: rebellion had to be seen to be punished or it might spread. As the early-second-century historian Florus had put it, the continued possession of Britain was essential 'to the bearing of imperial power' (he considered the island otherwise worthless).

In 293, Constantius Caesar, the new junior emperor in the West, launched a second attack on the rebel regime. Boulogne and north-western Gaul fell swiftly and the rebel empire was reduced to Island Britain. Carausius, politically damaged by defeat, was overthrown, murdered and replaced by his finance minster Allectus. Then, for three years, both sides prepared themselves for the coming struggle. Constantius' invasion force, when it sailed in the summer of 296, must have been a vast armada, comparable with 54 BC, AD 43, 1066 and 1588. Hundreds of vessels had probably been commandeered or constructed in the Gallic ports, and thousands of men, veterans from the frontiers and new levies of provincials and mercenaries, embarked. The crossing was made in two divisions: one, under Asclepiodotus, heading for the Solent, the other, under Constantius himself, for the Thames. Asclepiodotus eluded the defending British fleet, made safe landfall, burned his boats, and then marched inland to confront and defeat the army of Allectus in a great battle somewhere in south-central Britain. The rebel emperor died in the fighting. His routed Frankish mercenaries threatened London. Constantius' division arrived in the Thames just in time to save the capital and complete the victory. A commemorative gold medallion found near Arras in France depicts Constantius Caesar, mounted and in armour, clutching a spear and wearing a victory-wreath, riding along the Thames towards the city to be greeted by a kneeling female figure representing *Britannia* or *Londinium*. The legend describes him as 'restorer of the eternal light' (*redditor lucis aeternae*). The ten-year-old British Empire was dissolved. The British provinces were returned to Rome. By now, though, the late Roman counter-revolution, long-prepared in the storm and strife of the third century, was coming to completion, and the Empire which Britain rejoined in 296 was very different from that of the Antonine emperors over a century before.

5

THE LATE ROMAN
COUNTER-REVOLUTION

The crisis of the 260s had been revolutionary. The Roman state had rotted so completely that a determined push would have crumbled it to dust. But the apocalypse was averted; the Empire survived. Rome's enemies failed to destroy her. The Germanic and Gothic barbarians of continental Europe lacked the will, the cohesion and the strength to conquer and settle the territories they repeatedly devastated. In the East, for all their vigour, the Sassanid kings were hamstrung by the very vastness of their sprawling, makeshift, rebellious empire; their offensive power was easily soaked up by these sandy wastelands. At home, the Roman ruling class, however unpopular, faced no effective challenge from below. Neither gentry nor peasantry were truly national classes able to contend for state power. The gentry were organised in a thousand towns, the peasantry in a hundred thousand villages; thus atomised, their outlooks were essentially local and limited, their ability to influence imperial politics dependent on the mediation of others. The provincial gentry might back a regional usurper. The local peasantry might lynch the tax-collector or ambush the press-gang. But however degraded and demoralised by the crisis, however hostile to the state power, these two principal subordinate classes of the late empire could not threaten revolution. Each lacked the collective organisation, the all-empire perspective, and that essential ingredient of successful revolt from below: a grand vision of how the future might be recast for the better. The only truly national class was the imperial aristocracy. Overthrown neither by foreign military conquest nor by internal revolution in the 260s, it survived as arbiter of its own history. And the abortive revolution thus culminated in its nemesis: a late Roman counter-revolution to shore up the privilege and power of the imperial grandees for an entire epoch.

The crisis of the imperial state has been discussed above: a compound of military defeat, foreign invasion, palace coup and secessionist revolt, rooted in the central government's lack of sufficient resources for frontier defence. The solution was simple enough: to increase the amount of surplus wealth siphoned from the provinces to the central state – that is, to enrich further the court at the expense of the towns, the soldiers at the expense of the peasants, and the grandees at the expense of the gentry. Military monarchism writ large. Not, then, as it was called by Peter Brown, a 'late Roman revolution', but the reverse of this: a counter-revolution, in which state power was intensified to guarantee the survival of the established order. In the years 268-337, the Roman Empire was reformed so radically by a succession of strong soldier-emperors that the European world of the mid-fourth century was as different from that of the mid-third as the latter had been from that of the mid-second. Every aspect of the state's operations was affected, from the way taxes were collected at the most remote farmstead, to the career prospects of the most highly placed courtier. The result was an empire, an economic system and a late antique world which were, to the limits imposed by pre-industrial existence, despotic, totalitarian and militaristic.

Diocletian (284-305) symbolised the new order. Like all conservative reformers – as so many emperors were – he claimed to be a traditionalist. But, like Claudius Gothicus, Aurelian and Probus, he was a tough soldier-emperor risen from the ranks, a practical man of action, a defender of the established order by whatever means necessary. His successor, Constantine the Great (306–37) was somewhat different: as a son of the junior emperor Caesar Constantius, he was, in a sense, born to the purple, but this, if anything, gave him the personal confidence and political security to carry the reforms to far more radical conclusions. Constantine brought the late Roman counter-revolution to completion, and by the end of his reign a new, as it were, post-classical and proto-medieval world had come into existence. In reviewing its principal features, we shall start at the top, with the emperor and his court.

The early imperial court had been static and palatial: the emperors had usually resided at Rome, their palace complexes dominating the Palatine Hill overlooking the Forum, so that the city was the political centre of the Graeco-Roman world. The late imperial court, on the other hand, was mobile: the emperors moved around the Empire, from one administrative centre or army-base to another, accompanied by an ever-changing entourage of courtiers, officials, soldiers, clerks and flunkies. The *Pax Romana* had been irrevocably shattered, and Rome's commander-in-chief was needed at the front. If he preferred the fleshpots of the Palatine, the soldiers could give allegiance to other men – hard men more like themselves, bred in the army-camps of the frontier. War drove the emperors from the ease of the palace-courts of Rome to the rigours of the ever-moving, ever-changing, peripatetic courts of the late empire – from *palatium* ('palace') to *comitatus* ('retinue'). But if the relationship between emperor and soldier was recharged by physical proximity, it was also reformulated. The early emperors had cast themselves as *principes* ('leading men'), maintaining the fiction they were old-style republican magistrates holding office under the authority of Senate and People; most were tactful enough to avoid offending aristocratic sensibilities. They were not constitutional monarchs – military autocrats better describes them – but, true to their Graeco-Roman cultural inheritance, they eschewed the paraphernalia of an 'oriental despotism'. But there were dangers here. The succession was determined by merit not birth, the divine sanction fell only on the deserving, and the legitimacy of these men who were merely 'first among equals' was ever open to question. A slip or two and one might seem no longer 'the best man'; there were always others, possible alternatives, as yet untried and unsullied.

The third century, of course, was a testing time: the vicissitudes of war and revolution ripped away the cover from each mistake and mishap, exposing every flaw and failing. Half-hearted claims to divine status had been made for emperors since the time of Augustus, but this hardly squared with traditional emphasis on republican propriety. The emperor, in practice, had remained firmly rooted in the world of men, and the reputation of any who had in their time aspired to a higher station – Caligula, Nero, Domitian, Commodus – had afterwards been drowned in abuse and ridicule. Emperors in troubled times needed a mystique of power and an aura of divinity – a touch of the royal – to lift them clear of the blame attributable to mortal men. Dress, decorum and distance now separated monarch from people. Those who entered the serene presence were required to debase themselves in worship (*adoratio*). The imperial bedchamber (*sacrum cubiculum*) became an important court department, the imperial eunuch-chamberlains important court officials (*cubicularii*). The rulers openly proclaimed their descent from the gods – Diocletian from Jupiter, his co-emperor Maximian from Hercules. The royalism latent in the military dictatorship had long been held in check by the reality of imperial power: where there was substance, there was no need of fiction. But the crisis – the defeats, the secessions and the coups – had degraded and diminished the purple office. So the emperors floated off into the stratosphere, where, elevated to heaven, weakness could masquerade as strength. At the highest pinnacle, the alienated politics of crisis and counter-revolution found true expression in royal mysticism: the embattled dictator became an invincible god.

In part, it was the tense equilibrium of competing forces within the Empire that permitted this 'orientalising' of the monarchy: the emperor was lifting himself above the warring factions below. In other respects, too, the crisis was reshaping the monarchy. Regional secessionism had created in the third century a series of usurper-emperors dedicated to local defence. This dangerous centrifugalism was now neutralised in a multiple-monarchy: henceforward, there would be not one emperor, remote and pre-occupied, but two, three, or four, so that every region would have its own supreme ruler. Sometimes in the past there had been such multiple-monarchs – whether by agreement, in awkward co-existence, or open conflict. But now, as in so many things, past practice *ad hoc* became regular system. In 286, Diocletian took Maximian as his colleague and divided the government of the empire in two, himself keeping the East, his co-emperor receiving the West. In 293, each senior emperor (*Augustus*) adopted a junior (*Caesar*), Galerius in the East, Constantius in the West, and government was thereby further divided into four distinct geographical spheres. Thus was the Tetrarchy, the Rule of Four, created, and though it survived barely a moment beyond the retirement of its founder in 305, it converted the episodic occurrence of multiple-monarchies in the third century into a constitutional principle to be revisited in the fourth. This had its downside: the usurpers of the third century had had to build their political infrastructures from scratch; those of the fourth would find them ready-made. The first such political crisis in the new century, the one which brought down Diocletian's carefully-crafted Tetrarchic system, broke out in Britain – and not by accident, of course, since the island was a well established centre of regionalist disaffection.

In 305, the Augusti, Diocletian and Maximian had retired, ceding senior place to their juniors, the two Caesars, Galerius and Constantius, who now themselves adopted juniors – the intention being that things would continue in this way and thus produce a seamless sequence of successions. It was not to be. The emperor Constantius, campaigning in north Britain, died prematurely at York in 306, and there, refusing to honour the Tetrarchy and hail his Caesar as the new Augustus in the West, the British army reverted to the former system whereby the soldiers chose their own emperors: Constantine, son of Constantius, was acclaimed. The year yielded other illicit fruit: Maxentius, son of Maximian, was elevated in Rome and Italy, and so, with the East still under Galerius, the Empire was for a time divided into three. Twice in the next generation the tensions exploded in civil war. In 312, Constantine invaded Italy and destroyed Maxentius and his army at the battle of the Milvian Bridge, making himself master of the West. Then, in 324, he attacked the East, where Licinius had succeeded Galerius in 311-3, and at the battle of Chrysopolis destroyed his rival's army and reunited the Empire under his sole rule. Multiple-monarchism was briefly in abeyance, but after 337, with the strong hand lifted, it was chaotically reasserted in the struggles between Constantine's sons and successors. Britain, meantime, remained a key Constantinian power-base. London-minted coins seem to record imperial visits in 307, 312 and 314, and the title *Britannicus Maximus* ('Conqueror of the Britons') implies successful war in Britain between 315-8. Constantine was a usurper from the north-west – a victorious Carausius – and he no doubt took care to succour his base as the struggle for supreme power raged on. The true form of the fourth-century monarchy still showed behind the momentary supremacy of Constantine the Great: it was a mobile, military, multi-headed despotism.

THE DEFENCE OF BRITAIN

In 293-6, the Roman Imperial Army had crushed the revolt in the north-western provinces led by the rebel-emperors Carausius and Allectus. It had been one in a decade-long series of campaigns by which the Tetrarchs had re-established central control over the troubled regions of Britain, Gaul, the Rhineland, the Danube, the East, and Egypt. These campaigns included extensive frontier restoration-work. Constantius may have been involved in frontier fighting in Britain in 296-7 after the defeat of Allectus. He was certainly leading a campaign against the northern barbarians on the eve of his death in 306:

> In that last great expedition of his, he did not seek ... merely British trophies; when the gods were calling him, he attained the farthest limit of the Earth. So many and such great things were achieved. But he did not occupy the forests and swamps of the Caledonians and other Picts, nor neighbouring Ireland, or the far-distant Shetlands, nor yet the Fortunate Isles, if such there be.

Thus the words of an unknown poet at the court of Constantine, who identifies the seat of war as the far north, and perhaps lets slip that, as so often in the past, there were strict limits to Roman success: punitive columns went in, but no new territory was occupied. (Such panegyrical poetry – a debased literary genre whose dominant characteristic of obsequiousness enabled it to flourish in the despotic courts of the period – is often our only source for events in the fourth century.) In the following decade, as noted above, the new emperor Constantine's coin legends and titles probably indicate further fighting in Britain – in 307, 312, 314 and 315-8. Our written sources, moreover, can be expected to record only imperial interventions; there may have been other small-scale frontier wars conducted by local commanders. It would seem that, as in the late second and early third century, the northern frontier was unstable from c.296-318. Certainly, much new building work was undertaken. At Birdoswald, a fort in the central sector of Hadrian's Wall, an inscription dated c.296-305 records the restoration of the commandant's house ('covered with earth and fallen into ruin'), the headquarters-building, and the bath-house. Stone epigraphy was unusual in this period, so mostly we must rely on pots and coins in foundation deposits to date military construction-work to the Tetrarchic or Constantinian period. On this evidence, there were greater changes at Housesteads around 300 than at any time since it was first built: a large, two-storey, double-aisled store-building was constructed; parts of the old headquarters-building and granary were partitioned off for domestic accommodation; the soldiers' barrack-blocks were completely remodelled; and central-heating was installed in the commandant's house. Much contemporary work is evident at other northern sites, too, where sometimes forts were rescued from third-century dilapidation, and elsewhere new ones were built from scratch on virgin ground.

The threat now, though, was not just in the far north. A central issue in the civil war between Carausius and Constantius had been the strengthening attacks of Saxon sea-raiders on the south-east coast. It was as a great sea-lord who kept the Channel free of pirates that Carausius had built a base of support in the north-west provinces, and Constantius, his conqueror, was obliged to assume the same role. The court poet, Eumenius, lauding the victory over Carausius, stressed the restorationist regime's policy of peace and security on the high seas:

What a manifold victory, won by so many triumphs! By it Britain was restored; the strength of the Franks utterly wasted; obedience imposed on many other guilty tribes; and the seas cleared for a lasting security. You may boast, invincible Caesar, that you discovered another world; for in restoring naval renown to Rome's might you added to your empire an element greater than all lands. In a word, you have concluded, invincible Caesar, a war which seemed to threaten all provinces and could have spread and flared up over an area as wide as that which the whole ocean and gulfs of the inland seas wash with their waters.

Around this time – whether under Carausius or Constantius – the south-coast defensive screen built up earlier in the third century was greatly improved (*21*). The original coastal forts had been designed on traditional lines: they were rectangles with rounded corners, where the walls were low and narrow, the gateways wide and unsophisticated, and the only towers were observation turrets set flush with the exterior wall-line. Thus, Brancaster, Caister-on-Sea and Reculver were more like secure barrack-compounds than defensible strong-points; the idea was that the army went out to fight. Now, though, a new defence-minded military architecture was coming in. Oddly, it seems to have had no impact on the north British frontier – in contrast to many of the Empire's other land frontiers – but on the Saxon Shore change was apparent by the end of the third century. Bradwell and Burgh Castle seem to represent this transition. The evidence at the latter is clearest. The lower half of a new-style projecting tower is found butting against a rounded corner, but the upper half is bonded into the main wall; moreover, the tower has an elongated pear-shape, as if stretching to peer round the corner of the fort and facilitate enfilade (i.e. shooting into the enemy's flanks) – purpose-built defensive forts had square corners to avoid this problem. Burgh Castle is, then, a curious hybrid, as if, mid-construction, a young military architect trained in the latest thinking had arrived on the scene. Later forts, some replacing old ones, others on fresh ground, were all in the new style from the outset: they had square corners, projecting towers, small heavily-defended gateways, and thick high walls (which made an internal bank redundant, but encouraged the use of tile bonding-courses to pin the structure together). Richborough, Dover and Portchester were of this type, while Pevensey and possibly Lympne had the additional defensive feature of having their walls curve along the line of a natural contour. These places were built as fighting platforms from which to stop people breaking in; unlike the old 'playing-card' forts, they were siege-resistant.

The towns too were put in a state of readiness. The barbarians had shown they could penetrate deeply into the Empire's interior. The war had now come home and nowhere was safe. Most large towns had received earth-and-timber defences in the late second century and masonry ones in the mid-late third, but these administrative centres, mainly *civitas*-capitals, were few and far between in the relatively un-urbanised British provinces – perhaps 22 in all, giving an urban density only about a quarter of that in southern Gaul, for instance. These gaps in the urban infrastructure mattered, not least now that towns were part of a fast-evolving strategy of defence-in-depth, and not least in Britain, as much a front-line territory as anywhere in the Empire. The gaps were plugged by some of the hundred or so 'small towns'. These had long been growing up beside the main centres – most had origins in the early empire – but their heyday was in the third and fourth centuries. They differed from the administrative towns not only in being generally smaller, but in having a variety of morphological forms and little evidence for systematic town-planning, monumental public architecture, or elite town-houses. Typically, a Romano-British small town was an irregular web of winding, narrow, muddy streets dominated by the simple strip-houses of artisans and tradesmen, a workaday sort of place which had grown up bit by bit in response to local need. Many were simply market centres for rural hinterlands remote from the nearest administrative town; others were important roadside settlements built around official travel-lodges, like Godmanchester discussed above; some were industrial centres, such as Water Newton, built amidst the Nene Valley potteries, or Droitwich, famous for its salt-springs; a few were centres of pilgrimage, notably Bath, with its temple and bathing complex built around the hot springs of Sulis-Minerva; and often several roles were combined in a single place. There was no fixed order, no general pattern. It was all quite different from the administrative towns, places under close official supervision, laid out military-style, and dominated by grand monuments and houses; here, the gentry resided, the town councils met, and magistrates laid down law and collected taxes (*20*). The small towns, by contrast, had remained largely outside this official society. Maybe, indeed, it was just because they were free of control, places where anyone could set up and do business, that they were thriving. Now, though, they acquired a new role.

About forty small towns had, by this time, like the *civitas*-capitals, been at least part-enclosed within defensive circuits. Dating evidence is often poor or non-existent, but where something is known, it seems that earth-and-timber circuits were usually constructed between the mid-second and early third century, masonry ones in the late third or early fourth; that is, around the same time as, or just a little later than, the *civitas*-capitals. The result was a network of fortified outposts across the hinterland (*22*), mostly strung along major roads like the Fosse Way (running diagonally across the country from Exeter in the south-west to Lincoln and York in the north-east), Watling Street (following an opposite diagonal from London to Wroxeter and Chester in the north-west), or Ermine Street (linking London and the south-east with the far north). Had you, for instance, headed out from London towards Wroxeter along Watling Street in late Roman times, you would have passed through eight walled settlements on the way: *Verulamium*, Towcester, Whilton Lodge, Cave's Inn, Mancetter, Wall, Penkridge, and Redhill. At Wall, situated on an important crossroads, a series of first- and early-second-century forts had been replaced in the Hadrianic period by a travel-lodge (*mansio*) with bath-house, by which time the civil settlement was a ribbon-development stretching almost 2 miles (3km) along Watling Street; a place much like contemporary Godmanchester, in fact. Much later, probably in the fourth century, a walled enclosure was constructed astride the main road and around part of the settlement: approximately 210 by 130m in extent, the walls were nearly 3m thick and backed by an earth rampart, and there were three defensive ditches around the outside. Sites like this were an important addition to the late empire's system of defence-in-depth: a series of strong-points and supply-depots along the major communication-lines likely to be used by both raiders and defenders. The barbarians would have had neither the time nor the means to capture such places – Fritigern the Goth is reputed to have said, 'I am at peace with walls'. Yet they would have been highly disruptive of enemy operations: blocking the main access roads, they would have slowed down their movements; giving safe storage to supplies, they would have threatened their ability to 'live off the land'; and as refuges, assembly-points and stores-bases, they would have maximised the strategic mobility and tactical security of defending forces. And the deeper the barbarians penetrated, the greater their danger: they could, with difficulty, bypass the strong-points, but these were then lodged in their rear threatening to cut off escape. Above all, the strong-points would buy time for the defenders: time to concentrate for the counter-attack. The ruthless efficiency of small elite Roman strike-forces in the late empire (we shall consider some examples in chapter 7) owed much to these strings of 'hedgehogs' along the main roads of the provincial hinterland.

That is not to say the old administrative towns were neglected: they were vital to late Roman military infrastructure, and their defences were maintained and improved. Some, of course, were more important than others, whether through strategic location, political status, or both. Canterbury, for instance, was centrally positioned in relation to the Saxon Shore forts of Kent – Reculver, Richborough, Dover and Lympne – and may well have functioned as a command centre, supply-depot and reserve base (21). London, whose masonry defensive circuit was completed with the construction of a riverside wall in c.255-70, is likely to have had a key military role, quite apart from its importance as a provincial and diocesan capital: it was the only fortress on the Thames able to block a seaborne raider's passage upstream into

▲	fort
⬤	provincial capital
●	major town
•	walled small town
+	signal station

200 kilometres

22 Defence-in-depth: the walled sites of late Roman Britain. Distinct zones are apparent: the strong line of forts along Hadrian's Wall; the hinterland forts in northern England and Wales; the coastal and estuarine forts of the Saxon Shore; and the dense network of walled towns in the south-east

the heart of central England. Most major towns had recently finished construction of their masonry circuits, and little new work
was needed in the Tetrarchic and Constantinian periods. Where
weaknesses were detected, however, Constantius and his successors sought to remedy them – as at York. A legionary fortress had
been established on the north side of the river Ouse in the 70s,
and a civil settlement had in due course developed on the south
bank. By 237 at the latest, this settlement had achieved urban status as a citizen-colony (*colonia*), for Roman York had by then
become the greatest political and military centre in the north. In
208-11, when Severus, Caracalla and Geta were in Britain, York
had been a temporary imperial capital, and soon afterwards it had
become the permanent provincial capital of Lower Britain. It was
important again in 306, hosting the court and headquarters of
Constantius and Constantine, and now, moreover, with the shift to
defence-in-depth, its traditional status as the main Roman military base in the north was augmented by a new role as major
front-line strong-point. Though little is known of the defences on
the south bank, the walls of the legionary fortress to the north
were substantially reconstructed around this time. Eight projecting towers were built along the river-front facing the civil
settlement, including two huge polygonal ones at either end of
the wall, one of which, the 'Multangular Tower', survives today.
Constantinian York was rebuilt in the new late Roman style of
military architecture.

In *c.*150, there had been but a handful of defended sites in the
south-eastern half of Britain: in the golden age of Antoninus
Pius, it had been the *Pax Romana* that had protected the settlements and farms of the Romano-British, not walls and
militia-men. Even in *c.*250, there had been only three or four
coastal forts and three or four towns with masonry walls; other
defended settlements had had only earth-and-timber circuits. By
*c.*350, the aspect of south-eastern Britain had been transformed:
counting shore forts, defended major towns, and smaller walled

settlements and enclosures, the south-east was protected by about 75 stone-built strong-points – roughly the same number as the forts of the north and west (*22*). All of Britain was now part of the military zone. This Roman system for the defence of *Britannia* in the fourth century bears a strong resemblance to the burghal system of King Alfred's Wessex in the ninth. The parallel is worth exploring, since the better recorded late-Saxon experience sheds light on the late Roman one: similar crises often produce similar responses. The Vikings were highly mobile bands of raiders, occasionally coalescing into large invasion armies, and they were capable of repeated, devastating, long-ranging attacks. Alfred's *burhs* were intended as a network of fortified central places which would protect vital government infrastructure and stores, provide military bases for the West Saxon militia, offer places of refuge to the rural population, and facilitate a strategy of defence-in-depth which would make deep-penetration attacks by enemy forces extremely dangerous. The *burhs* were distributed so that nowhere was more than about 20 miles (a day's forced march) away from one, and to create such a dense network a number of different types of site were used – old Iron-Age hillforts, Roman forts and walled towns, Saxon royal manors and new towns, and newly fortified promontories. The system would seem to have been astonishingly successful: whereas in the campaigns of 865-78 the Vikings had succeeded in invading Wessex on three separate occasions, in the war of 892-6 they failed completely to do so. In view of the oft-repeated claim that late Roman walls were motivated by civic pride – a claim for which there is not a shred of evidence – two features of the Alfredian system are worth emphasising: the whole programme was state-directed, and the defences were constructed and manned by local forces. Even without equivalent written testimony, we can assume the same for the Constantinian system. Fourth-century Britain, like ninth-century Wessex, wore the aspect of an embattled military monarchy.

A NEW MODEL ARMY

Our knowledge of the late Roman army is much less than that of late Roman fortifications. The literature of the period usually records only a bare outline of the bigger campaigns. Military inscriptions – building records, religious dedications, and tomb memorials – can be helpful, but these were fewer in the late empire than before. Some clues arise when fort excavations reveal changes in the layout of barrack-blocks or the fills of rubbish-pits, but here the evidence for what the army itself was like is indirect and open to conflicting interpretations. One class of information for the late Roman army stands out, however, as supremely important: that contained in a document known as the *Notitia Dignitatum* ('Directory of High Offices'). The subject of intensive study and debate, much about the *Notitia* nonetheless remains obscure, but its value as an historical source is beyond doubt. It comprises a series of lists, each giving the principal civil and military officials in different parts of the Empire, along with the staffs, units and places under their control. It was probably compiled from returns submitted periodically by locally based subordinates to the office of the *primicerius notariorum* ('secretary-general') for the Western Empire. The document (which survives somewhat incomplete) dates essentially to *c*.395, but some parts may have been out-of-date by this time, and other parts were subject to corrections up to *c*.425 (whether by official hand or for some amateur purpose we cannot be sure). Much *Notitia* information throws light on the situation earlier in the fourth century and even before; it all depends how far organisation and deployment changed in this period. The *Notitia* certainly shows something of the evolution of the late Roman army from the third century onwards, and, from corroborative evidence, we know that many of the garrison postings recorded, not least for Britain, date back that far. Let us summarise the key points known from the *Notitia* and other late Roman sources.

The army of Constantine was profoundly different from that of Augustus. The increased risk of frontier penetrations had caused a strategic shift to defence-in-depth based on networks of hinterland strong-points and the use of mobile field-armies. Zosimus, a pagan Greek historian of *c.*500, expressed it thus in an oft-quoted passage:

> By the foresight of Diocletian, the frontiers of the Roman Empire were everywhere studded with cities and forts and towers ... and the whole army was stationed along them, so that it was impossible for the barbarians to break through, as the attackers were everywhere blocked by an opposing force. But Constantine ruined this defensive system by withdrawing the majority of the troops from the frontiers, and stationing them in cities which did not require protection.

Zosimus had his own agenda: rejection of the pagan gods had brought down the Western Roman Empire, and Constantine, the first Christian emperor, was cast as the architect of catastrophe. In fact, static frontier-defences had repeatedly collapsed in the third century, and the strategic shift to defence-in-depth was a feature of the period as a whole; it is likely, though, that in this, as in so many things, Constantine carried reform far beyond its Diocletianic limits.

Central to the new system was a distinction between lower grade garrison-troops in permanent posts on or near the frontier (*limitanei*), and crack campaigning troops attached to various mobile field-armies (*comitatenses*). The old army had stationed all its men close to the frontiers; there had been no reserve, and when expeditions were formed, troops had been pulled out of the line to make them up. The key distinction then had been that between the legions of elite citizen heavy-infantry (*legiones*) stationed in huge fortresses, and units of auxiliary and specialist support-troops (*alae* and *cohortes*) strung out along the frontier in small garrison-posts. This system had broken down during the crisis of the third century. The emperor Gallienus had been forced to create a small cavalry army under his personal command, able to shift rapidly from one threatened point to another; it was, indeed, precisely this centralised control of military striking-power which had enabled the Empire to defeat its disparate enemies. This practice was later enlarged and institutionalised: permanent field-armies were formed out of detachments seconded from existing frontier units and through the raising of wholly new regiments. A notable pro-portion of men were recruited from among Germanic barbarians and other warrior-peoples, and cavalry regiments were especially numerous, mainly newly-raised units equipped, organised and trained to operate on the battlefield as crack armoured forces. In war, as in other things, the Middle Ages had begun: for a thousand years of antiquity, from archaic Greece to imperial Rome, the cit-izen heavy infantryman had dominated the battlefield; now and for the next thousand years, elite armoured cavalry would be decisive.

As important to the efficiency of the army as its organisational structure was its command system, and this too was changing shape in the fires of war. The professionalisation of the officer corps, a process begun under the Severan military monarchy, now reached completion with the full separation of civil and military posts and the creation of alternative army and civil-service careers. Gone were the days when the self-same Roman gentle-man – convinced that talent was inherited along with wealth, and that the exercise of *imperium* was a birthright – might manage his estates, practise the law, administer justice, command a legion, and write a history book, all with equal accomplishment. Now the state required its servants to specialise, to train, to gain experience, and to achieve elevation through merit. This was especially so in the army: here the demands of war readily exposed incompetence and failure, and the claims of birth and favour must needs count for little; here was the best chance for the ambitious and upwardly mobile. The officers and generals of the late Roman army were full-time professional soldiers, and the rungs of their career ladder we find listed in the *Notitia*. The British army, for instance, belonged to the command of the Master of Horse for the Gallic Provinces (*magister equitum per Gallias*), and under him there were three officers with a rank equivalent to general in post on the island. The Duke of the British Provinces (*dux Britanniarum*) commanded 37 regiments on the northern frontier, some on the Wall itself, others in the hinterland forts, while the Count of the Saxon Shore (*comes litoris Saxonici*) controlled nine coastal forts in the south-east. Archaeological evidence suggests the lists are incomplete (additional forts appear to have been occupied in the late fourth century), but the overall system of command and control implied here is supported by other written sources for late Roman Britain. These two commands were both of 'limitanean' or permanent garrison-troops. The third general-officer, on the other hand, commanded 'comitatensian' troops, and he is likely therefore to have been in Britain only for a short period at the end of the fourth century (around the time the *Notitia* was written): this was the Count of the British Provinces (*comes Britanniarum*), whose field-army of nine crack units, six of them cavalry, were probably dispatched to deal with a specific military crisis. The Roman historian Ammianus Marcellinus records the presence in Britain of similar expeditionary forces earlier in the fourth century.

The *Notitia* does not provide information about the size, composition and equipment of late Roman army units, so we must turn to the archaeology of forts for help with this, especially if we want to form some estimate of overall fighting-power. The evidence we have implies smaller, more settled, more locally-rooted garrisons than formerly. Housesteads on Hadrian's Wall is a key site in this respect. Excavations here have shown that around 300 the design of the barracks was radically altered. Previously, a barrack-block had consisted of a range of ten double-room units, each providing accommodation for a *contubernium* ('section') of eight men, with a veranda running along the front, and a semi-detached junior officers' house at one end; thus, a full century of eighty men (*sic*) could be housed in one long single-roofed building. Now, however, the barracks were reconstructed as a series of small separate buildings (or 'chalets') with narrow alleyways between – like rows of beach-huts – each with its own hearth or brazier, and each showing slight differences of plan, such as might be due to individual preference. Other contemporary changes may be connected. Some of the fort's communal buildings, the granary and the hospital, were converted to domestic use, and, somewhat later in the fourth century, a small bath-house was constructed over the demolished end of a large store-building. It may also be significant that the civilian *vicus* outside the fort had largely been abandoned by *c.*320. How might these changes be interpreted? The conditions of military service had steadily improved under the Empire: forts had been rebuilt in stone, the luxuries of piped water and military bath-houses provided, pay and perks increased, the right to marry and have families during service granted. It was a good life in the army – relatively speaking. The chalet-barracks of the fourth century were perhaps part of this process of amelioration. Perhaps, too, as the barriers between soldier and civilian broke down in centuries-old garrison towns where military discipline was lax, soldiers' families moved out of the *vicus*-settlements to enjoy the security and comfort of the forts themselves. There may have been plenty of space: army recruitment was perennially difficult in the third and fourth centuries, the pay of existing men was often delayed by financial and logistical crises, there was the widespread practice of forming new regiments by dividing up old ones, and casualties and desertions could be high when the frontiers were attacked in force. Late Roman sources indicate that field-army units commonly numbered a few hundred; frontier units are likely to have been less well maintained and may often therefore have numbered even less. If it was one soldier per chalet in fourth-century Housesteads (with or without family), then the garrison, the First Tungrian Cohort, could have numbered as few as a hundred or so.

Military organisation reflects the circumstances of conflict. The soldiers of the early empire had been grouped into huge units and concentrated in a few places for the purpose of attack. The highly trained and heavily armoured infantry of Rome, massed in this way, had easily crushed whatever disorderly gatherings of barbarian tribesmen had stood in their path. Thus the offensive in war concentrates its forces at the point of decision. The soldiers of the late empire, by contrast, were grouped in many small units widely dispersed: their role was to cover all points of entry and every possible target across the whole great expanse of empire. Each unit needed to be a tight, tough, specialist team, able to move fast and strike hard: a compact nugget of military power in a flexible system of defence-in-depth. The massed offensive had given way to the dispersed defensive. The image we should have of the late Roman army is of highly trained, well equipped, wholly professional units of a few hundred men, often operating independently, or brigaded with only a handful of others, and geared to delivering fast and lethal retaliation for enemy provocation – something more like the hired mercenary armies of late medieval Christendom than the citizen mass levies of classical antiquity.

GRANDEES, GENTRY AND PEASANTS

The Roman state was a war-making machine, and this involved it in two principal types of activity. It was the job of generals and soldiers to maintain the security of the Empire by conducting military campaigns and guarding frontier defences. But of equal importance were the officials, clerks and policemen of the civil service whose role was to appropriate the resources necessary to sustain this war effort. Military operations and military supply were two faces of the same coin, and, although professional specialisation and alternative career paths were features of late imperial state service, civil servants remained as much a part of the war machine as army officers. In the style of Mussolini's Italy or Hitler's Germany, the functionaries of civil society were harnessed to the war-god's chariot. Legally, civil servants were soldiers of the emperor, subject to strict ranking and tight discipline, and their markedly military character was symbolised by their attire: paramilitary uniform was *de rigueur* in government offices, and one turned up for work wearing the official-issue tunic (*vestis*) and military belt *(cingulum)*. This militarised administration was the state's instrument for jacking up the amount of surplus extracted from civil society – in essence, for raising the rate of exploitation in the Roman countryside – a necessary precondition for the improvement of imperial defence.

One aspect of this was an attempt to bring the central state closer to the point of exploitation – that is, to the point where tribute and labour were directly extracted from the rural peasantry – by creating smaller provinces and interposing new tiers of administrative authority between the *civitates* and the emperor. Surveillance and supervision from above thus became more immediate. Britain had already been divided into two provinces by the Severan emperors; now it was made into four: Lower Britain was divided between *Britannia Secunda* in the far north (governed from York) and *Flavia Caesariensis* in the north Midlands (Lincoln), while Upper Britain became *Britannia Prima* in the west (Cirencester) and *Maxima Caesariensis* in the south-east (London). These four new provinces formed the diocese of Britain, governed by a *vicarius* ('viceroy'). This in turn formed part of the prefecture of the Gauls, which covered much of the West (Britain, Germany, France and Spain), one of four major administrative sub-divisions of the late Roman empire corresponding to the fourfold division of imperial power under the Diocletianic

Tetrarchy. *Maxima Caesariensis* had primacy among the British provinces: all governors were originally *praeses* ('protectors'), but the *Notitia* later shows *Maxima* ruled by a higher ranking *consularis* ('consular'), and London, the province's main centre, doubled as the diocesan capital. In addition to these five top men – diocesan viceroy and four provincial governors – there were four other senior officials listed for Britain in the *Notitia*. There were two financial secretaries (*rationales*), one for government revenues, the other for the emperor's estates, a director of the treasury (*praepositus*), and the managing-director (*procurator*) of a state cloth-factory. The three finance officials are likely to have been based in London, the director of the treasury definitely so, but the cloth factory was at a place called *Venta* (presumably a provincial town in good sheep-rearing country). The centrally appointed officials listed in the *Notitia* represent only the visible tip of a labyrinthine bureaucracy spreading downwards into the fat of civil society. London was clearly the main administrative centre, but we can assume large establishments in each of the provincial capitals (with the governors' staff and regional finance-offices), and there were probably government officials in all the *civitas*-capitals and many other local centres. The 'Guardians of the Community' (*curatores civitatis*) referred to above – local agents of the central state – seem to have become permanent and universal in towns from the time of Diocletian onwards. Here, at *civitas* level, were the synapses of the late Roman imperial system, where the power-lines of the state bureaucracy extending downwards from the court fused with those of the local gentry stretching out across the countryside. Here, a minority of army officers, civil servants and urban power-brokers, all endowed with great wealth and honour, their privilege and corruption under state protection, confronted a mass of lesser landowners, locally rooted, without connections, open to abuse, and much put upon to sustain the military-supply system which fuelled the war machine. The towns, then, were not just strong-points in a strategy of defence-in-depth; they were vital points of articulation linking the imperial grandees with the municipal gentry – those who gave orders, that is, with those who carried them out.

The gap between the two – giving orders and carrying them out – was getting wider. At the top, systematisation, efficiency drives and prescriptive edicts attempted to deliver fourth-century order from third-century chaos. At the bottom, there was the bedrock of peasant resistance to rising demands. The regime over-hauled the whole fiscal and monetary system. Disorder, recession and inflation had wrought havoc with tax-revenues, and every device government economists could contrive to rectify the shortfall was attempted. Sometimes these devices collided. To tackle inflation, new coins with higher silver-content were intro-duced to replace the debased issues of the previous generation; but the government soon gave into temptation and debased its own coins to increase their yield, a one-off, short-term benefit which was the ancient equivalent of 'printing money'. Another attempt at counter-inflation, this time by diktat and threat, was Diocletian's Price Edict, a government tariff of fixed prices for a long list of commodities; it was wholly abortive. If long-term price stability was unattainable (even though inflation was less in the fourth century than in the third), then the method of levying taxes would have to change. If money could not be trusted, or if the monetary cycle broke down, then one could collect in kind, taking the goods themselves. The Roman Empire seems always to have collected some taxes in this way, but the practice became dominant in the later third and early fourth centuries, and it seems to have continued on a considerable scale thereafter. The logistics were a nightmare: the variety of goods in which taxes were levied, the need to check both quantity and quality when they were paid, and the sheer bulk of material needing to be transported and stored necessitated a huge interlocking mecha-nism of officials, clerks, police, drivers, warehousemen, dockers and boatmen.

Either way, though, whether taxes were collected in kind or in coin, the state sought protection against inadequate receipts. There are two ways of looking at taxation: how much should the producer pay, or how much does the consumer want? The Diocletianic system shifted the balance towards the latter: a new, uniform, empire-wide system of tax-assessment was introduced which could yield variable amounts to the exchequer. A unit of tax (*annona*) was due on each area of cultivable land (*iugum*) which could be worked by one man (*caput*) and provide his subsistence. The total due therefore depended on the extent of one's ownership of land and control over labour; it was a combined property and poll tax. Crucially, however, the amount of *annona* payable on each unit could be varied annually according to the changing needs of the state. Tax increases became an automatic corollary of falling or inadequate receipts. The producer, meantime, never knew what was coming. Nor was this his only problem; he also had to deliver his dues to their destination. This might involve transporting tax-in-kind over long distances at great expense, or obtaining high-denomination coin for payment in bullion. In either case, many will have opted (or perhaps were required) not to make payment directly to officers of the imperial state (who were distant and inaccessible), but indirectly to local *decuriones* (one of whose roles was supervision of tax-collection), who would then assume responsibility for forwarding tax-receipts from their estates in bulk at an appropriate time. It is easy to imagine how, in the hands of skilful estate-managers and accountants, the boundaries between the tax obligations of lord and peasant could become obscured, especially if rent payments and other local dues were conflated with state taxes in a single levy. We do not know how much was taken; for what it is worth, limited evidence from elsewhere in the late empire suggests that as much as a quarter or a third of produce was paid in taxes; if so, once rents were also deducted, the peasant-producer may have retained barely half the fruits of his and his family's labour.

The late Roman tax-system was, of course, an exercise in class warfare. As such, it was tested in a million encounters between collector and producer, and often these would flare into scuffles and skirmishes, or even, sometimes, into banditry and rebellion. There had always been tension, but this was now ratcheted up by the rising and unpredictable demands inherent in the Diocletianic system. A spiralling disaster was latent. Peasant resistance and non-payment would produce compensatory increases in the rate of the *annona* in succeeding years, and this would provoke yet stronger defiance of the tax-collector and further shortfalls in anticipated receipts. The very simplicity of the system was problematic: its uniformity across the Empire and the highly standardised way in which the productivity of land and labour were assessed meant that countless local variations and generations of custom and prac-tice were simply blotted out. Farms just viable under the old tax-system, or those blighted by accidents of nature or human fail-ure, would pay the same as others running in milk and honey. Moreover, the burden was distributed unevenly – indeed, regres-sively – between social classes, and this reflected the distribution of social power within the imperial system. Roman society was cor-rupt. Grandees could buy immunity or call in a favour – a generous tax-assessment, a sympathetic court-hearing, a blind eye or a year's grace – and they would get richer. The gentry were vul-nerable to the machinations of the well-connected, but they could, as we have seen, dump on their own dependants. The peas-antry, on the other hand, without resources or connections, were fully exposed to plunder by more powerful men. Something of the fear and hopelessness felt by the humble in the presence of the great comes through in this contemporary description of late Roman tax-collectors:

When such an investigator comes to some frightened province, accompanied by purveyors of false information and borne aloft by costly services, he is all arrogance. He demands the assistance of the governor's staff; he also often joins to his service the imperial guardsmen; and with his men and offices thus multiplied, terror extorts whatever greed pleases. To introduce himself, the visitor publishes and reiterates fearful commands concerning many and varied tax categories. He unrolls clouds of minute computations jumbled in unintelligible obscurity, which are the more effective as they are the less understood by persons ignorant of the arts of deceit. They are required to show tax-receipts consumed by length of years and age which, in the simplicity and trust of owing nothing, they have not the wit to preserve ... The palace official, his accomplice in robbery, encourages him, the flunkies rowdily join the attack, and the soldiers press ruthlessly for action.

It is a statement issued by the court of Valentinian III, ruler of the Western Roman Empire, in c.450; there are many others in the same vein. Power in the late empire had recrystallised around the state, and power attracted wealth. The imperial grandees used their position to enrich themselves, as they were bound to do, as all ruling classes do given the chance. The boundary between what was legal and what was extortionate was, at best, hazy, and sharp practice and vested interest made it more so. Those at the bottom, for whom the law was an impenetrable fog anyway, lacked the resources for a challenge; in their encounters with the great, they were victims pure and simple. Here is the real meaning behind the late Roman legal distinction between *honestiores* ('the honourable') and *humiliores* ('the humble'). It was not just that the humble could be mutilated and murdered under the law if unlucky enough to be dragged before the courts; it was also that they lacked the knowledge, the means and the contacts ever to be able to seek legal redress themselves.

As well as tax-revenues, the system also needed to mobilise labour. Slaves and convicts could do some of the work, but they were no longer available in sufficient quantity; successful foreign war was the main source of slaves, and there was not enough of this now; local labour had to be used much more. The state needed public buildings maintained, defensive walls constructed, roads and bridges repaired, military supplies transported. That this work was done is obvious enough from the material remains recovered, and that it was done mainly by forced-labour corvées is an entirely reasonable supposition, supported as it is by written references to this practice elsewhere in the Empire. Tacitus referred on more than one occasion to forced labour in first-century Britain, and, though there are no explicit references surviving for later periods, one or two pieces of evidence are suggestive. Eumenius, the panegyrical court poet, mentions that Constantius Caesar, in 297-8, sent British artisans to assist the restoration of Autun in Gaul, and this may have been a compulsory service. Several short and crude inscriptions from Hadrian's Wall record building work by tribal communities (*civitates*), probably dating to the fourth century, and these very likely refer to drafts of forced labour: two mention the Dumnonii (from the far south-west), two the Durotriges (of Dorset), one the Catuvellauni (of Hertfordshire), and one the otherwise unknown 'Bricic'. Perhaps the best evidence is provided by the so-called 'milestones' of Roman Britain: these very rarely refer to distances or destinations, but they are found beside major thoroughfares, always have a dedication to the reigning emperor, and sometimes mention the *civitas* involved, so they are best interpreted as commemorative inscriptions to record remetallings and other roadworks. A large number were erected in the mid-third century and again in the early fourth, and these late Roman examples were especially crude. They conjure a picture of the press-ganged quota, dispatched by the municipal magistrates for a month-or-so's heavy labour on the roads, roughing it for a while in a wilderness encampment, and then recording their relief (with perhaps a touch of pride) by carving an amateurish dedication when their stint was done.

The difficulty for the state was to keep track of everyone. The tax-collector and the recruiting-officer could only be efficient if the census was up-to-date. If people moved, they were lost to the system. The solution was to stop them moving: to tie people to their farms and jobs; indeed, to tie them to those of their fathers and their fathers' fathers. Under the late empire, not only was there impressment, there was also compulsory residence, direction of labour, and the inheritance of occupational status. Peasants were designated *coloni*, a word which, whatever its earlier significance, came to mean someone who not only worked on the land but worked one particular part of it which he was not permitted to leave – a serf, in short. This had many advantages for late Roman *honestiores*: census and assessment records were simpler because less changed; tax and labour dues were easier to collect because you knew where to go; rents could be racked up because tenants could not seek better terms elsewhere; marginal (but taxable) land was kept in cultivation because impoverished crofters had to stick it out; the policing of the countryside was more cut-and-dried because people were either in the right place or they were not. The same regime applied to other occupations: river boatmen and cross-Channel shippers found themselves in controlled occupations; soldiers' sons born in a garrison-town were expected to follow their fathers into the army; town councillors were compelled to attend meetings, stand for office, and carry out local government duties. Society was being regimented, dragooned, controlled; turned into an appendage of the military state. The counter-revolutionary grandees were straining towards an antique totalitarianism.

STATE AND PARTY

In 312, before fighting the battle of the Milvian Bridge against rival-emperor Maxentius, Constantine ordered his soldiers to paint the cross of Christ on their shields. The new god gave victory to these born-again converts, and the following year the two remaining Roman emperors, Constantine in the West and Licinius in the East, issued the Edict of Milan legalising Christianity throughout the Empire and ending three centuries of persecution. The year after that, Constantine himself presided over the Council of Arles, an all-empire episcopal assembly meeting to settle a divisive theological dispute. Pagan emperors had united temple and state in a powerfully charged ideological nexus. The Christian emperors inherited this tradition and transformed it. The polytheistic diversity and religious tolerance of the early empire fitted a world in which a large, prosperous, culturally diverse gentry ruled a thousand towns spread out between the Yorkshire dales and the Egyptian cataracts. Things were different now. The Empire was embattled and retrenched, the gentry in retreat, the towns in decay; civil society was wilting in the shadow of oriental despotism, imperial aristocracy and military state. A new god was needed, and it was part of the counter-revolutionary radicalism of Constantine, part of his programme to discard whatever of the old order was out-of-date and inefficient, that he rejected Jupiter for Christ. There were clear advantages. Christianity, though riven by sectarianism and schism, was monotheistic, aimed at uniformity, and was intolerant of paganism and heresy. Also, it possessed a universal ecclesiastical organisation staffed by men who were often of the highest administrative and intellectual calibre. Potentially, then, the Church was an immensely powerful ideological machine, able to beam its message across the Empire and have it echo in the farthest recesses. The message, moreover, was subtle, relevant and stirring: it was God's work to extirpate evil and win souls for salvation, and those who did this work exercised the highest idealism and would be rewarded with purity, grace and eternal life; the emperors represented this struggle on a cosmic scale, and the faithful should honour them with loyalty, obedience and self-sacrifice; the emperor's army was God's army, waging holy war against the massed forces of barbarism, paganism and darkness.

The Church, in short, could counteract men's alienation from the state, mask the power and greed of the imperial grandees, and endow the war effort with the aura of a crusade. As ever, religion mystified reality so that men would continue to obey the orders of their masters.

Constantine's religious reformation was rapid. From *c.*320 a massive redistribution of wealth in the Church's favour began. Traditionally, town councils and guilds, local magistrates and priests, and various private patron–benefactors had, whether voluntarily or by obligation, paid for the erection, improvement and repair of urban public buildings. The whole *ensemble* of monumental architecture had been a matter of ambition, prestige and pride. Now, suddenly, this political energy was transformed and redirected. Wealth flowed into the Church from private bequests and imperial gifts. To grant estates for the maintenance of churches, to present gold and silver plate for holy service, to give Christian aid by succouring the poor; these were now the ways to gain the esteem of fellow citizens, the favour of political superiors, and, of course, the grace of God. The example was set at the top. Constantine ordered the 'dissolution' of pagan temple estates and a direct transfer of wealth to the Church as a way of consolidating the ecclesiastical infrastructure. But he and his successors also endowed the Church out of the imperial estate itself, and many courtiers, civil servants and generals followed suit. The great benefactors now were the emperors and the grandees, the main beneficiaries were the leading cities where court and government were based, and the principal focus of such generosity was the Church.

This sudden accretion of ecclesiastical wealth created a new corps of the Roman imperial elite: the bishops. Their position was further enhanced by direct government support in the form of imperial legislation, political preferment and financial subsidy. An ecclesiastical hierarchy arose in parallel with that of the imperial state: provincial capitals had their metropolitan bishops and cathedral churches; *civitas*-capitals had local bishops and *titulus*-churches; and groups of canons (*canonici* or *cardinales*) attached to each bishop would carry the message out into the hinterland. The bishop would take his place among the local grandees, and many in due course acquired the roles and manners of old-style pagan magistrates, some eventually to provide the final rallying-points of disintegrating *Romanitas* as the Empire in the West went down. The clergy were exempt from taxes and public duties, travelled at state expense, and acquired judicial powers alongside secular officials. Church and state were marching together, the former empowered, enriched and protected by its secular ally, the latter legitimised and sanctified by the most effective ideological apparatus in antiquity. Of special importance was Christianity's role in welding courtiers and officers into a more united ruling class, and the army generally into a more effective instrument of imperial power. The army, of course, was more open to advancement from below, so Christians could more easily rise to the top, and Christian confession was more likely to be advantageous. The Church, too, now that it was rich and powerful, became another ladder for rapid upward social mobility – though, for the same reason, its effectiveness in this respect was limited as established aristocrats moved sideways to occupy and block its higher rungs. Even so, court, army and Church formed a distinct, dominant faction within the wider late Roman ruling class. Christian confession came to have important career implications for members of this faction and those who aspired to join it: it was like a party card – a testimonial of political loyalty, and a promise of conformity, obedience and good service. As such, it earned preferment. And this, of course, provoked resentment and opposition.

All aristocracies are divided against themselves. They compete for the wealth and rank that provide individual families with prestige, privilege and protection. Aristocracies are bands of warring brothers, united against outsiders, bitterly feuding within. It had always been so among the Roman aristocracy, but the form of this traditional conflict had changed as the Empire evolved. Now it changed again, to pit Christian against pagan. The aristocracy of late Roman grandees wore a double aspect. The demands of war in the third and fourth centuries had opened the army high-command to rising talent; the peripatetic courts of the soldier-emperors breathed this freer air of service, achievement and merit; and the Church's message of salvation for all, regardless of birth and station, through faith and good works, gave the matter a heady spirituality. The old senatorial aristocracy, from whom many civil grandees continued to be recruited, was different. These men of the established elite had received a traditional education in rhetoric, law and the classics, and their world was dominated by the assembly-room, the court-house, the arts of administration, and the upper-class salon. Their education and experience were valuable in many departments of the late Roman state, so they still formed part of the aristocracy-of-office. But many posts expected by birthright in the past were now shut off, and they resented these exclusions by uncouth soldiers and upstart courtiers. As ever, old rich hated new rich. Now, though, it was expressed as pagan against Christian, old Rome against new Constantinople, time-hallowed tradition against new-fangled theory. The courtiers and the soldiers worshipped Christ, a crucified criminal, the god of slaves, rebels and barbarians; that was fitting enough. Cicero, Virgil and the Stoics, by contrast, had marched with the old gods in defence of rank, order and traditional values, so the marks of a true gentleman clearly included pagan faith and temple sacrifice. Can we hear any echoes of this conflict of ideals in late Roman Britain?

The island was a distant, marginal, underdeveloped diocese, so it is no surprise that evidence for fourth-century Christianity is limited. Equally, though, the strength of the bond between Church and state in the late empire, and the centrality of party allegiance to career advancement, should guarantee a mark. This we find. The Canons of the Council of Arles (314) record the presence of four British delegations: Bishop Eborius of York; Bishop Restitutus of London; Bishop Adelphius, who may have been from Lincoln; and Father Sacerdos and Deacon Arminius, who were possibly from Cirencester. Thus, it seems, the four provincial metropolitan bishops we might anticipate were represented. Further British delegations are recorded at later church councils, at Nicaea (Turkey) in 325, at Serdica (Bulgaria) in 343, and at Ariminum (northern Italy) in 360, when three British bishops accepted free travel using the imperial post-service. We have definite evidence, then, for developed church organisation in Britain during the fourth century – but with a suggestion that it was somewhat impoverished and dependent on official subsidy. Furthermore, at least one prominent late Roman cleric was British, and his career suggests that the island's Christians, or some of them, were, by the end of the fourth century at least, networked into an international ecclesiastical community. Pelagius seems to have received a thorough education at home in Britain before setting off to study law at Rome in *c.*380, where he later emerged as a leading theologian, promoting, in opposition to Augustine, the 'heretical' view that human beings had free will, were captains of their souls, and could be architects of their own salvation. The Pelagian heresy was widespread and powerful in the early fifth century, not least in Britain, to which an orthodox mission was dispatched from the continent in 429 charged with stamping it out. Patrick may have been another illustrious product of early British Christianity. As a young man, he escaped from slavery in Ireland, entered the Church, received a higher education in the monasteries of Gaul, and then returned to Ireland to carry out his great work of Christian conversion. But the dating of Patrick's life is uncertain. He may have been the son of a Romanised gentleman with estates in western Britain in the late fourth century – or he may have lived a century later.

Despite the uncertainties about Patrick, there is good evidence in the written sources for a fourth-century Romano-British

Church whose organisation paralleled that of the secular administration and whose functionaries participated in ecclesiastical affairs
internationally. Archaeology confirms this impression of a state-
backed, town-based, rather elitist institution. A small number of
possible late Roman churches have been found or are strongly
suspected, notably at the major towns of London, Colchester,
Verulamium, Lincoln, Silchester and Wroxeter, at the small town of
Icklingham, and at the Saxon Shore fort of Richborough. The
Silchester example, though particularly small, is otherwise typical:
located in the town centre and dating to the late third or early
fourth century, the remains comprised a nave with an apsed west
end and a mosaic where the altar may have stood, an aisle on
either side of the nave with two tiny transepts, a narthex or
enclosed entrance-lobby at the east end, and the foundation for a
possible baptistery just in front of the main building. Elsewhere,
when large, late Roman inhumation cemeteries have been excavated outside towns, evidence for Christian practice has
sometimes been encountered, either in the form of possible associated cemetery-churches, or in some aspect of the burial rite
itself. At Poundbury outside Dorchester (Dorset), for example, not
only were the burials west-east aligned and usually without grave-
goods (normal late Roman practice), but great care had been
taken both to avoid the site of an earlier pagan cemetery nearby
(because it was profane?), and to ensure that later burials did not
disturb earlier ones (perhaps in deference to the contemporary
Christian belief in literal resurrection of the body). Moreover,
among the objects found in the cemetery was a coin pierced for
suspension and bearing the *chi-rho* motif (the first two letters of
Christ's name in the Greek alphabet; a traditional Christian symbol). Outside the towns, the evidence for Romano-British
Christianity is limited. Some villas appear to have had Christian
chapels. Apsidal rooms with rectangular antechambers were decorated with Christian mosaics at the villas of Hinton St Mary and
Frampton in Dorset, while fallen wall-plaster in a basement room

at Lullingstone villa in Kent showed an image of figures praying in the traditional *orans*-style of the early church (arms outstretched and hands upraised) and another of a *chi-rho* symbol within a wreath. Often we have no comparable surviving evidence to help us identify the function of a room; there were perhaps many such villa-chapels in late Roman Britain. A number of Christian objects have been found as parts of precious-metal hoards. The most spectacular example is the Water Newton hoard, comprising nine vessels or parts of vessels, eighteen votive silver plaques, a gold disk, and some odd fragments; among these, four vessels and ten plaques bore the *chi-rho* motif, sometimes also with *alpha* and *omega* (the first and last letters of the Greek alphabet, symbolising Christ's claim to be 'the beginning and the end'). A hoard such as this is clearly Christian, though its ownership and purpose can only be guessed at: the church plate of a well-heeled local Christian congregation?

The archaeology of Romano-British Christianity is modest. No doubt many churches, chapels and improvised places of worship have gone unrecognised; our sample is a small fraction of what once was. Even so, the character and distribution of the evidence we can identify confirms the impression conveyed by the written sources: Christianity was not widespread and deep-rooted; it was not a mass popular movement; it had not won over the country people (the *pagani* in Latin). Christianity was limited mainly to the towns, where it enjoyed official support and subsidy, to certain forts, where evangelical officers perhaps tried to convert their men, and to some villas, where the local grandees or gentry happened to be 'members of the party'. The richness of some Christian objects – the Hinton St Mary mosaic or the Water Newton silver plate – is further testimony to the exclusive, upper-class flavour of the cult in far-flung Britain. What seems clear, too, is that the conflict with paganism, so well attested in the literary sources for other parts of the Empire, could erupt violently even in Britain. Where this happened, it is likely to have been a struggle within the elite – for favour, for influence, for advancement – but quite possibly with orchestrated mob violence playing a role. The evidence is circumstantial but compelling. In the late third or early fourth century, the three known temples of Mithras (*mithraea*) on Hadrian's Wall seem to have been vandalised in a similar way: the main relief sculptures depicting Mithras slaying the bull were demolished. Around the same time, the London *mithraeum* was partly dismantled and a rich collection of pagan images – some mithraic, some Dionysian or of other cults – were buried, presumably for safe-keeping, though not before the head of Mithras had taken a heavy blow. Perhaps the Constantinian religious reformation had given a green light to the bigots – especially in strongly Constantinian Britain – and Christian mobs had gone on the rampage, attacking pagan temples and smashing their holy images. The beneficiaries, of course, would have been 'card-carrying' imperial grandees, their pagan peers intimidated and compromised by a pogrom which will have marked them out as politically suspect.

Even so, beyond the Romanised centres, most people were probably as culturally and ideologically distant from state-backed Christianity in the fourth century as they had been from the state-backed cult of Rome and Augustus in the second. Now, as then, beneath the Romanised veneer – urban, cosmopolitan, sophisticated – there survived an ancient culture rooted in the landscape, in the native soil, and in the ancestral farmlands, much of it older than the Celts, older even than the Beaker folk, some indeed going back to the myth-time when the whole world was a wooded wilderness. A strong, submerged undercurrent of cultural continuity; a resource for expressing difference, opposition, resistance. Let us turn our view 180 degrees. Instead of looking down from above, where the plans of the embattled military monarchy and the greed and power of the imperial grandees predominate, let us look up from below and try to see the impact of the late Roman counter-revolution on civil society in Roman Britain. We have some hypotheses to test. Can we detect, in the material evidence from towns, villas and the countryside generally, the social changes predicted in this chapter: the rise of the imperial grandees, the decline of the municipal gentry, and a worsening struggle for life among the peasant majority? And, more than this, can we detect in the cultural remains of the period, in its religion and its art, evidence of continuity, resistance and survival in those dark peasant masses otherwise hidden from history?

6

GRANDEES, GENTRY AND PEASANTS IN LATER ROMAN BRITAIN

THE DECLINE OF CLASSICAL URBANISM

In the crisis of the mid-third century, civil construction-work in the major towns of Roman Britain all but collapsed. Urban communities made do with their existing suites of public buildings. Few of the urban gentry built new town houses. Even basic maintenance and repair of the existing stock were sometimes neglected. Instead, at colossal expense, second-century earth-and-timber defensive circuits were replaced by new masonry ones (8). Parts of the Romano-British towns, some of whose buildings were more than a century old, came to look dilapidated and ruinous. At Leicester, the east wing of the civic centre was falling down, some of the porticoes were clogged up with street filth, and rubble and refuse were accumulating in the courtyard outside. In London's civic centre, an equally ruinous east range was pulled down – presumably for safety reasons and to salvage building materials – but neglect and decay soon spread to other parts of the complex. Towards the end of the third century, Silchester's town-hall was taken over by metalworkers, and Wroxeter's was destroyed by fire, never to be rebuilt. Urban oligarchies, driven by competitive

Romanitas, had provided themselves with a superfluity of public monuments in the golden age of the Antonines, but in the grimmer circumstances of late antiquity there was neither the will nor the means to sustain them. Living in towns seems to have lost its appeal. Though there is no evidence for falling population – those who owned town-houses continued to occupy them, cracked and crumbling though some of them no doubt were – urban growth ceased. At *Verulamium*, we know of at least eleven new town-houses built in the years *c.*150-200, but only two in *c.*225-75. Between *c.*125 and 225, the number of rooms occupied in private houses in Romano-British towns roughly doubled; from then until the end of the third century it remained static (*7*). The implication is that there was considerable urban population growth in the second century, but none in the third. The Romano-British gentry's early enthusiasm for urban life had collapsed beneath a growing burden of public service under the military monarchy. Many sought refuge on their country estates from the too-persistent attentions of imperial officials. The towns were left stagnant or decaying.

This was not a state of affairs the late Roman state could happily endure. The towns remained central to the infrastructure of military supply. They were the local centres for census surveys and property assessments, for levying tribute and organising labour-services, for the surveillance and policing of the local countryside, for the maintenance of roads and travel-lodges, and, increasingly, for the storage of tribute collected in kind and of the supplies needed by the new mobile field-armies. The late Roman empire was a centralised command-economy founded on a hundred thousand scattered rural communities. It was a tiny cog-wheel trying to turn a very large one; it needed an intermediate wheel to transmit power through the mechanism. Without the towns, the countryside could not be controlled – and the state would be starved of resources by the primeval indifference of the peasant to life outside his village. In their new role as strong-points in a strategy of defence-in-depth, it was enough that the town walls stood ready for use when needed.

But as nodes of military supply, the towns needed a full-time staff of magistrates, councillors, officials, clerks and police. Late Roman towns had to be something more than a mere physical presence. For the Empire to be healthy, towns had to pulsate with civic energy.

But urban life could not simply be rebuilt by orders and threats. In holding together the human infrastructure of imperial power, force and fear were not enough. The Roman law codes threatened dire retribution on *decuriones* who abandoned their posts and neglected their public duties, but the repetitiveness, stridency and severity of such enactments implies their ineffectiveness. To work well, force and fear had to be allied with propaganda and persuasion. The ability of the imperial grandees to command the respect, consent and obedience of the municipal gentry depended on ideology: people had to be convinced that the cause whose burdens and sacrifices they bore was a worthy one. Rome's rulers claimed legitimacy as heirs of the imperial tradition, as defenders of classical culture and the Christian Church, and as founts of a divinely sanctioned authority whose greatness and permanence were assured. This ideological paradigm found expression in an archaic, monumental, Christianised classicism, and, since Graeco-Roman culture was quintessentially urban, its main showcases were the towns. The ideals and values that bound together the imperial elite and its client-groups found their fullest expression in the town planning, public architecture, classical art, and traditional offices and rituals of urban life. The towns continued as pre-eminent symbols of enduring *Romanitas*.

Fortified strong-points, organisational nerve-centres and ideological stage-platforms: the towns were indispensable to the late empire. No less than their predecessors, late Roman emperors actively promoted urban life. But the fruits of their labours were small, hard and sour – not the rich spontaneous growths of the second century, rooted in local conditions and succoured by peace and prosperity under the *Pax Romana*, but urbanism by diktat and favour from above. Roman imperial towns of the second century

AD had been direct descendants of the independent city-states of the fifth century BC. They had by then lost the sovereign decision-making powers that had once made separate states of a thousand urban settlements; towns had been yoked to the service of Rome. But so long as order was kept and taxes paid, the imperial bureaucracy, minimalist anyway, had left well alone. The municipal gentry had been free to raise public monuments, organise community festivals, administer local justice, and in other ways affirm and enjoy their status as men of property and power in the regions. Town government may have been exclusive and oligarchic, but it had remained in local hands. The Roman order had been an alliance between imperial state and local landowners, its well-being and the vigour of its urban civilisation dependent upon the active support of a large, prosperous, enthusiastic municipal gentry. This type of urbanism had decayed in the third century, and it could not be revived by imperial decree in the fourth. The soil in which it had grown was exhausted.

Between 286 and 312, Britain was the subject of close imperial supervision and a sustained attempt to restore its military and civil infrastructure – first by the rebel emperors Carausius and Allectus, then by Constantius Caesar after the restoration, and finally by Constantine the Great in a period when his domain was confined to the north-western provinces. To modernise an ageing infrastructure, many ambitious new construction-projects were launched in the Romano-British towns (8). The *Verulamium* theatre was badly in need of attention. Built in the mid-second century on a prime town-centre site, much enlarged and improved over the succeeding 75 years, it was, by the later third century, disused, dilapidated and rubbish-strewn. Shortly after 300, contractors were hired, scaffolding went up, and for several years the whole area was a major construction-site. The stage and dressing-rooms were rebuilt, the auditorium was enlarged, and new seating was installed throughout. When the theatre reopened, it was bigger and better than ever. A symbol of urban blight and '*Romanitas* Lost' had been transformed into one of hope and renewal. But it did not last. When Kathleen Kenyon excavated the theatre in 1933-4, she found the central *orchestra* filled with 1.5m of 'rich organic earth' – the remains of what had been, in the fourth century, a great dump of rotting vegetables and broken crockery. At some point the new theatre had shut down and the site been turned into an urban tip – it was probably used by traders from the market-hall located just over the road. *Romanitas* Lost Again. The story is similar in other towns: baths, theatres and amphitheatres restored in the so-called 'Constantian renaissance' at the start of the century were little used and soon abandoned. In a survey of fifteen urban baths, for instance, nine were still in use in *c*.300, but none as late as *c*.400. The archaeology of town-houses reveals a similar picture: an early fourth-century mini-boom, reversing late third-century decline, was followed by abandonment and ruination in the succeeding decades (*8*). Urban population levels seem to have declined sharply through the century: as measured by rooms occupied in excavated houses, they were down by almost 30 per cent in *c*.350, 65 per cent in *c*.375, and as much as 90 per cent by the end of the century (*7*). *Verulamium* was typical, with 16 known town-houses at the beginning of the fourth century, but only three at its end (*20, 23*).

Official and upper-class urbanism recovered for a moment and then slumped back again. What of plebeian urbanism? Some of the more prosperous artisans and petty-traders continued to live in strip-houses, just as their forebears had done since the first century. The *insula* XIV shops at *Verulamium* – four times rebuilt in timber and clay between *c*.75 and 150 – were reconstructed in masonry around 275 and continued in use well into the fourth century. Six substantial residences have been excavated, each with several rooms extending back from the street front, some with such decorative refinement as painted wall-plaster and even a mosaic floor. These, surely, were the residences of the most prosperous of the petty-trading class. Others were less fortunate. Many examples have been found, at *Verulamium* and other towns, of tiny late Roman hovels.

Sometimes a flimsy one- or two-roomed hut was built in timber. Sometimes the ruins of an empty town-house were held up with roof props, or perhaps a lean-to was erected against an outside wall. Sometimes the only evidence was that of tessellated floors overlain by rough new surfaces of clay or gravel, maybe with associated fires, hearths and ovens, while domestic rubbish was dumped in vacant rooms nearby. In all, more than a dozen examples of this sort of development have been found at *Verulamium* alone (*23*). Given the low archaeological visibility of such evidence – the material is less substantial, less likely to survive, and less likely to be noticed in excavation than the stone walls and mortared floors of the second century – it may attest a widespread phenomenon: an urban under-class of impoverished artisans, petty-traders, general labourers, street-hawkers, petty criminals and prostitutes living in a shanty town of huts and shelters.

This so-called 'squatter-occupation' is one distinctive feature of late Roman urban archaeology; 'dark earth' is another. Deposits up to 2m deep of dark-grey loamy soil, often rich in animal bones, plant remains, charcoal, and sometimes artefacts, are often found directly overlying the latest Roman walls and floors. Once routinely dug away without record, now increasingly the subject of careful excavation and scientific analysis, there is much debate about what dark earth represents. The answer, though, is probably quite simple: a prolonged process of urban decay. The disintegration and demolition of buildings, most of them comprising a high proportion of clay and timber, coupled with regular rubbish-dumping by a still-substantial urban population, could produce a rapid accumulation of deep deposits of decomposing organic material, degraded building debris and much cultural bric-a-brac. Most likely, municipal regulations governing refuse disposal had become unenforceable by the fourth century, and rubbish previously burnt, buried in pits or carted out of town was now being dumped on any conveniently close waste-ground. The consequences cannot have been pleasant. Contemporary descriptions of medieval cities reveal how foul the pre-industrial urban environment could be. In four-teenth-century London, on the eve of the Black Death, waterways were clogged up with stinking sludge from latrines and sewers emptying into them, open street-drains were blocked by piles of household refuse tipped out of doors and windows, and along the banks of the Thames and in adjoining lanes there were great dumps of rubbish and animal dung. The medieval authorities fought a los-ing battle against garbage and sewage: the sheer quantities involved meant that refuse could not be carted or piped very far, and, since someone had to pay even for this, most people simply dumped waste on the nearest bit of ground they could find beyond their own property boundary. It required consistent, rigorous and expen-sive municipal action to keep the urban environment clean. In fourth-century towns, with the gentry disillusioned and the popu-lation declining, the authorities were overwhelmed by the task. Detailed study of pottery assemblages at York has revealed a fourth-century increase in rubbish dumping within the town, especially after *c*.360, indicating what local archaeologist Jason Monaghan has described as a 'breakdown of civic pride' and the failure of 'organ-ised rubbish disposal practices'. *Verulamium* provides some instructive contrasts. The *insula* XIV shops were burnt down in *c*.155 and the site was undeveloped waste-ground from then until *c*.275. Yet, although in a prime town-centre location next to the main markets, there was no accumulation of rubbish, and the exca-vator guessed that the whole area had been enclosed by hoardings. During the following century, on the other hand, when the theatre on the other side of the road shut down, it became a massive dump; as we have seen, excavators in the 1930s dug through some 1.5m of 'dark earth' filled with the debris of human occupation.

The old view that the Romano-British towns flourished to the end of the fourth century and even beyond must be rejected in the light of such clear evidence of civic decline. In *Verulamium* after about 350 (*23*), there were numerous grand old houses empty, boarded-up and derelict, their grounds rubbish-strewn, the streets

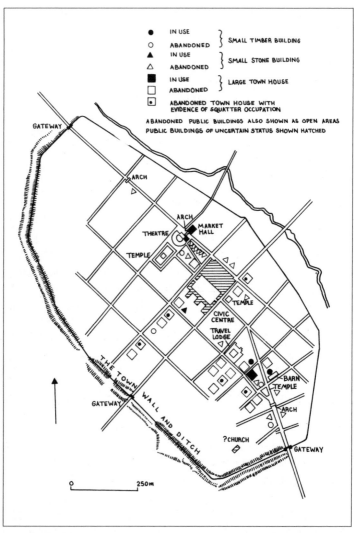

Legend:
- ● IN USE ⎫
- ○ ABANDONED ⎬ SMALL TIMBER BUILDING
- ▲ IN USE ⎫
- △ ABANDONED ⎬ SMALL STONE BUILDING
- ■ IN USE ⎫
- □ ABANDONED ⎬ LARGE TOWN HOUSE
- ⊡ ABANDONED TOWN HOUSE WITH EVIDENCE OF SQUATTER OCCUPATION

ABANDONED PUBLIC BUILDINGS ALSO SHOWN AS OPEN AREAS
PUBLIC BUILDINGS OF UNCERTAIN STATUS SHOWN HATCHED

GATEWAY

ARCH

ARCH
MARKET HALL
THEATRE
TEMPLE

TEMPLE

CIVIC CENTRE

TRAVEL LODGE

BARN TEMPLE

ARCH

GATEWAY

THE TOWN WALL AND DITCH

?CHURCH

GATEWAY

0 — 250m

23 Verulamium in c.375. Plans labelled simply 'fourth-century Verulamium' are highly misleading: in c.325, many buildings had been recently restored, and only a few had yet been abandoned (20); 50 years later, most of the town was a wasteland of disused civic buildings, empty houses, overgrown plots, and heaps of filth and rubbish outside pitted and ankle-deep in filth. Elsewhere, impoverished plebs had colonised parts of the decaying townscape, erecting squalid little huts on open ground, or taking over two or three rooms of an abandoned town-house, where they would light cooking-fires on the tessellated floors. Refuse and sewage were everywhere. The place stank. The hoped-for renaissance of classical urbanism was stillborn. The late Roman counter-revolution had raised up the monarchy, the army and the grandees by turning local gentry into conscript clerks and emptying local coffers into the central treasury. It could not conjure from this a new golden age of urban *Romanitas*. Nonetheless, the towns, though much decayed, did survive – but in the image of the late Roman imperial order of which they were now a part.

THE MILITARY TOWNS OF LATE ROMAN BRITAIN

The Roman Empire was not a façade behind which the 'hidden hand' of some sort of proto-capitalism operated: ancient towns were never an organic growth of free-market enterprise. Urbanism was something ordained, planned and imposed from above. Towns were founded by an act of state, their councils constituted before a stone was laid, and public buildings erected by elite patrons. Most aspects of urban life were regulated. Little was spontaneous. It is because of this that towns were in crisis in the later third century. They were no longer sustained by a vigorous country gentry eager to raise their standing and advance their careers in spectacular architectural displays of *Romanitas*. The gentry were in retreat from public life, forsaking their town houses to seek refuge on their country estates. Their physical presence at council meetings could be ordered. A skeleton of municipal government could be operated. But the Romanising enthusiasm which had built the towns in the second century could not be forced back into being by government order in the fourth. To the extent that towns and town life continued in the late Roman empire, this happened through the intervention not of the municipal gentry, but of the imperial grandees. Looked at up close, the towns of fourth-century Britain bear the hallmarks of the militarised command-economy and bureaucratised state-apparatus of late antiquity.

One vital element in fourth-century urbanism was, as we have seen, the maintenance and improvement of town defences. The earth banks of second-century circuits were cut back to receive masonry walls, commonly between 2.5 and 3m wide, probably over twice that in height, their gateways guarded by tall projecting towers. These circuits ranged in extent from less than a mile (1.5km) at small administrative towns like Caerwent and Caistor to more than 2 miles (3.5km) at large ones like Cirencester and *Verulamium*. This huge construction-programme was more or less finished in the major towns by the end of the third century – though comparable work continued at some of the small towns – so the focus of the early-fourth-century urban renaissance was on rebuilding inside the walls (*8*). We have noted already the decay of the old civic centres – about half the excavated sites have revealed clear evidence of this. Gross in scale and baroque in decoration, these complexes had always been a liability, and now, in the straitened circumstances of the late empire, parts of them were scrapped as too expensive to maintain. But this was not the whole story. The state still needed office accommodation. Many sites show occupation continuing on a reduced scale – there was retrenchment and downsizing, but a leaner administration carried on its work. At Caerwent, most of the town hall was demolished in the mid-fourth century, but a skeleton staff seem to have operated out of some rear-range offices left standing. At Leicester, while parts of the complex were heaped up with rubble, refuse and street filth, elsewhere old offices were reconditioned with new floors and partition-walls. At Silchester, though the town-hall was filled with industrial plant, a hypocaust was installed in part of the west range, presumably to provide central-heating for offices. In some towns, there is no evidence for civic-centre decline at all. At Cirencester, the forum buildings were first partially reconstructed and refurbished, probably early in the fourth century, perhaps to accommodate the government of the newly constituted province of Lower Britain, and then, at the end of the century, an extension was put up to link the town-hall with a building over the road. The fourth-century provincial capitals – London, Lincoln and York as well as Cirencester – would have been prime recipients of official patronage. These were smaller versions of the great imperial capitals on the continent – Trier, Arles, Milan, Ravenna – which, as residential and administrative centres, occasional or permanent, for large contingents of imperial aristocracy, attracted the lion's share of investment in monumental architecture and works of art. Urbanism by diktat and largesse from above increased the differences between one town and another. A few achieved unprecedented grandeur; most declined, some slowly, others abruptly.

The central importance of official patronage is very clear in the case of the Church. The Constantinian reformation had made Christianity a state religion: it was protected by law, enriched by temple dissolutions, and dignified by obvious imperial favour. The politically suspect became, more or less overnight, the politically correct. The Church was strengthened by an influx of new fair-weather converts among career-minded officers and civil servants, and the flow of elite patronage became a torrent – to endow a church became a precise measure of one's orthodoxy and reliability. The main terrain of Christian advance was in the towns. Urban paganism was in decline, and temple renovations featured little in fourth-century construction programmes. In a survey of 24 pagan temples in Romano-British towns, only 13 remained in use after $c.300$, five after $c.350$, and there were just two left in $c.375$. Some appear to have been deconsecrated – or desecrated – and converted to other uses, like Building 52 at Balkerne Lane in Colchester, a conventional Romano-Celtic temple whose central shrine was retained for some unknown purpose when the surrounding ambulatory was demolished. There were exceptions, but they counted for little. A new town-centre temple complex was opened at Caerwent in *c.*330, for instance, but it was a rare case in one of the most remote corners of the Empire. In contrast, while pagan temples were vandalised by sectarian mobs, despoiled by imperial commissioners, and left to tumble into ruin for lack of patrons, new urban churches and cathedrals were being founded. The evidence from Britain is slight, but we know of perhaps half a dozen examples. A notable recent addition to our knowledge comes from an excavation at Tower Hill near the south-east corner of Roman London. Evidence was found for a massive masonry basilica, erected in the second half of the fourth century, with double aisles, marble wall-veneers, painted wall-plaster, a floor of cemented tile-fragments, and a well in the centre of the nave. The design, the monumental scale, the quality of decoration, the date and location, and contemporary continental parallels, all argue for this being the diocesan cathedral.

Religion could inspire men to fight, but they needed the hardware with which to do so. Towns replaced forts and *vici* as military workshops. At Silchester, bronze- and pewter-smiths were employed in the town hall from *c.*275, and iron-workers from *c.*330. Similar evidence, though on a smaller scale, for late Roman metalworking in parts of the old civic centres has been recovered at Caerwent, Leicester and London – contemporary, it seems, with continued use of some rooms as government offices. What does this signify? We might expect the imperial state – controlling authority of a pre-industrial total war economy hampered by slow and expensive long-distance communications – to set up its own arms factories in defended towns close to frontier troop concentrations. This is what the *Notitia Dignitatum* tells us was done. It records a state cloth-factory at 'Venta' in Britain (presumably Caerwent, Caistor or Winchester), and, since the *Notitia* is an incomplete list of *c.*400, we need not assume this was the only government plant in fourth-century Britain. The civic centres, however rundown, were still public property, and the metalworkers based within them, even if private contractors, are likely to have been in government service and part of the late Roman military-supply system.

The towns were also store-depots. The fourth-century historian Ammianus Marcellinus, recording preparations for the emperor Julian's campaign in Germany in 359, wrote,

[Julian] decided ... that before engaging in hostilities one thing above all imperatively demanded his attention. This was to enter and recover towns long since destroyed and abandoned, and repair their defences; also to build granaries in place of those which had been burnt, to store the corn regularly brought from Britain ... The granaries were quickly built and stored with ample supplies of food, and seven towns were reoccupied ... After this one vital task remained, the restoration of the walls of the reoccupied towns while it could be carried out without obstruction ... The [client] kings, in accordance with the agreement of the preceding year, sent a quantity of building material in their own carts, while the auxiliary troops ... were of the greatest service in building operations.

The central role of the emperor and the army in fourth-century urban renewal, at least in a devastated frontier region, could not be clearer. Two priorities were paramount: the reconstruction of town defences, and the provision of military storage facilities. Since taxes were now frequently collected in kind, and since late imperial armies often campaigned deep inside home territory, government stockyards and warehouses were needed at local centres, and these, as protection against thieves, bandits and raiders, had to be located in forts and walled towns. Half a dozen large warehouses, basilical or similar in design and of late Roman date, have been excavated in Romano-British towns. That at Colchester, known as Building 127, is typical: a large, rectangular, masonry hall, comprising a nave and two aisles, at least 45m long and 17m wide, it was probably erected in the late third or early fourth century and remained in use for a hundred years or more. Lacking any of the fittings and finish we would expect of a high-status building, and standing alone on the site of a demolished town-house near the south wall surrounded by allotments and waste-ground, its excavator's conclusion that it was some sort of store-building seems certain. Moreover, though unproven, its interpretation as a government facility is compelling. Large, urban, basilical warehouses were something new in the late empire – both in Britain and on the continent – and they would have been ideal for storing taxes paid in kind and military supplies. Ancillary buildings associated with private residences, on the other hand, were generally smaller, of simple design, and occurred in all periods.

Also characteristic of late Roman towns were extensive, open, gravelled piazzas. Many were laid out in the early empire and simply continued in use, but others were established later, sometimes on town-centre sites that had previously been built on. Towards the end of the fourth century, part of the civic centre at Gloucester was demolished and a large area extending across the *forum* courtyard, *forum* ranges and surrounding streets and buildings was metalled over. Such open ground with good hardstanding would have been ideal for stock-pens. No less important were facilities for moving goods. Though the scale of development on London's waterfront, for instance, was much reduced in the fourth century, there is no evidence that the port ceased to function, despite the construction of a riverside wall in *c.*255-70 which must have greatly inconvenienced access to and from the docks. A central feature, then, of late Romano-British towns was the large-scale movement and storage of government property. Grain and other foodstuffs arrived by barge and cart. Cattle, sheep and pigs were driven in on the hoof. These goods flowed through urban networks of roadways, dockyards, warehouses and stock-pens. Such was the circulatory system of the imperial order: an endless process, mediated by the towns, of accumulating and redistributing agricultural surpluses.

Important, too, in the fourth century were urban markets. The old municipal market-halls (*macella*) known at many Romano-British towns – usually four short ranges of shops or offices around an open central courtyard – were often rebuilt and repaired, generally well maintained, and continued very much in use throughout the century. That at *Verulamium* was reconstructed in grand style some time in the years *c*.300-20 – its monumental street-front façade a symbol of the new *Romanitas* – and the market-traders who used it were still dumping their refuse in the theatre over the road at the end of the century. Sometimes new market facilities were added. At Canterbury, though the main public baths went out of use early in the fourth century, an adjoining street-front portico was first reconstructed in stone, several times thereafter modified in timber, and then continued in use as a row of shops and stalls well into the fifth century. These urban markets were probably places of private commerce – not state enterprise – but they were no less dependent on the military-supply economy for that. The shopping arcades and malls would empty of traders and fast fall into ruin at the end of Roman rule; no free-market capitalism sustained them. The state was both pump-primer and prime mover. The urban markets provided goods and services to the grandees and their entourages of officials and clerks, guards and police, flunkies, servants and call-girls; also to those gentry households that chose to remain in occasional or permanent residence; and to country people coming into town to pay taxes, do labour-service, or seek redress of some grievance by appeal to the high and mighty. The fourth-century urban markets were busy places – yet mere contrivances of the imperial order.

Late Roman urban life, then, revolved around the imperial grandees. Some were simply the greatest of the local lords, the 'leading men' (*principales*), now elevated high above the mass of ordinary gentry. Others were professional career civil-servants, part of an aristocracy-of-office, a pool of men available to central government for service in long-term administrative postings in the regions. Like the sheriffs of medieval England or the prefects of absolutist France, they ruled as local incarnations of the central power, transmitting its orders, imposing its demands, personifying its dictatorship. Such men required accommodation in the grand style. Though the town-house was in decline during the fourth century, some remained in use, a few new ones were built, and the size and embellishment of these establishments could be spectacular. Cirencester, probable capital of the province of Lower Britain, may have been more heavily populated in the mid-to-late fourth century than at any time previously. The townscape was open-plan, with large houses sitting in ample grounds, and it was these private residences, not town-centre public buildings, which enjoyed the luxuries of mosaic floors, painted walls, fine architectural decoration and sculpture, and even domestic bath-suites. Urban luxury had been thoroughly privatised. Building XII.1, a house perhaps first built in the late-third or early-fourth century and reaching its fullest development around 350, had 16 rooms, 12 decorated with mosaics, and its own bath-house. At least six other comparable grand houses of this period are known at Cirencester. Even in more depressed urban centres, some elite residences remained. Although excavations have revealed only one small town house surviving at *Verulamium* in *c.*375, two others are known to have been built shortly afterwards, one of just five rooms, the other, Building XXVII.2, a true urban mansion. It comprised at least 22 rooms, organised in three ranges (there may have been a fourth) around a central courtyard, with tessellated floors in half the rooms, mosaics in three, and a central-heating system in one. Elite urban residences may have been far fewer than in former times, but the grandeur of those there were was undiminished – just the pattern we might expect, in fact, if power were now concentrated among a minority of grandees.

The fourth century, from *c.*325 at least, was a period of decline for the broad-based urbanism of the municipal gentry. By its end, virtually all civic amenities and private houses had been abandoned and were in ruins if not demolished (*23*). But in places, amid the wasteland of roofless structures, collapsed building-debris, shanty-town slums, heaps of rotting garbage and pools of stinking sewage, one would have seen little oases of civilisation. There were a few well-maintained cottages belonging to the better sort of artisan or trader, and, more rarely, a grand old mansion still kept up in traditional style, whether by one of the ancient gentry families still left in town, or by a state *apparatchik* appointed to the district on a long-term posting. Bath house, theatre and temple were in ruins, and parts of the civic centre had been demolished, but still there were government offices and a municipal authority. Taxes were collected, labour gangs organised, warehouses and stock-pens filled, armaments manufactured and dispatched, military supplies hoarded in readiness, town walls repaired and patrolled, churches built and decorated. The booming civil towns of the golden age had been superseded by the gloomy police towns of an age of blood and iron.

LANDLORDS, ESTATES AND VILLAS

In the high empire, between *c.*150 and 225, those with money to spare were more likely to have built grand town houses than to have embellished their country seats. Fewer than ten villas are known to have had mosaic floors in the second century; more than three dozen town houses did so. But the third-century crisis shattered the structure of classical urbanism in Britain. That structure had always been fragile, since town life was more a matter of preference than of necessity. If it became burdensome, one could simply leave to live elsewhere. Wealth in Roman Britain derived from landed estates, not town property; control over the labour of rural slaves, serfs and tenants, not that of urban plebs, was the essence of class power. What is more remarkable, in a way, is not the decline of the Romano-British towns in the fourth century, but the momentary preference of the landowning elite for urban residence in the second. Otherwise, from the Bronze Age to the Civil War, the owners of the British countryside generally lived in it. Indeed, even at the peak of the urban craze, many villas were constructed. Figure *18*, based on a sample of 78 sites for which detailed excavation evidence is available, shows high and rising investment in villas between the late first and late second century. Some rich gentry may have maintained both rural and urban residences. Most, though, probably had only one. None of the British towns appear to have had sufficient grand houses for all its gentry. At Silchester, where we have a complete town plan, there were about 30, and it is only by adding a similar number of villas in the surrounding *civitas*-territory that we can assemble a respectable-sized town council. Some town-houses, then – those that were sole residences – must have served as estate-centres; some landowners, in other words, had their 'villas' in town. Either way, wherever they were resident in the second century, the gentry retained their rural roots. Towns were fashionable places to be, but a gentleman could live well enough in the countryside.

It was no great matter, therefore, to 'retreat to the countryside' (as modern scholars have sometimes expressed it). A small shift in the balance of advantage could empty the towns as quickly as they had filled. Urban life was a Roman bauble, momentarily dazzling, but soon discarded once the shine had gone. One then returned to one's ancestral seat. Changes there, in contrast to new-fangled towns, were more to do with form than substance. One's ancestors had lived in huge round-huts, where, after a feast cooked on the central hearth, before walls decorated with glinting armaments, and as Gallic wine was served to retainers and squires, the bard would sing of Celtic heroes and battles long ago. Now, in the late third century, as many villas were vastly extended and richly decorated, status found expression in Mediterranean architecture, classical art, and (no doubt) Italian manners. This was now *de rigueur* for Romano-British sophisticates – in the south-east at least. But the substance of lordly power was in fact unchanged: a centuries-old inheritance of the right to rule the land and those who toiled on it.

Too much emphasis on the 'Romanisation' of the British elite has sometimes obscured this. Changes in material culture – the data-base of archaeology – are often confused with changes in social processes, whereas new ways of displaying wealth, power and status are often simply a matter of conforming to the prevailing fashion. The decline of the towns and the rise of the villas meant, in a sense, a return to normality.

A villa we know much about is that at Bignor in Sussex. It had a prime location on the highly-fertile Upper Greensands just north of the South Downs. This would have provided prime arable close to the estate-centre, more marginal arable and rough grazing on the chalkland to the south, better quality grazing in the water-meadows of the Arun valley to the east, and woodland resources on the Wealden clays to the north. Excellent communications would have permitted efficient marketing of surpluses: the villa lay close to Stane Street, the main road between London and the south coast, and this linked it with the small town of Hardham 3 miles (5km) to the north-east, and the *civitas*-capital of Chichester about 15 miles (24km) to the south-west. A tentative reconstruction of the villa economy has been worked out from a study of farmyard buildings and the surrounding landscape. The estate, running to perhaps 2,500 acres (1,000ha) in all, may have had cereals and other crops on about 750 acres (300ha) of good arable, 50-plus cattle out to pasture in valley-bottom meadows, 200 sheep up on the downland, and an unknown number of pigs in the woods, where perhaps there was also timber-cutting, coppicing and charcoal-burning. The mixed-farming regime was probably essential to long-term success: animals grazing on post-harvest stubble would have fertilised the arable with their dung. A workforce of between 30 and 50 hands is likely, and, if we allow for dependants at the common ratio of 1:1.5, we get a total of 75-125 for the estate peasantry as a whole. The esti-mates involve a series of uncertain leaps, but they perhaps give an order of magnitude, and suggest that the lords of Bignor were great landowners who dominated the lives of all around them.

At first, however, the Iron Age farmstead on the site of the later villa continued little changed into the Roman period. The first villa-like structure was not put up until the late second century, and this was built of timber. Even its mid-third-century masonry replacement was modest in scale compared with what was to follow. Perhaps the owners had resided previously at Chichester, and only later did they join the exodus from a town in severe recession and invest serious money in their country seat. The original five-roomed masonry house was at first extended a little at a time, but then, around 300, a massive reconstruction was undertaken, supplemented by further major works perhaps a generation later (*24*). The old house became the west range of a much grander complex as its small north and south wings were lengthened into full ranges on either side of a large rectangular courtyard. This was enclosed by a covered walkway on the east, shutting out the farmyard and working areas, and thereby creating a high-status residence which looked in on itself across a garden likely to have been laid out in a formal Mediterranean style. The finished villa comprised some 60 rooms and corridors, 15 with mosaic floors, including ample bath-blocks in both the south and west ranges, and a magnificent suite of large, heated and superbly decorated living-rooms on the north side. Among the latter was a large apsidal room whose floor mosaic depicted a bust of Venus and a frieze of cupid-gladiators. Another large room, this with hexagonal basin and fountain in the centre, was decorated with an image of Ganymede being carried off to Olympus by Jupiter. The richness of the mosaics is perhaps the best indication of the wealth and taste of the owners. We can only guess at the more portable (and so less enduring) valuables and *objets d'art* which filled the villa in its heyday. There is a clue, perhaps, in the spectacular hoards of fourth-century metalwork which are occasionally recovered from isolated spots – from places, that is, where villa owners in troubled times may have stashed their household plate for safety. The Mildenhall treasure from Suffolk, dated sometime after *c*.360, comprised 34 silver items, including spoons, platters, bowls, and, most notably, a great dish of 24in (60cm) diameter and almost 4lbs (8.3kg) in weight; some of the vessels were superbly decorated to the highest standards of classical art.

Clearly, not all rural landlords could afford a villa as extensive as Bignor or treasure as rich as that found at Mildenhall. Such discoveries attest the presence in fourth-century Britain of the imperial grandees: a minority of big landowners networked into the top echelons of the state. Sometimes this *apparatchik*-landlord nexus is directly confirmed when the badges of rank known to have been worn by late Roman officials turn up on villa sites. Contemporary visual images show grandees wearing tunics and cloaks decorated with jewellery and dress-fittings appropriate to their status. Signet-rings had distinctive designs on their bezels to allow important documents to be sealed with a unique mark as proof of authority. Brooches, notably of crossbow design, were worn prominently on

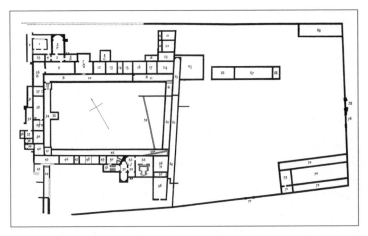

24 Bignor villa, Sussex, c.325. One of the great courtyard villas of late Roman Britain. The enclosure shown on the right of the main residence contained the farmyard and agricultural outbuildings. Note that the central courtyard is about 60m across on its longest side. (Some details of this plan, based on the work of Samuel Lysons in the early nineteenth century, have been modified in the light of recent fieldwork.)

the shoulder to pin cloaks in place and at the same time signify status (25). Belt-fittings in the form of buckles and decorative plates were worn as part of the *cingulum* (the wide leather belt which was part of the military-style uniform of late Roman officials). The right to wear precious-metal versions of these items was probably a prerogative of rank. Examples of all three types have been found in Roman Britain.

We can picture the late Roman grandee as a man dressed in richly coloured and embroidered garments decorated with gold jewellery and fittings. At home and at ease, the central-heating lit against the evening chill, he, his family and a few close friends might recline on ornamented dining-couches to eat Italian-style dishes off silver plate, the meal washed down with an imported vintage. A mosaic image of the gods at their feet, mock marble-veneers painted on the walls, they might look out across the neatly clipped trees, shrubs and box-hedges of a formal garden. A new illuminated copy of Virgil resting on a side-table might become a talking-point later in the evening. But we should imagine the grandee's neighbours rather differently. Ordinary gentry lived in single-range houses overlooking their farmyards, with only a couple of rooms well-decorated and heated. They wore silver badges, ate off pewter, and probably thought Virgil rather high-brow. Gorhambury in Hertfordshire was more typical of ordinary villas (17). The grand house here had been completely rebuilt in the late second and early third centuries as a large, well-appointed 'double-winged corridor' villa of 14 rooms. It grew no larger, however: despite much refurbishment after a period of decay, there were no further extensions, and the owners of Gorhambury were clearly lesser lords than those of Bignor. Other villas could be smaller still. The late-third-century house at Rock on the Isle of Wight was just six rooms with a connecting corridor; walls were painted, but there was no floor tessellation or central-heating. Small corridor-houses like Rock merge down into the three- and four-roomed cottages of prosperous peasants like those at the Romano-British village of Heybridge in Essex (see below). We should not, then, think in terms of a single, unified ruling class in late Roman Britain, but of a highly stratified landowning elite, graded finely from top to bottom by differences of rank, wealth and culture. At the heights were high imperial officials with fat-cat salaries, expense accounts, perks and bonuses, with multiple holdings and multifarious business arrangements; in the middle range were the solid respectable gentry of secure status but only local repute; at the depths were decayed gentlemen struggling to maintain themselves above the level of plebeian tenant-farmers.

Bignor, Gorhambury, Rock: high, middle and low. There are signs, moreover, that the gap between grandee and gentry was increasing in the late empire. When Romano-British villas (from our sample of 78) are ranked by size into four categories and analysed by period, we can see this change. The number in the two lower-value categories, having reached a peak in the early third century, fluctuated around an average of about 20 between $c.225$ and 350. By contrast, the number in the two higher-value categories continued to increase, rising from 11 in $c.225$ to a peak of 18 in $c.300$. In other words, in the late empire, the proportion of large villas compared with small increased sharply. Not only, then, was the landowning elite of late Roman Britain internally stratified, but the gap was growing wider between grandee and gentry. The tensions implicit in this situation cannot have added to the cohesion and efficiency of the state – least of all now, in the middle years of the fourth century, when all the economic indicators point to an agricultural depression in the Romano-British countryside.

PEASANTS, VILLAGES AND AGRICULTURAL DEPRESSION

Whatever differences of status existed among Romano-British landlords, the gulf between all of them and those who actually worked the land was far wider. Landlords were gentlemen, classed by the law as *honestiores* ('men of honourable rank'): property-owners who need not work because they controlled the labour of others. These others were the slaves, serfs and peasants who formed the great mass of people in Roman Britain. Compelled to toil in the fields in order to live, they endured traditional agriculture's endless cycle of back-breaking physical labour. *Humiliores*, they were called, 'men of humble station'. Many country people in the villa-dominated south-east must have worked for all or part of their time on landlord estates. Most villa excavations have concentrated on the high-status residence, but a few have looked in detail at the farmyards and associated buildings nearby. Sometimes evidence has been found for worker accommodation, often in large rectangular buildings divided into a nave and two aisles (thus known as 'aisled-houses'), often with internal partition-walls, hearths and domestic debris. Columella, a Romano-Hispanic army officer who

25 Insignia of the late Roman grandee: gold crossbow brooch from the Moray Firth, Scotland

wrote a lengthy treatise on farming, described the typical Italian villa of the first century AD as having three main elements: a high-status residence (*pars urbana*), a farmhouse and working areas (*pars rustica*), and store-buildings (*pars fructuaria*). Part of the farmhouse, he explained, should be divided into individual rooms for the accommodation of slaves, and the layout of the complex as a whole should be compact to facilitate effective supervision by overseers. Gorhambury conforms closely to this pattern (*17*). The complex was divided by boundary-ditches into two separate compounds, the inner one containing the main residence, the outer one a farmyard with a large timber aisled-house and a fine stone-built bath-block for the use of the labourers.

The Gorhambury workers may have been slaves. Not far away, at Hambleden villa in Buckinghamshire, 97 infant burials were exca-vated. If mass infanticide is indicated (it may not be), then this would be strong circumstantial evidence for slavery – the rearing of child-chattels may not have been cost-effective. But the use of slave labour in productive work was always contingent upon supply. In the years 43-84, when those taken captive in the wars of conquest were being sold, supply may have been high and slaves fairly cheap. For most of the next three centuries, however, supply is likely to have been a trickle, pushing up the price to a level where slaves were bought only as luxury goods, not as an investment in 'tools which speak' (*instrumenta vocalia*). The discussion of this subject has, anyway, been somewhat oversimplified: whether labour was slave or free was only one of a number of variables. The Gorhambury estate would have needed a core workforce for year-round duties, and an additional temporary workforce for busy times like ploughing and harvest. The former, if not actually slaves, may have been depend-ent, tied or indentured labourers – though the employment of free workers on contract is also possible. The seasonal workers, on the other hand, may have been local peasants under obligation to their lord, an arrangement perhaps implied when villas and villages are found, medieval-style, in close association. At the Romano-British village of Catsgore in Somerset, one exceptional building was classed by its excavator as a 'villa' because it was larger than the others and set apart from them; and some 800m to the south-west was another, larger, more definite villa (26). There is no way of knowing, of course, but one interpretation could be that we have a house for the bailiff in the village itself – for effective supervision – while the lord's residence was located a socially comfortable distance away.

Generally, however, such native settlements – whether villages, hamlets or isolated farmsteads – are found at a greater distance from villas, and this has sometimes been taken to mean a two-tiered economy: the farms of independent peasants co-existing with villa estates worked by tied labour. We cannot know, but it must be stressed that the settlement evidence is wholly inconclusive. Social domination does not depend on physical proximity. Landlord power was never limited to line of sight. Eighteenth-century English aristocracy surrounded their stately homes with acres of landscaped parkland. Many had multiple estates and drew revenues from distant villages and farms. Few of the common people were truly free: most were tenants and rent-payers, or labourers in search of work. Probably, Roman Britain was much the same, at least in the south-east. Free men perhaps survived in the interstices: tilling poor ground in woodland clearings between the great estates, herding sheep on remote upland pastures, working in rural industries making pots or smelting iron, living as itinerants odd-jobbing or hawking trinkets from settlement to settlement. But most men on good land were likely to be obliged to a lord. Even so, competition for labour at harvest time might have induced some gentry to build aisled-houses and bath-blocks, like those at Gorhambury, to attract workers free to pick and choose. In 1931, George Orwell joined the hop-pickers in Kent and found them 'to be of three types: East Enders (mostly costermongers), gypsies, and itinerant agricultural labourers with a sprinkling of tramps'. One can imagine that an equally disparate bunch was sometimes assembled for seasonal work on the big estates of Roman Britain.

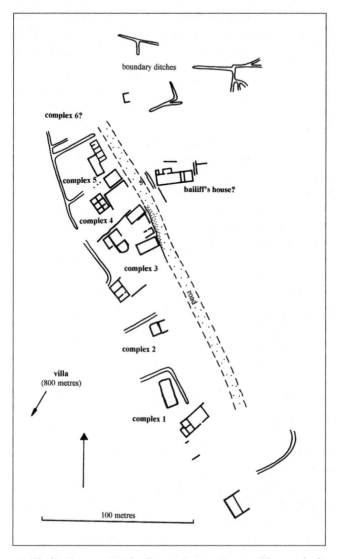

26 The late Romano-British village at Catsgore, Somerset. The growth of the village may be related to the manorialisation of the countryside in the late Roman period. After Leech

A controlled countryside, then, where most land and labour were held in lordship. Naturally, the degree to which men were locally rooted, tied to the land, and obliged to their masters varied. Landlordism probably bore hardest on those who lived on imperial estates or where villas were numerous (*16*). These were the areas of good arable, easy communications and handy markets – most of the south-east, in fact – and pollen analysis has shown that heavy forest clearance had created an open landscape of fields and pasture by the early Roman period. The government, moreover, had built many long straight roads across this countryside, roads that were metalled, well-maintained and good for commerce. Rural settlements were soon linked with these by countless winding trackways bounded by ditches and embankments. These gave a thousand or so villas access to the ready markets of the military-supply economy. It meant also, for better or worse, the integration of much larger numbers of vil-lages, hamlets and farmsteads: down the roads and trackways of Roman Britain came the landlord's bailiff, the tax-collector and the recruiting-sergeant. Native rural settlements were evenly and densely scattered across this landscape. Evidence from air-photo-graphs and fieldwalking surveys on the river gravels of the upper Thames valley in Oxfordshire shows one Romano-British settle-ment every 1-1.5km. Travelling through the countryside of south-eastern Britain in Roman times, you would have seen little more woodland than today, and you could have gone no great dis-tance without passing human habitation and the sight of men and women at work in field and farmyard. An open landscape teeming with life and labour.

Many lived in individual farmsteads – like Woodcuts, situated on the chalk downland of Dorset. A 100m-wide circular farmyard bounded by bank and ditch was established here in the late Iron Age. Over the following 150 years, two irregular 'working hollows' and dozens of wattle-lined pits were dug, presumably for processing and storing grain. No evidence for a house was found in excava-tion, but a clear space in the centre of the compound could have accommodated a sizeable round-hut of traditional type. Romanised artefacts at this period were few. Change was slow, but from the late second century onwards the site had sub-enclosures for specialised activities, one containing a well, another two corn-drying ovens (to improve long-term grain preservation), and elsewhere there were such Roman domestic refinements as wall-plaster. A high degree of self-sufficiency is implied by finds of quernstones, spindle-whorls and loom-weights. Woodcuts – in the late Roman period anyway – was the farm of an enterprising, prosperous and independent peasant household.

Others lived in nucleated settlements. These could range from tiny hamlets of two or three farms clustered together to large organised village communities of two, three or four hundred people – like that recently excavated at Heybridge in Essex. Here, too, settlement began in the late Iron Age and continued into the Roman period. Originally, clusters of round-huts grouped in compounds marked out by boundary ditches were ranged along several unmade trackways. The Heybridge pattern – where each farm comprised a number of enclosures and buildings – seems a common one at Romano-British native sites. The typical peasant household may have been quite large – perhaps an extended family plus other dependants. The original trackways were eventually turned into gravel-surfaced roads, and along the sides of these, within some 50 family compounds, the old hut clusters were gradually replaced by new-style rectangular long-houses. About 20m in length and subdivided into three or four rooms, these had timber frames, wattle-and-daub walls, clay floors, thatched roofs, and centrally placed cooking-hearths. Finds from the site imply a lifestyle very much like that at Woodcuts: a mixed-farming economy, much cottage industry, and a high degree of self-sufficiency. The villagers cultivated wheat and ground their own bread-flour on rotary querns. Animal bones show they reared cattle, sheep and pigs to supply meat, hides, wool, dairy products and bone. Nearby woodland was exploited for timber, withies and charcoal. The local estuary yielded fish, oysters and sea-salt. Various crafts were practised. Several kilns produced coarse greyware pottery for everyday use in the home. Iron was smelted and smithied to produce hammers, chisels, awls, axes, knives, shears and saws. Numerous spindle-whorls and loom-weights attest much spinning and weaving to produce cloth. Wood, leather and bone were also worked. Nothing was wasted – neither resource nor skill. Roman Heybridge had little need of the outside world. Imports were mainly luxuries: cooking oil, fancy tableware, glass trinkets, pretty brooches – rarely anything vital.

The outside world, on the other hand, had need of Heybridge. What the evidence indicates is not independence from the Roman world system, but an utterly one-sided relationship with it. The great superstructure of courtiers, officers and landlords – that which is recorded archaeologically by forts, towns and villas – was entirely dependent on agricultural surpluses pumped out of places like Heybridge. The return on this, as we have just seen, can be measured in handfuls of knick-knacks. The outside world, moreover, was in crisis, and the weight of the superstructure pressed down ever more heavily on the countryside during the fourth century. The consequence – much scholarly opinion to the contrary notwithstanding – was an agricultural depression.

Our review of the evidence for this can begin with the villas. The villa-building craze seems to have peaked as early as *c*.300, and thereafter the fall was abrupt: by *c*.325 the construction rate had almost halved, and by *c*.350, at barely a third as much, the rate had fallen below that during the third-century crisis (*18*). With fewer villas built and others lacking renovation, the villa population, measured by rooms occupied, fell steadily from its *c*.325 peak: down 15 per cent in *c*.350, 35 per cent in *c*.375, and 70 per cent by the end of the century (*19*). Bignor's golden age may have been very short. It was a generation or so after the great rebuilding of *c*.300 that the grand living-rooms with their splendid mosaic floors were added to the north range, but there are signs of decline only a decade or two after that. The amount of material – pottery and coins – recovered in excavation is much lower for the mid-fourth century than for earlier, and there seems to be nothing at all after $c.360$-70. A litter of broken roof-tiles was excavated where it had fallen through the rotted rafters above. There is no evidence that this did not happen decades before the Romans left Britain. It was similar elsewhere. At Gorhambury, probably early in the fourth century, the grand house fell into ruin and seems to have been incorporated into the farmyard when two barns were constructed close to it. At Rock on the Isle of Wight, a corn-drier was built in the last quarter of the fourth century, but the villa itself was by then dilapidated, some of its stone probably already carted off for reuse by local farmers. At Ditchley in Oxfordshire, fires were lit on a living-room floor, and at King's Weston in Gloucestershire, occupation had been reduced to a few rooms. There seems to be a pattern: the grand old houses could not be maintained, but agricultural activity continued, represented by 'squatter-occupation' – similar to that in once-grand town-houses – and an enlargement of farmyards and working areas. A glittering villa civilisation had arisen in the years $c.275$-325, but within a generation it was in crisis, and between $c.350$ and 400 it virtually vanished. It had lasted a mere moment – a will-o'-the-wisp, it seems.

The villa evidence allows only one possible conclusion: in the mid-late fourth century, agriculture was depressed and landlord surpluses were being squeezed hard. Moreover, this was no short-term crisis due to crop blight, transport failure or disrupted markets. It was a long-term structural collapse from which no escape was possible: a full-blown systems failure. The most likely explanation is an intensified struggle for control of a shrinking surplus. The landlords had retreated to the countryside to protect themselves and their property from the demands of state officials. This decentralisation of power may well have been of some effect. The logistics of state surplus-accumulation must have been much more difficult with the gentry dispersed, obstructive and hard-to-get-at. The villas may have collapsed, but so too did the army, and we might guess from this that, while possibly successful in resisting state power, the gentry succumbed to something more deep-rooted. If the pressure from above had become too great, the peasant economy would be unable to reproduce itself, and in this case the surplus available for appropriation by both state and gentry would shrink. This would encourage efforts to increase the rate of exploitation and pump out more surplus, but this policy could only worsen the crisis in peasant agriculture. The economic foundations of the imperial order would then be collapsing beneath it. The struggle for control of the surplus extracted might become more bitter, but whatever the outcome, the end result would be the ruin of both state and gentry. There is every indication that this is precisely what was happening in late Roman Britain.

The historical and archaeological records imply a tightening of landlord control over the peasantry. The late Roman law-codes refer frequently to *coloni* ('cultivators'), peasants who were tied to a single lord's estate in the manner of feudal serfs. These references signal an erosion of peasant freedom and more efficient exploitation of rural labour: the right to move in search of lower rents or higher wages was the peasant's principal defence against the landlords – deprived of this right, the peasant would be forced to accept whatever terms were imposed. On the other hand, to maximise the benefit from legal serfdom, landlords needed to ensure close supervision of their workforces – just as Columella had urged in relation to slaves – and a more nucleated settlement pattern might therefore be expected. The labour of a remote homesteader was less easily managed than that of a villager under the bailiff's gaze. There is some evidence that such a change towards greater nucleation did in fact occur: villages may have become larger and more numerous in the late Roman period. A good example is the Romano-British agricultural village at Catsgore in Somerset (*26*). In the early second century, only three embanked farm-compounds and four round-huts are known to have existed here (and the latter may not all have been contemporary). In the fourth century, by contrast, there were at least 12 compounds, now bounded by stone-walls, and 16 buildings, most of them rectangular with stone-footings, all broadly contemporary. As noted above, two associated buildings may imply control by a landlord: the large house in the village which perhaps belonged to a bailiff, and the villa 800m away which may have been the manor-house. If the change in the wider settlement pattern implicit at Catsgore – from dispersion in separate homesteads and small hamlets to nucleation in a single main centre – can be interpreted sociologically, we might guess that pressure from villa-owning landlords had converted relatively free peasant smallholders into more tightly controlled serfs.

A process of manorialisation was perhaps under way. Certainly, the whole Romano-British settlement pattern suggests decentralisation of power from town to country during the fourth century. As the major towns declined, never recovering fully from the dark days of the mid-third century, villas, small towns and rural industries developed apace. Things levelled out: instead of a sharp hierarchy with a few big towns at the top, many tiny homesteads at the bottom, and not much in between, the pattern now was for a more even distribution across the landscape of settlements similar in size, wealth and culture. One consequence may have been that villas developed in place of towns as tax-collection centres. From where the peasant stood, rent to the lord or tribute to the emperor, labour-service on private land or public roads, would have come to seem pretty much the same – if, indeed, they did not already. Villa, it seems, dominated village as never before. Fourth-century Britain may have looked much as eleventh-century England one day would. Out of the crisis of the late antique state and the decay of classical civilisation, a new medieval order seemed to be emerging.

Serf-like legal status, stronger landlordism, and the embattled condition of the state: these factors increased the renders of produce and labour demanded of the late Romano-British peasant and drove him into an economic depression. The best measure of this is the abandonment of marginal land and a decline in the number of agricultural settlements. The mechanism was simple enough. When the rural economy expanded, second-rate land was reclaimed from the wilderness and cleared for cultivation; though returns were low, they were still sufficient for a living. But each time rents, taxes and labour-services were ratcheted up, returns on the most marginal land then in use would fall below the viability threshold – and this land would have to be given up. A host of variables affected which parcels of land were affected – soil erosion, harvest failure, an outbreak of plague, corrupt tax-officers, a barbarian raid – but this had no bearing on the iron rule: for each increase in exploitation and surplus-accumulation, a proportion of peasant farms would fail and the land return to waste. The amount of abandoned land (*agri deserti*) may have been as high as 20 per cent in some areas of the late empire. The authorities made it illegal to withdraw land from cultivation. They settled barbarians as farmers in depopulated frontier districts. The issue was vital and the government knew it: land and labour were the foundation blocks of state power. How far can a process of land and settlement abandonment be detected archaeologically in late Roman Britain?

Figure **27** shows the results of one of two major surveys of native rural sites. It is based on a random sample of almost 200 sites where fieldwork projects were carried out between 1969 and 1996. This shows that settlement density was highest in the second century, dropped only modestly in the third, and then fell quite heavily in the fourth so that the total number of sites was 35 per cent down by the later fourth century. This conclusion is confirmed by Kate Meheux's survey of a sample of over 300 sites in the Severn Valley and Welsh Marches region: here again the number of occupied sites had dropped by around 30 per cent by the later fourth century compared with peak levels in the second and third. In some cases, the change might be explained as part of the process of manorialisation and nucleation proposed above: a landscape of villas and villages would mean fewer settlements as outlying homesteads and hamlets were given up. Often, though, it seems that the land itself was being abandoned, especially later in the fourth century, when villa estates were also failing.

The chalk downland farmed at Woodcuts may have been marginal land – the thin eroded soils of the higher slopes were perhaps worked out by the fourth century – and the site was abandoned some time shortly before *c*.375. South-central England is one area where pollen analysis has indicated woodland regeneration during and after the late Roman period. The native village at Heybridge may have been marginal, too. The site was very low-lying and prone to flooding. It was also, by the fourth century, in a frontier district open to seaborne attack. Stratigraphic and environmental evidence from excavations here has revealed a village at war with nature: soil and rubbish were dumped on roads and building-plots to raise the level clear of flood water, and this, mixed with animal-dung, created a foul-smelling mud across much of the site. The village lost its war, however: some peripheral areas were abandoned to returning countryside as early as 200, and even in the heart of the settlement, activity was greatly reduced in the third and fourth centuries. Though some Romano-British still lived at Heybridge when Saxon settlers arrived in the fifth century, the village was by then a shadow of its second-century prime.

By and large, however, we might expect sites in the prosperous south-east to fare better in troubled times than those in the more marginal north-west. Although land clearance in the Iron Age and early Roman period had increased the area under cultivation, farmland in the north-west was often surrounded by extensive tracts of upland wilderness, and the rough arable and grazing that had been wrested from nature yielded a poor living. Air-photographs show the average farm near Hadrian's Wall to have been a mean-sized plot of barren ground: enough for subsistence and not much more. The main cereal crop was barley, not wheat, and the herding of sheep and cattle loomed large. Houses were small and of traditional type, Roman-style pots and trinkets were few, and people lived a timeless existence of hard and unrewarding toil in a desolate land-

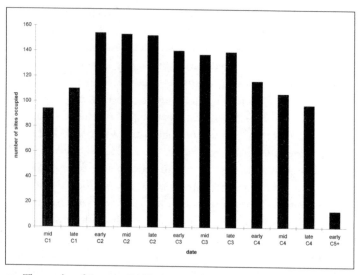

27 The number of Romano-British native rural sites recorded in fieldwork, 1969-96, organised by period. A clear pattern of contraction is apparent in the late Roman period. Sample: 177. Source: Britannia

scape. Here, in north and west, beyond the villa line which extended roughly south-west from Exeter to north-east at York, the impact of the agricultural depression on marginal upland farms seems to have been severe. A typical site lies at Chysauster in Cornwall (*28*). The settlement consisted of nine households. Each family lived in a courtyard house approximately 20m across and oval in plan, with a thick stone wall around the edge, a central open space, and usually three or four roughly-circular rooms built into the boundary wall. The largest of these usually faced the main gateway, contained a hearth, and would have functioned as the main dwelling. The others were perhaps used mainly for animal-stalling and food-storage. Outside each house was an attached farmyard enclosure with working areas and stock-pens. Beyond the settlement site lay a field system, the remains of which indicate a mixed-farming regime. Chysauster seems to exist outside history. Founded in the first century BC, it appears not to have changed at all in the next four centuries. It was beyond the pale of civilisation and nothing recognisably Roman ever happened here. But around 300, the village was abandoned. We cannot know why, but, like many other marginal north-western farming communities, the settlement perhaps had too narrow a threshold of survival to weather the troubled times of late antiquity. Certainly, its fate was shared by many others: in a random sample of 30 Cornish sites, 22 were occupied in the late Iron Age, 15 in the second century, and just 7 in the fourth. Timeless they may seem, but these remote sites do have a history – albeit mostly lost to us – and it seems likely that their demise now was intimately connected with the crisis of the world system of which they formed, however peripherally, a part.

Villas and villages were in decline. Romano-British agriculture was in recession. The same appears to have been true of rural industries. The potteries provide the fullest evidence. In the early Roman period, coarseware pottery had been provided by local, often town-based, producers, while most fineware was imported, principally from the Samian industries of Gaul. Subsequently, some Romano-British potteries diversified into fineware manufacture, expanded their product range, and established market dominance across large areas. Although there was a recession in the mid-third century, the virtual cessation of imports (in particular of Samian) meant that the fineware market became dominated afterwards by a small number of Romano-British producers. Detailed studies have been made of several of these industries – Nene Valley, Oxfordshire and New Forest especially – and these have revealed a clear trajectory of expansion and contraction. Key measures of vitality are the number of new forms introduced and the number of forms in the current product range (29). Innovation and repertoire were limited in the second century, there was some recession in the middle years of the third, and then the Romano-British potteries expanded dramatically in the late third and early fourth. By the mid-fourth century,

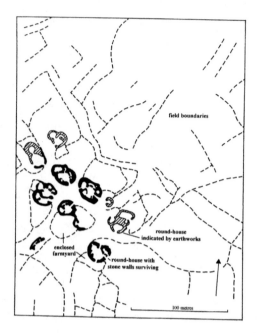

field boundaries

round-house
indicated by earthworks

enclosed
farmyard

round-house with
stone walls surviving

100 metres

*28 The Romano-
British village at
Chysauster, Cornwall.*
After Christie

however, there were signs of recession: the number of new forms introduced fell by well over 50 per cent in *c.*325, and then dropped to almost nothing in *c.*375, by which time the total product range was also down sharply. For a time, long-distance marketing networks seem to have held up, despite shrinkage in the size of the overall market, but after *c.*370 a sharper contraction began the terminal decline of the major potteries. By the end of the Roman period, assemblages were looking distinctly shabby. The latest in south-eastern Britain included rough shell-tempered wares, a fair proportion of local handmade pottery, and a range of forms restricted to a few simple jars, bowls and dishes.

Put simply, in the Romano-British countryside of the fourth century, four things happened: power was decentralised when the gentry decamped from the towns to their country estates; the wealth gap between state grandee and local gentry grew wider; the exploitation of the peasantry increased and many peasant households were pushed close to or over the edge; and the rural economy as a whole went from boom to bust as settlements were abandoned and land returned to wilderness. The 'retreat to the countryside' turned out to be abortive – the gentry reduced its exposure to the state authority and tightened its grip on landed property, but it could not, even so, sustain itself for more than a generation or two. The late Roman countryside bears a superficial resemblance to medieval feudalism. But the Norman lords of the eleventh century combined both economic *and* military power: the medieval fiefdoms directly supported warrior knights whose armed might guaranteed their

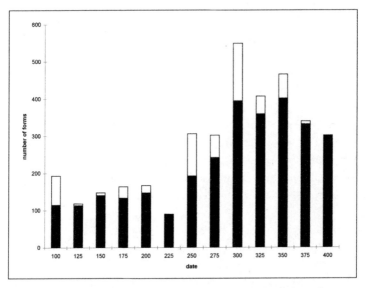

29 The rise and fall of the Romano-British potteries. The graph combines the evidence from detailed studies of the Nene Valley, New Forest and Oxfordshire fineware industries. The black areas show the number of forms in use at the time, the open ones the number of new forms being introduced. The results clearly indicate fourth-century decline. After Fulford, Howe et al. and Young

property against both state power and peasant revolt. In the late empire, though landlords might hire mafia-like gangs to maintain order on their estates, they lacked serious military resources. Facing state demands backed by armed force, or collective acts of peasant resistance, they were vulnerable. But this separation of economic and military power worked to the state's disadvantage also, for the grandees remained dependent on gentry co-operation to extract the surpluses needed by the army. Grandees and gentry were divided over their spoils, and while the former controlled the army, the latter had most of the land and labour. The contradictions implicit in a situation that was both conflict of interest and division of power were fatal for the property-owning classes as a whole. Not only was the late antique civilisation defended by the grandees doomed, so too was the bastardised feudalism of the gentry.

But how were these struggles of Roman Britain's decline and fall understood by contemporaries? As class tensions increased – between soldier and civilian, grandee and gentry, lord and peasant – alternative cultural identities must have formed to articulate differences and oppositions. For, in contrast to traditional claims for a general process of Romanisation, what the archaeological record indicates is great variety and sometimes sharp dichotomy. In particular, a cultural chasm separated 'men of honourable rank' from those 'of humble station': on one side, the Romanised world of lords, villas and high culture, and on the other, a British tribal world of native people and ancient custom.

CLASS AND CULTURE: ROMAN LORDS AND BRITISH PEOPLE

In archaeological writing, the term 'culture' has two principal meanings. First, it is used about the collections of material objects that survive from the past and form what is, in a sense, the database of the discipline. Secondly, it refers to the particular *ensembles* of belief and practice by which past communities defined themselves in contradistinction to others. The former is a matter of things, the latter mainly one of thoughts. Though these two concepts – material culture in an archaeological sense, and past culture as a lived experience – are quite different, they are often confused. It is perhaps only natural that archaeologists – working on a sample of material, but trying to understand the whole past it represents – should be tempted to fuse the two concepts and produce what has sometimes been called 'culture history'. To understand Roman Britain properly, we must untangle this knot.

There is a relationship between material culture and culture-as-lived, but it is not a direct one; there are various distortions. For one thing, because ancient ruling classes controlled productive resources and shaped dominant ideologies, a much higher proportion of surviving material evidence relates to their activities than to those of working people. Secondly, irrespective of who controls them, the *forms* of material culture may tell us nothing about the *content* of past practice and belief. There is a vital distinction between appearance and substance, which, though linked, can to a large extent change independently of each other. In the days of the Raj, India was flooded with cheap cloth from British mills, and native village industries were destroyed. Machine-made replaced homespun. But the dominance of British capitalism in Indian textile markets – a major branch of contemporary material culture – did little to alter the thought-world of the native peasantry. The Indian countryside was not 'Anglicised' any more than we need assume the British countryside was 'Romanised' by Samian pottery. A third complication arises from the multi-layered and contradictory nature of much of the symbolism embodied in material culture. The more prominent and public a cultural symbol – a temple dedication, say – the more likely it is to be 'politically correct'. Private symbols, on the other hand – such as prayers uttered before household shrines – are more likely to express personal belief, non-conformity and even opposition. But these two realms of belief and practice, public and private, leave differential traces. The medieval episcopate – spiritually desiccated, morally bankrupt, yet officially approved – is represented today by the most monumental and beautiful architecture of the age. The enthusiasm and militancy of the heretical sects are, by contrast, archaeologically invisible. In addition, even when material culture survives as evidence, its interpretation is fraught with difficulty, for the same symbol can be read differently, both now and in the past. Most real consciousness is mixed, containing, in relation to dominant ideas, elements of conformity *and* opposition. The symbols which articulate consciousness reflect this. Take the medieval image of Christ. He was both Christ Pantocrator and Christ the Crucified: the ruler of a cosmic hierarchy who gave divine sanction to kings, lords and bishops, and the simple carpenter murdered by the rich because he gave hope to the poor. Material culture is a magic jigsaw. Its countless pieces are no sooner fitted into place than they have changed into something else. Nothing is fixed and frozen, all is flux and process – like society itself. No simple, uniform, linear concept of 'Romanisation' will do. Behind the few unrepresentative scraps of Romano-British culture that survive, we must imagine a material assemblage and a thought-world of kaleidoscopic complexity.

There was no single culture in Roman Britain. Contrasting and conflicting cultures co-existed. They were rooted in different economic circumstances, and these were perhaps becoming more pronounced in the late empire. Though there is little evidence for changes in farming practices and agricultural technologies in the early empire, the late third and early fourth century was a period of innovation and increased productivity – the economic basis for the contemporary flowering of villa civilisation. Many big estates introduced a new type of heavy plough which used an iron coulter, an asymmetrical plough-share and a mould-board to cut through and overturn the sod. Buried nutrients in deep heavy soils could now be exploited to the full and wheat yields greatly increased. A late Roman shift from arable cultivation to sheep and cattle ranching is also detectable. A general increase in the proportion of cattle bones in site assemblages (perhaps because sheep were now reared for wool rather than meat), finds of wool-combs on high-status late Roman sites, and references to British woollen goods and a state-owned cloth factory in late antique sources, all combine to suggest this. Perhaps there was growing commercialisation of agriculture by big landlords producing for the market, and the emergence in some areas of 'cash-crop' regimes based either on a combination of corn and sheep – like eighteenth-century East Anglia under the Enclosure Acts – or animal husbandry alone – as in the Highland Clearances of the nineteenth century when 'men were replaced by sheep'.

By contrast, native farming was always essentially a subsistence affair. An intermediate category of rich peasants producing a significant marketable surplus – like English yeomen or Russian kulaks – may have existed in the late Roman countryside, but if so they were greatly outnumbered by a mass of middle and poor peasants. Most native farms were still worked with light ploughs (or ards) – essentially an iron-tipped wooden beam – since the capital cost of the heavy plough (mainly in animal-power for traction) was beyond most peasant households. This restricted peasant agriculture to lighter soils, where soil exhaustion was a danger and the yield only modest. A detailed study of animal-bone assemblages from Romano-British sites by Anthony King is also instructive. High sheep-bone counts are characteristic of low-status native sites, whereas highly Romanised fort, town and villa sites have more cattle, pigs and deer. Two-thirds of native sites have 30 per cent or more sheep bones in their assemblages, compared with less than a third of high-status sites. The high sheep-counts seem to be diagnostic of traditional peasant agriculture, where sheep were raised for mutton as part of a mixed subsistence-farming regime. The low sheep-counts, on the other hand, are associated with elite consumption and production for the market, with beef, pork and venison the preferred meats, and sheep being raised more for their wool and possibly their milk.

Two economic systems co-existed side by side: villa production for the market, and village production for subsistence. Two different ways of life corresponded to these two economic systems. The life of *honestiores* – grandees and gentry – revolved around two poles: their round of public duties, and the management of their estates and property. It was a genteel life of what Romans called *negotium et otium* ('business and leisure'), a life which brought these 'men of honourable rank' into regular contact with their peers and integrated them into the wider world of imperial affairs and classical culture. The world of peasant *humiliores*, by contrast, revolved around the cycle of the seasons and the demands of agricultural labour; it was a world of farm, field and woods, where the structures of everyday life – its routines and customs, its cultural bric-a-brac, its mind-sets – were long-rooted and slow to change. In Roman Britain, the 'men of honourable rank' and those 'of humble station' had different class positions, life patterns and thought-worlds. These overlapped, collided and interacted to produce an immensely rich range of culture-as-lived. Religion is the key measure of this, for it was the main focus of thought and cultural activity in ancient society.

The dominance of religious ways of thinking about the world is easy enough to understand. Nature was unpredictable and inexplicable. Society was oppressive and cruel. Life was ruled by the terrible tyranny of fate. So men and women imagined all human experience to be governed by a great pantheon of spirit beings. There were thousands of minor sprites who guarded a household, a spring or a clearing in the woods. There were hundreds of more powerful deities who protected whole cities or commanded far-reaching magic powers. There was a handful of super-gods, like the great mother-goddesses who presided over the harvest, or the mighty lords of the universe who controlled the elements and the fates. These many gods were quick to anger, but they could be appeased by appropriate ritual and a suitable offering. The simplest human act required knowledge of holy lore and the performance of sacred rite. To live safely, let alone well, the good favour of the gods had to be eternally renewed; the dangers attendant upon neglect and misconduct – on sacrilege of any sort – were acute. For these reasons, how the gods were represented and honoured is the most important signifier of changing cultural identities in antiquity.

Our main evidence is provided by religious dedications on inscriptions, but these must be analysed critically. The sample is heavily skewed, since more than three-quarters of known inscriptions are from military sites in the north-west. Fortunately, many inscriptions allow us to identify both deity and dedicator, and this evidence can be used to study the range of religious belief and practice in Roman Britain in relation to differences in social status. Figures *30*, *31* and *32* summarise the evidence. They show clearly that the lower we reach in the social scale, the stronger traditional religion seems to be – Celtic cults feature in only 15 per cent of corporate (or, as it were, 'establishment') dedications, but in over 50 per cent of those made by unranked soldiers, civilians or unknowns (i.e. by those who were probably commoners rather than members of the elite). These results, moreover, are bound to understate greatly the strength of popular religion, partly because the commoners represented were relatively affluent and Romanised – soldiers, *vicus*-dwellers and petty-traders rather than peasants – and partly because all stone inscriptions were *public* statements subject to self-censorship in pursuit of respectability. The private beliefs and practices of the peasant hinterland hardly figure at all in the corpus of Romano-British inscriptions.

A hidden strength to native religion is indicated in other ways, too. Just as stone-cut inscriptions attest an immensely diverse pantheon – from anonymous local nymphs to masters of the universe – so too the holy places of Roman Britain ranged from the smallest wayside shrines to great civic monuments and pilgrimage centres. Each *civitas*-capital is likely to have had two official shrines, perhaps located in the civic centre, one dedicated to the patron deities of the Roman state, the Capitoline Triad of Jupiter, Juno and Minerva, the other to the imperial house and the deified emperors of the past. Likewise, each fort had its chapel (*aedes* or *sacellum*), located centrally inside the headquarters building (*principia*), where the image of the emperor and the military standards were kept; and around the edge of the parade-ground outside the fort there were altars and shrines dedicated to Mars, Victory and especially Jupiter. This is the archaeological face of official religion. Its context was the civic pageant and military tournament; its purpose was to encourage conformity with the imperial order, its rituals being inextricably bound up with obedience to political authority. Correct behaviour was really all that mattered; Rome had no use for 'windows into men's souls'. We learn from such evidence almost nothing about belief and devotion.

If it is religious passion we want, we must seek it elsewhere. Sometimes it is glimpsed when we look closely at the evidence for private practice – as opposed to that of state and army – at well-excavated sites. At Carrawburgh, one of the forts in the central sector of Hadrian's Wall, three different shrines have been found close together just outside the fort. One was a small temple (or *mithraeum*) dedicated to the Persian god Mithras. This was an 'eastern mystery cult' whose adherents believed that Mithras, in a primeval act of creation, had released the world's life-force by slaughtering a mythic bull. The god was thereafter engaged in an epic struggle between the forces of good and evil, and he offered salvation and eternal life to those who joined him. Holy rites took place in gloomy, subterranean, lamp-lit rooms – imitating the cave of the bull sacrifice – attended by small and rather well-heeled congregations. The mithraists organised themselves as an exclusive club: applications were heavily vetted, elaborate initiation ordeals were imposed, and the cult acquired a rather 'middle class' tone – it was especially popular among army officers and merchants. Temples of Mithras, like Christian churches at this time, were invariably small. That at Carrawburgh was 5 by 12m. Two dozen people in here would have been a squash. Mithraism – a 'weird' and 'posh' foreign cult imported into Britain by Roman soldiers and traders – was never a mass religion.

Outside the mithraic temple, on the other hand, was a minor shrine of a kind typical of thousands that must once have existed across Roman Britain. It comprised nothing more than a stone-lined well, a semi-circular stone seat, and a small stone altar, and it was dedicated to the anonymous nymphs and spirit of the place. But there was something of greater importance nearby: the temple and sacred spring of the Celtic water-goddess Coventina. There was a small square building, the interior floor of which was raised up, and in the middle of this there was a rectangular stone-lined basin, forming a reservoir for natural spring-water which welled to the surface at this point. Around the sacred pool were numerous altars and inscribed stones, and within it were thousands of coins and other small objects cast as holy offerings by generations of worshippers. Of the 30 altar dedications found at Carrawburgh, only four were to Roman gods and three to Mithras, but there were no less than 14 to Coventina, and at least five more to other Celtic deities.

Equally compelling is the evidence from major cult centres in the south-east. It is hard to imagine a place more Romanised in appearance than ancient Bath. One of the most important centres of pilgrimage and healing in Roman Britain, its geographical location placed it amid the richest flowering of villa civilisation on the island. A small town had grown up around an elaborate cult complex consisting of a classical-style temple set within a large walled enclosure, a huge covered pool filled with naturally heated water, and two sets of bathing rooms, each with hot, warm and cold facilities. The whole *ensemble* was a masterpiece of hydraulic engineering, architectural design and classical art. At its centre, forming an architectural hinge between temple complex and bathing establishment, was a vaulted reservoir filled with hot spring-water: the bubbling, steaming water-palace of the Celtic goddess Sulis. Although she had been 'interpreted' as the Roman Minerva – and the magnificent bronze head from the cult statue in

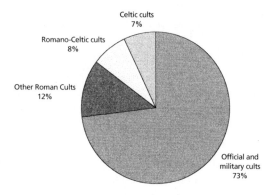

Celtic cults
7%

Romano-Celtic cults
8%

Other Roman Cults
12%

Official and
military cults
73%

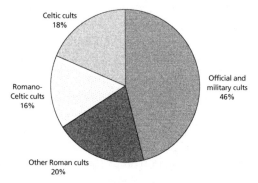

Celtic cults
18%

Official and
military cults
46%

Romano-
Celtic cults
16%

Other Roman cults
20%

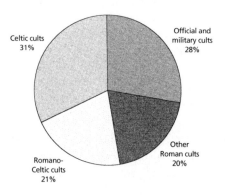

Celtic cults
31%

Official and
military cults
28%

Romano-
Celtic cults
21%

Other
Roman cults
20%

her temple was a wholly classical representation – it is clear that Roman Bath represents the continuation of a native religious tradition, and that Celtic Sulis was the real object of veneration. Many inscribed dedications to the goddess have been found at the site – some on stone, many on lead curse-tablets or offerings thrown into the Sacred Pool – and these provide our best evidence for the mind-set of the worshippers. Where the goddess is named, she is often referred to as 'Sulis', sometimes as 'Sulis-Minerva', but never, it seems, simply as 'Minerva'. The popular conception of the goddess was – despite her repackaging in fashionable Graeco-Roman style – still essentially that of the Iron Age Sulis.

This brief review of two religious sites – one in the north-western military zone, the other in the 'civilised' south-east – raises again the vexed question of 'Romanisation'. The loaded term used to define the debate is itself significant: 'Romanisation' rather than something more neutral – say, 'Romano-British acculturation' – which would leave open to debate the direction of the flows of influence and change. The bias arises because, in historical discussion generally, societies tend to be viewed from the top down – the Romans ruled the British – but also because, in the study of classical antiquity, the Roman Empire is seen as a superior civilisation offering 'progress' in place of 'backwardness' and 'underdevelopment'. This perspective has had the unfortunate effect of reinforcing the distortion inherent in the evidence which, naturally, represents

Opposite page:

30 Top: *Religious dedications in stone by corporate bodies (mainly military) in Roman Britain. Sample: 156. Source:* RIB

31 Middle: *Religious dedications in stone by army officers in Roman Britain. Sample: 173. Source:* RIB

32 Bottom: *Religious dedications in stone by unranked soldiers, civilians and unknown others in Roman Britain. Sample: 248. Source:* RIB

official and elite activity much more fully than that of the masses. We need a self-conscious 'archaeology from below' which attempts to reconstruct the fabric of everyday life and thought *at the base of society*. I have suggested that, even when looking at mainly elite evidence like stone inscriptions and highly Romanised sites like Carrawburgh and Bath, there are many clues to aid such reconstruction.

If we look further afield, the evidence may be slight, but what we see confirms the impression of half-buried cultural worlds hardly touched at all by Roman imperialism. Ammianus Marcellinus, a late fourth-century army officer and historian, wrote of the Gallic Celts that, though now 'civilised', they retained their Druidic religious philosophy, their musical traditions, and 'the bards [who] celebrated the brave deeds of famous men in epic verse to the accompaniment of the sweet strains of the lyre'. Many artistic images from Roman Britain, especially representations of the divine in stone and bronze, display strong native characteristics, having simple forms, stylised features, and much use of curving lines and rounded shapes in the detail. In these images, alongside mysterious native deities unknown in the classical world, we encounter Graeco-Roman deities given native form – not so much *interpretatio Romana* as *interpretatio Celtica*. Important, too, are art objects of low value, especially items of personal adornment like brooches – items which probably often had totemic and magical significance now lost to us – since these bring us close to the preferred taste of the common people. Romano-British brooches were essentially Celtic in design. Derived from archetypal 'safety-pin' brooches of the continental Iron Age, they took on a bewildering variety of curving forms, often richly decorated with intricate mouldings and enamel-work, and occasionally incorporating highly stylised animal-motifs (*33*). Although developing hugely during the Roman period, most types owed nothing at all to any detectable classical influence. (The term 'Celtic' to describe them may or may not be appropriate: it has become a controversial word for reasons there is not space to discuss here. What remains true, however, is that a distinctive material culture traditionally called 'Celtic' can be seen in the archaeological record – however we might choose to interpret that. Romano-British brooches seem to represent a development of that 'Celtic' culture rather than a Graeco-Roman one.)

These British brooches were truly popular artefacts. They are found in large quantities on sites of all kinds. The 1955-61 excavations at *Verulamium* recovered 47 bronze brooches – compared with only 10 mosaic floors. During excavations at Gorhambury villa in 1972-82, the haul of brooches was 46 complete and 12 fragments – compared with three mosaics. The 1970-3 excavations at Catsgore Romano-British village found 35 brooches – and no mosaics at all. Broadly, whereas mosaics were rare luxury items of highly Roman design, brooches were numerous, popular and Celtic in style. Brooches tell us something about far more Romano-British people than mosaics ever could.

Roman civilisation may, therefore, have been little more than a veneer of elite culture. In the villages, hamlets and farmsteads where most people lived, a traditional, pre-Roman, indigenous culture seems to have endured, one only partly visible in an archaeological record dominated by the rich and powerful. Fourth-century *Roman* Britain was also very much a *Celtic* (or at least a *British*) Britain. It still contained the raw materials for preserving – or refashioning – a

33 People's art?: Romano-British bronze brooches, Sedgeford, Norfolk, mid-first to early second century. Artefacts like these seem to lie beyond the reach of Graeco-Roman cultural influence. Drawn by Ray Ludford

different cultural identity from that of the conquerors: the Celtic language with its bards, myths and fairy-tales; the native landscape with its local gods and sacred groves; the traditional patterns and motifs of folk-art; even the taken-for-granted routines and customs of everyday life in peasant settlements. The archaic classicism of the imperial grandees was the culture of an embattled civilisation imposing on its people economic distress and social injustice. We can well imagine how, in these circumstances, surviving indigenous culture forms may have been used to forge alternative group-identities among ordinary Britons – in opposition to the Roman ruling class and its war effort.

7

THE FALL OF
ROMAN BRITAIN

The historian Ammianus Marcellinus records that in 367 Britain was assailed by devastating barbarian raids. The tribes of the Pictish confederation attacked the northern frontier. The Attacotti of the Western Isles and the Scotti of Ireland struck at the western coasts. The Rangers (*areani*) – units of frontier scouts and spies – were corrupted and supplied information about Roman troop movements to the enemy. General Fullofaudes, commander of the northern forts, was surprised, outflanked and cut off. In the southeast, coastal settlements were raided by Frankish and Saxon pirates, and Nectaridus, Count of the Coastal Region, was defeated and killed. Ammianus describes these events as a 'barbarian conspiracy' (*coniuratio barbarica*) which aimed at a co-ordinated attack to break through overstretched Roman defences and bring 'the provinces of Britain to the verge of ruin'. The barbarians penetrated deeply into the soft, rich hinterland of the Romanised south-east. Here they broke up into small bands to plunder at will, and then, when sated, headed home with herds of cattle, columns of slaves, and wagons piled high with booty. Many Roman units disintegrated in the chaos of defeat, and the countryside filled with deserters and bandits.

Or so the story goes. Unfortunately, the integrity of our source is uncertain. Ammianus wrote his history in retirement at Rome during the reign of Theodosius the Great (379-95). The emperor's father, Count Theodosius, had been dispatched to Britain with a field army to wrest back control of the island from the barbarians. It would have been most impolitic not to celebrate this as a great achievement, and Ammianus' account of British events in 367-9 is hagiographical in tone. To be convinced of the seriousness of the 'conspiracy' – and of the difficulties overcome in the 'restoration' – we must seek corroborative evidence. I think this is of several kinds, all circumstantial, but adding up to a strong 'contextual' case for the essential authenticity of Ammianus' account. Although our literary evidence is heavily skewed towards the period 354-78 – the years covered by the surviving portions of Ammianus' history – barbarian attacks on Roman Britain do appear to be more frequent and dangerous from the mid-fourth century onwards. No historical event of any kind is recorded in Britain between 306, when Constantius Caesar campaigned on the northern frontier, and 343, when the emperor Constans (337-50) paid a winter visit (for reasons which remain obscure). The next we hear is of a sinister official intervention in 354 after the collapse of a revolt by the usurper-emperor Magnentius the year before. Paul 'the Chain', a Gestapo-like police chief and executioner, was sent by the emperor Constantius (337-61) to investigate, purge and destroy the remnants of the faction in Britain which had supported the rebellion. But there was no mention of the frontiers. Only in 360 does Ammianus testify to a renewed barbarian threat. The Picts and Scotti were raiding Britain, and the junior emperor in the west, the Caesar Julian (355-63), dispatched one of his top marshals, Master of Horse (*magister equitum*) Lupicinus, with a field-army brigade of four light regiments, to shore up the diocesan defences. A few years later, at the joint accession of Valentinian (364-75) and Valens (364-78), we are told that among 'the most savage nations' in arms against Rome were to be counted 'the Picts, Saxons, Scotti and Attacotti [who] harassed Britain in a never-ending series of disasters'. Though we have no details of the Roman military action taken on either occasion, a serious deterioration on the British frontiers in the 360s is implied. This seems to be confirmed, as we shall shortly see, by occasional references to events later in the century, by the military archaeology of late Roman Britain, and by what appears to have been happening in the Empire generally at this time. Before considering these matters, however, let us review what is known of these barbarian enemies of late Roman Britain.

Later history teaches that island Britain is a natural fortress protected by the Channel from the worst horrors of war periodically visited upon continental neighbours with land frontiers. But ancient Britain was deeply divided by geography, social organisation and political authority. The south-east had become a Romanised enclave integrated into an empire centred on the Mediterranean. Beyond this was an arc of territory to the north and west which, though under direct Roman control, had remained essentially 'uncivilised' – a Roman *barbaricum*. Beyond this again was an outer arc of territory yet more distant and wild, and wholly outside the empire. This was true *barbaria*, an unconquered land of inhospitable mountains, trackless forests and bogs, and grey windswept islands. The people who lived here were poor but tough, and Roman booty would buy renown, status and power at home. Roman Britain was therefore surrounded by enemies: traditional ones in the north, where the tribes of the Southern Uplands, Central Lowlands and Highlands had coalesced into a loose Pictish nation; new ones in the west, where a coastline riddled with inlets, estuaries and small peninsulas was exposed to attack by seaborne Attacotti and Scotti; and others in the south-east, Saxon raiders from Free Germany beyond the Roman border on the Rhine (*34*). The British frontier was now a thousand miles long. None of the enemies who threatened it formed regular mass armies that could be brought to decisive pitched battle – the bloody carnage favoured by Roman commanders that Victor Davis Hanson has called 'the western way of war'. Rather, they were loose, fluid, mobile hordes, able to leak through a hundred small gaps, concentrate against a major weakness, or disperse and disappear in the face of superior force. The defenders may have packed the hardest punch. But where to punch?

We examined the possible causes of Saxon piracy in chapter 4: barricaded into the far north-west of mainland Europe by more powerful neighbours, the Saxons' watery homeland was fast sinking beneath the sea, coastal settlements were being abandoned to the elements, and a class of seaborne warlords had arisen who offered an escape through violence and robbery to those willing to hazard the dangers. All evidence points to an increase in these social stresses between the late third century (when we first hear of Saxon piracy) and the mid-fifth (when the earliest English settlements were founded). The sea-level continued to rise and ever more coastal settlements were deserted. The continental folk-migrations of Germans, Goths and Huns, which had the Saxons corralled into the north-west, grew larger and more threatening. And the prominence of the Saxons and their aggressions in the accounts of contemporary historians increased significantly during this period.

Our knowledge of the other barbarian enemies of late Roman Britain is rather less. Like the term 'Saxon' as used by Roman writers, the term 'Pict' (or 'Painted Man') was imprecise and generic, yet its appearance in the texts seems to symbolise a process of political centralisation observable among barbarian peoples on other frontiers. At the time of Agricola, Hadrian and Antoninus Pius, there had been five major tribal groupings between the Tyne-Solway line and the Great Glen. Only two groups (the Caledonians and Maeatae) are named in connection with the early-third-century campaigns of Severus, and just one (the Picts) in relation to those of Constantius Caesar in 306

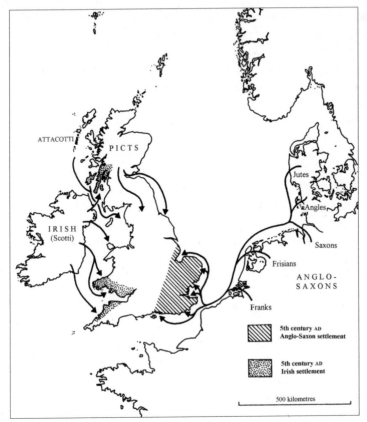

34 The barbarian enemies of late Roman Britain

(though Ammianus refers to a continuing division of the confederation into two main tribes, the Dicalydones and the Verturiones, when describing the events of 367-9). Attempts to define the Picts closely and to see them represented by a distinctive and diagnostic material assemblage may be misplaced. A Pictish core perhaps existed in the Central Lowlands and Highlands, but the organisation and composition of the confeder-

225

ation was probably loose and changeable, often no doubt including strong contingents from the Southern Uplands. There is no evidence in the archaeology – which is dominated by very small settlements with few signs of social stratification – for a developed political hierarchy and state structures. Compelled to combine for effective military action against Rome, the people of the north otherwise remained essentially primitive – their enemies, in defining all 'hostiles' as part of a uniform Pictish threat, perhaps implied a higher degree of political centralisation than in fact existed. A Pictish mobilisation was an occasional gathering of the clans – not the levying of a regular militia – and each band of men within the horde was out for the booty it could bring back. The paraphernalia of war were simple (35). Each man carried a small square shield and a spear. Only the better-off had swords, and only the chiefs wore helmets and rode to war mounted on small ponies. But with numbers, speed and surprise, they could break through the depleted and demoralised Roman frontier-regiments, and then pan out to plunder at will.

About the Attacotti, nothing at all is known; it is only a guess that they came from the Western Isles. The Scotti, on the other hand, are known to have come from Ireland (whence some migrated to north Britain to found the kingdom that would eventually overturn the Picts). The ancient Irish settlement pattern was dominated by single-farmstead enclosures – earthen 'raths' and stone-built 'cashels' – of which more than 30,000 are known dating from the late Neolithic onwards. High-status sites, by contrast, were few and small, principally hillforts associated with the families of Irish kings, of which the most famous is the royal capital at Tara in Meath. Genealogical myth-making by medieval Irish rulers has obscured the truth about many of these sites, but Tara and some others were certainly occupied in the third and fourth centuries. Links with the Roman world at this time can be established archaeologically – indeed, finds of Roman material are the basis on which Irish sites are dated. Of particular interest are two precious-metal hoards of similar composition from Balline and Coleraine in Ulster. That at Coleraine contained, apart from some scrap silver, over 1,500 late Roman coins, and seven silver ingots of a type used for special payments by the Roman government. It hardly matters whether such material was acquired through successful raiding, demands for 'protection money', or services as a client-king – all possible contexts for the movement of Roman bullion across the frontier. One way or another, it shows that Ireland had become some sort of threat. Again, though, as in the homelands of the Saxons and the Picts, the overall settlement pattern does not indicate much social stratification or political sophistication. Later Irish medieval records confirm this. They describe a society in which 'high kings' demanded allegiance from huge numbers of sub-kings and lesser nobles, but this power, and that of the ruling class as a whole over the common people, was based on the personal ties of man to man rather than on property rights – a clan society, not a feudal one. Precisely that, though, could make Roman Britain attractive: it was the place, perhaps, where a scruffy chieftain could win for himself the means of patronage and the renown for valiant deeds which might turn him into a real king. Remote from the centres of modern war on the continent, Irish military technology was primitive even by the standards of the British Isles. Nobles fought on foot, unprotected by armour and equipped with small swords of third-rate iron. Commoners carried spears and clubs. Though warfare was endemic, often linked with cattle-rustling, it was of the crudest kind. But against the long exposed coastline across the Irish Sea, the Scottish kinglets deployed some advantages: they could concentrate their forces at landing-places of their choosing, surprise the enemy at their first descent, and, once abroad, move fast to evade him in the difficult upland country of the far west.

These, then, were the barbarian enemies of late Roman Britain. If, as I suspect, their violence became more persistent from the mid-fourth century onwards, this would fit an empire-wide pat-

35 *A Pictish warrior. The reconstruction is based on various fragments of evidence. He wears a cloak and kilt of woollen cloth with woven designs, and carries a small, square, metal-studded shield, two light javelins, and a long sword. His upper body is exposed to reveal tattoos with protective powers, and he wears a captured late Roman helmet on his head. The sword and the helmet would mark him out as a man of substance*

tern of increased frontier insecurity. Diocletian had brought the great wars of the third century to an end by 300, and he and his successor Constantine had remodelled the army and its defence-works in such a way that the frontiers were relatively undisturbed for much of the following fifty years. From the death of Constantine in 337, the Empire was ruled by his three sons, Constantine II (337-40), Constans (337-50), and Constantius II (337-61), but the fraternal triumvirate was weakened by coups and civil wars. Between 350 and 353, the House of Constantine faced a major challenge when Constans was assassinated and the usurper Magnentius was elevated to the imperial throne by the western generals. War raged across Gaul, northern Italy and the Balkans, and frontier garrisons were thinned out as men were fed into the mincing-machine of civil strife. Consequently, shortly after the defeat of Magnentius, the Empire faced war on each of its three main frontiers: against the Germanic Alamanni on the Rhine, the Sarmatians and Quadi on the Danube, and the Persians in the East. To help deal with the crisis, Constantius II made his young cousin Julian a junior emperor (or Caesar) and appointed him to com-mand of the West (355).

Julian quickly became a new lightning-rod for all the old ten-sions. Constantius had hoped that the appointment of a kinsman would ensure the loyalty of the West, but the regionalist sentiment of western officers and landowners easily moulded Julian to its purpose. Circumstances were making men, not men circum-stances. Between 356 and 359, Julian waged successful war in the Rhineland, won the pitched battle of Strasbourg, and restored broken frontier defences. In 360, the western army hailed him full emperor (Augustus), and he invaded the East to make good his claim against Constantius' opposition. His rival died before any final showdown, and the eastern army then gave its allegiance to Julian. Constantius' Persian campaign had become bogged down in a war of sieges, and Julian, who now inherited this campaign, sought to break the impasse in 363 by launching a full-scale invasion in overwhelming force with the aim of total conquest. Julian the Pagan was a reactionary who believed in the Old Rome, its traditional myths and values, its past glorious deeds. The ghost of Alexander tugged at his sleeve. As the great dream of eastern conquest marched out again, Julian's mailed fist punched through whatever stood in its path, but it was soon swallowed up by the vastness of the East. The Persian cities held firm, mounted guerrillas harassed the Roman column, the soldiers fried and rotted in the sun. Julian was fatally wounded, his army fell back, and the generals were forced to make an unhappy peace. But the effects of Julian's military adventurism would be felt across the Empire – even in far-off Britain.

In his account of Julian's career, Ammianus includes two illuminating scraps of information. First, we learn that Julian's usurpation was precipitated by Constantius' demand that thousands of western army troops should be transferred east to fight in the Persian war. Secondly, it is reported that Julian built a fleet of 600 ships in which to move corn from Britain to fill his Rhineland granaries during the German war. The value of the north-western provinces to the late empire is clearly revealed. They were important sources of military manpower and supplies. Their resources could be pumped out to feed the main mass of Roman imperial infrastructure defending the heartlands. But this could provoke resistance and revolt by those whose property was left vulnerable to attack. Land and labour: soldiers and grain: here was the very essence of the struggle for the north-west in the late empire. Julian's wars were but one dramatic expression of these contradictions. Britain must have been drained of troops in the 350s and early 360s, first by Magnentius' revolt, then by Julian's German war, his march into the Balkans, and the crusade against Persia. The barbarian incursions of 360, 364 and 367 were the bitter fruits of this programme, with Britain, by the end of the decade, on the brink of being lost to the Empire altogether. It took a major change of policy by the incoming government of 364 to prevent this.

A messy succession had eventually been resolved with the elevation of the Danubian soldier-emperor Valentinian I, a man of obscure origin, considerable military skill and a ruthless determination to succeed. While he took personal charge of the West, he made his brother Valens co-emperor and gave him control of the East. In contrast to Julian's imperial fantasies and pagan revivalism, the Valentinianic regime was a practical, rational, modernising government of party men. Civil and military career structures were streamlined, state expenditure was kept on tight rein, laws were enacted against corruption by government officials, and Julian's anti-Christian measures were reversed. Frontier wars were short, sharp shocks where it mattered, not Homeric crusades. Valentinian threw the barbarians back over the Rhine, pursued them into Free Germany, won a great victory in the Black Forest, and then spent seven years rebuilding the Rhine-Danube frontiers. The military crises of the recent past had underlined the need for further army reform and frontier improvement. The field army was permanently split into an eastern and western half, and each was further divided into 'palatine' units attached to the emperor himself, and others commanded by the imperial marshals (or *magistri*). The continental frontier was overhauled. The Valentinianic system comprised a line of rebuilt forts and strong-points, new watchtowers along the roads linking them, and the fortification of bridgeheads, landing-places, granaries and internal roads close to the frontiers. The result was a denser, more intensively watched, more heavily-guarded defensive line. In place of Julian's flamboyant offensive, there was now Valentinian's solid defensive. Trajan had been succeeded by Hadrian.

It was while on the march during one of his German campaigns that Valentinian 'was shocked to hear the serious news of a "barbarian conspiracy" which had reduced the British provinces to near-ruin'. The new emperor acted with customary vigour. He was not about to write off such a valuable asset as the diocese of Britain.

THE THEODOSIAN RESTORATION, AD 367-9

Early reports perhaps understated the scale of disaster. Dictatorship encourages cover-ups. Two senior officers were sent out in fast succession to investigate on the spot, but neither could retrieve the situation: troops were needed. Count Theodosius was given a field-army brigade of four crack units, and with these he crossed from Boulogne to Richborough, whence he marched overland to London. His army was divided into flying columns and sent in pursuit of raiding parties operating around the capital. The barbarians were greatly disadvantaged by their dispersal across the countryside, their encumbrance with wagon-loads of spoil, and their ineffectiveness in a head-on collision with well-trained and heavily armed Roman regulars. Early successes were considerable. But the zone of operations did not at first extend much beyond London, and Theodosius lacked the numbers to clear and pacify the up-country and the uplands beyond. Time was needed to rebuild the shattered Romano-British state so that it could fight for itself. New officers were appointed from the continent. Deserters who returned to the colours were granted pardon. The winter was spent drilling, re-equipping and raising morale. A large reconstituted army – part crack field-regiments, part reformed frontier-battalions – was then led out in 368-9 to complete the recovery of Britain. The loose hordes of lightly equipped barbarians, even with time to concentrate their forces and prepare for battle, could not have risked a clash with Theodosius' army. The enemy vanished from the Romans' path. The west and north were cleared, unreliable elements were purged, new garrisons were installed, and Theodosius inaugurated an ambitious programme of military reconstruction for the future security of the diocese.

Though Ammianus tells us that Theodosius 'completely restored towns and forts ... and protected the frontiers with guard-posts and defence-works', in trying to link archaeological evidence with the historical events of 367-9, we confront an insuperable problem: the imprecision of archaeological dating. Coins and pottery still provide the great majority of dates on Roman sites, and these are rarely more precise than a band of 25 years or so. There is not a single building in Roman Britain which we can attribute with certainty to Count Theodosius, and far too much scholarly ink has been wasted on the effort to define this or that group of structures as definitely 'Theodosian'. The issue, anyway, is not important: does it really matter which particular named Roman officer was in charge when a building was constructed? Large-scale construction projects were often protracted, sometimes subject to spurts of activity followed by long lulls, and calls on manpower and resources for restoration work at one fort or town may well have delayed the commencement of work at others. Theodosius undoubtedly kick-started essential military building-works which had been aborted by the war, but these are likely to have continued long after his departure. It is enough to know that around this time the Romans undertook their last sustained programme of military reconstruction-work in Britain – part of a wider programme of frontier improvement under Valentinian and Valens in the period 364-78.

Late-fourth-century Britain was threatened on land and sea by a protracted, dispersed, small-scale, low-tech guerrilla offensive. There were insufficient regular troops to defend the diocese, and linear defences were easily penetrated. A strategic shift was essential, and I think we can identify five principal elements, or bands of defence, in the 'Theodosian' system (22). North of the border, the Rangers were disbanded and the outpost forts beyond Hadrian's Wall abandoned. Treaty arrangements with the more friendly northern tribes were probably renewed. The rise of the Pictish confederation will have provided Rome with allies among those who stood in fear of it. A great hoard of late Roman silver at Traprain Law hillfort may represent payment of a subsidy to the traditionally friendly Votadini tribe. The use, according to medieval king-lists, of Roman names and titles by fourth-century, north-

British rulers may imply client status. Here, perhaps, was the first element of the reformed system: a buffer zone of pro-Roman chieftains.

The second was the Wall itself, where Valentinianic rebuilds are in evidence at some forts. Old-fashioned regimental pomp was now sacrificed to the military utility and soldiers' comforts of much-reduced garrisons. At Chesterholm, two latrines and a hypocaust were inserted in the offices of the old headquarters-building. At South Shields, the assembly hall was converted into a grain store. At Housesteads, a small bath-block was constructed in one end of an under-used warehouse. At Halton Chesters and Rudchester, largely ruined for a hundred years, wholesale reconstruction was undertaken – but on new alignments, using salvaged materials, and to shoddy standards. Defences were also improved: parts of the curtain wall appear to have been rebuilt, some milecastles and turrets certainly continued in use, and sometimes the circuit walls around forts were repaired. At Housesteads, the earth rampart was thickened in places (perhaps where the wall had actually collapsed), and at least one tower was rebuilt in timber.

A third band of defence was provided by the many forts in the hills south of the Wall, and here restoration work was generally more regular in plan and of higher quality in execution (a difference which may be related to alternative garrison arrangements). The fourth band lay further south still, beyond the northern hill-posts, where the heartlands of the diocese in the Romanised south-east were protected by a network of walled towns along the major routeways. Most circuits had been completed in the late third century, but major new work in the second half of the fourth added greatly to the towns' ability to resist attack. The best-dated evidence comes from the little town of Caerwent in south-east Wales, the *civitas*-capital of the Silures tribe. The town was enclosed by 3m-thick stone walls, the whole circuit measuring nearly a mile (1.5km), with centrally placed gateways on each of the four sides. Around 350, semi-octagonal projecting towers were added, six on the south, at least five on the north, and the defensive purpose seems clear: to provide shooting-platforms for defenders to enfilade the flanks of attackers approaching walls and gates. The addition of projecting towers necessitated the digging of new, wider ditches at a distance from the wall (lest the tower foundations be undermined). Later again (there is no precise dating) the north and south gates at Caerwent were blocked. Comparable late-fourth-century sequences are known at other Romano-British towns.

The final element of the reformed system was coastal defence. The Saxon Shore forts, despite a paucity of occupation evidence at some, were undoubtedly kept in commission, forming the core of a network which probably came to include many walled towns near the coast or on navigable estuaries (21). London may have been a linchpin of the Saxon Shore. Its eastward-looking defences were massively strengthened with the addition of up to 22 projecting towers (probably in the third quarter of the fourth century), and by the construction of what seems to have been a thick-walled projecting strong-point by the river's edge in the south-east corner of the town wall (perhaps in 390-400). But to the main 'coastal command' in the south-east must be added others that faced west and north. A semicircle of forts and towns ringed the coasts and estuaries around Wales: Gloucester, Caerwent, Caerleon, Cardiff, Carmarthen, Caernarvon, Caer Gybi, Caerhun and Chester. Some of these may have been integrated into a defensive screen to defend against Scottish raids across the Irish Sea. In the north, a line of forts on the Cumberland coast south-west of Hadrian's Wall – from Bowness-on-Solway to Ravenglass – had long formed part of Roman defensive arrangements. Other western forts, like Lancaster and Ribchester, covered possible landing-places further south. The east coast, by contrast, had been left more exposed, and a line of defended signal-stations was now established on the Yorkshire cliffs. The crudest of building-inscriptions has been recovered from the one at Ravenscar, telling us that 'Justinianus, commander (*praepositus*), and Vindicianus, marshal (*magister*), built this tower and fort from scratch'. Archaeologically better-known is the site at Scarborough, which comprised a central stone tower up to 30m high, an outer defensive wall with semi-circular corner-towers, and a ditch beyond: a secure platform for long-distance observation and the dissemination of messages by smoke and fire. There were, then, several 'coastal commands' within Roman Britain, though only the first appears to have been an independent one under its own general officer (the 'Count of the Saxon Shore'), while those in the north were probably subordinate to the 'Duke of the British Provinces'. We can only speculate about command and control in relation to the 'Irish Shore' in the west – the *Notitia Dignitatum* is silent.

It is silent about much else. Though a prime source for the late Roman army, it contains many gaps, the date of its various entries is uncertain, and much of the information is not contemporaneous. *Notitia* scholarship is a detailed business, and there is not space here to discuss arguments for and against different interpretations of the British lists. All I can do is to summarise the salient features in the context of some general comments about the garrisoning of late-fourth-century Britain. Under the Duke of the British Provinces, the *Notitia* lists 14 hinterland forts in the north-east mostly garrisoned by new formations, and 13 along the Wall and 10 in the north-western hinterland mostly garrisoned by old regiments. Under the Count of the Saxon Shore, nine south-eastern coastal forts and their garrisons are listed. Otherwise, the only troops recorded by the *Notitia* for Britain are nine field-army units under an officer called the 'Count of the British Provinces', but their presence is likely to have been temporary, and we can only guess at the occasion; they were not part of the regular frontier-garrison. The *Notitia* account is undoubtedly incomplete. About a dozen northern forts not listed are known to have been occupied after 369, and it is possible that unit detachments were outstationed (the *Notitia* recording only the main base), or that irregular units of *laeti* or *gentiles* were also deployed (and our copy of the *Notitia* does not record them). Parts of the Saxon Shore system may also have been omitted, and there is no doubt about the complete omission of the 'Irish Shore' forts and the 60 or so walled towns in the south-east. Nor has archaeology assisted us much. The relative lack of occupation evidence at many forts and the absence of any recognisable military structures in the towns have been taken to mean that they were never part of defensive strategy at all. This view must, however, be rejected.

The problem is that the late Roman army is archaeologically only semi-visible. There is nothing surprising about this. Its predecessor – the army of Hadrian, Marcus and Severus – is quite exceptional in being represented by the surviving remains of hundreds of stone-built forts. By contrast, the army of the Republic – that which conquered the Mediterranean world between 264 and 30 BC – is virtually invisible. The difference is that the former was committed to long-term military occupation and the defence of fixed positions, and it is this policy which created the impressive material remains associated with the Roman imperial army at its peak. By the fourth century, the army had been transformed again. Most units were now battalion-size, their active strengths anywhere between 100 and 500, with 300 pretty normal, and they were sometimes sub-divided into smaller detachments for specific duties. These units were immensely diverse in ethnic origin, in degree of training and experience, in equipment and fighting methods, in the way they were organised and commanded, and in their morale, commitment and reliability. Standardisation depends upon stability, and there had been little of this in the recent Roman past; a plethora of emergency measures had created a polyglot army. It was also a highly mobile army, operating a strategy of defence-in-depth, as the war of fixed lines became a war of

movement. Permanent bases counted for little; the army improvised billets and supply depots as it moved around on campaign.
Rather than build for itself, the army simply commandeered what
it needed. Comprising small units of diverse character which were
often on the move, the late Roman army generated comparatively
little diagnostically military archaeology. Given this, a little evidence must be allowed to go a long way. Literary references to the
billeting of late Roman troops in towns are frequent, and occasional finds of crossbow brooches, official-style belt fittings and
late Roman weaponry, especially when linked with improvements
in urban defences, constitute archaeological confirmation. At
Wroxeter, the town ditches were recut to heighten the earth rampart and create a single broad ditch with a counterscarp bank –
altogether a more formidable obstacle – and inside, during excavations in the town centre, several crossbow brooches were found,
along with six lead-weighted darts (*martiobarbuli*), used by late
Roman soldiers as close-range missile weapons. In the circumstances, such evidence seems conclusive enough: many more
defended sites than those listed in the *Notitia* were, at least occasionally, garrisoned by troops in late Roman Britain.

Such, in outline, was the Roman system for the defence of
Britain after 370. But could it hold? This depended, in large part,
on events outside the diocese.

THE REVOLT OF MAGNUS MAXIMUS, AD 383-8

On 9 August AD 378, on the battlefield of Adrianople, the Roman
army suffered its most catastrophic defeat for half a millennium.
Gothic settlers on the lower Danube were in revolt against
Roman maltreatment, and the emperor Valens led out the eastern
field-army of 60,000 men to crush them. When the armies collided, both were taken by surprise. The Gothic infantry formed a
defensive wagon-laager, and Fritigern, their leader, hastily recalled

his cavalry from their foraging expedition. Valens led his men in assault, but the attack was over-confident and badly controlled, and the Roman army was soon too heavily embroiled in the fight for the laager. The Gothic cavalry returned and plunged into the exposed Roman flanks, and the Gothic infantry surged down frontally into the now-disordered Roman mass. In the horrendous chaos of the melee which followed, the Roman army was compressed into a dense block of desperate men, hacking and stabbing, unable to escape, and doomed to die where they stood. When night fell, two-thirds of the eastern Roman army had been annihilated.

Adrianople sealed the fate of Roman Britain. The shortage of regular Roman troops was never made good. When the eastern Christian emperor Theodosius confronted his western pagan enemies, the usurper-emperor Eugenius and the field-marshal Arbogast, at the battle of the River Frigidus in 394, the eastern army was made up largely of barbarian federates from the Danube region. Twenty thousand Goths filled the Roman battle-line. These were not barbarians who had been recruited into regular Roman regiments, nor *laeti* or *gentiles*, barbarians settled under Roman authority with an obligation to do military service. The *foederati* employed by Theodosius (and his successors) were barbarians who retained their tribal organisation and served under their own kings and chieftains. They were allies and clients of Rome, not subjects. The distinction was crucial, since *foederati* represented separate barbarian polities within the Roman imperial set-up: states within a state, which could, in changed circumstances, overturn and replace the latter.

The 'barbarisation' of the Roman army was one part of Theodosius' management of the crisis after Adrianople. The other was his determination to keep the Empire united so that all its resources could be pooled. Desperately short of military manpower, especially highly trained and well-equipped regulars, the emperor needed to maintain control of the West and to suppress anti-government dissent within the aristocracy. To this end, the Theodosian regime promoted an evangelising, persecuting Christianity which delegitimised opposition and instilled a habit of unquestioning obedience. The West, especially the old Roman senatorial nobility, was eventually driven to revolt. The western emperor Valentinian II was murdered in 392, the pagan Eugenius usurped the throne, and the civil war which followed culminated in the battle of the River Frigidus, which, though a victory for Theodosius, was a pyrrhic blood-letting which drained further Rome's precious reserves of prime troops. It was in this context of manpower shortage, religious sectarianism and civil strife that, in the course of the preceding decade, Britain had again broken away from central Roman authority.

Magnus Maximus was a senior officer with strong western connections. A native of Spain, he had served in Britain under Count Theodosius in 367-9, and he was the holder of a high-ranking post in Britain in 383 (though it is not known which). After the death of Valentinian I, the latter's son Gratian (375-83) had succeeded as western emperor, but his government had made itself unpopular through its preferment of barbarian officers and its political repressiveness: career opportunities were being blocked by upstarts, and personal security and family property were threatened by judicial stitch-ups. The British officer-corps revolted and elevated Magnus Maximus to the throne. The new emperor assembled his army and crossed to the continent, where loyalist forces melted away, Gratian was caught and killed, and Maximus found himself master of Britain, Gaul and Spain. At first, the usurper regime was tolerated, since Theodosius was heavily committed in the East. But the relationship was tense. As discussed above, in framing an effective strategy for the defence of the Empire, the central government required exclusive control over imperial resources. It needed to be able to concentrate men and supplies at critical points, whereas a regionalisation of power prevented this: as long as Maximus controlled the West, Theodosius could not draw upon its reserves. Maximus was aware of the distrust and hostility, and he attempted to pre-empt his rival's move to crush him. Valentinian II (375-92), younger brother and junior emperor to Gratian, was still in control of Italy, and Maximus moved to eject him, driving him from the Po Valley across the Alps into the Balkans. Theodosius intervened from the East, counterattacking in full force, and defeated Maximus twice in Yugoslavia before catching up with and killing him at Aquileia in north-east Italy in 388. The rule of Theodosius and his western protégés was thus re-established – until, as we have seen, the challenge of Eugenius and Arbogast four years later. But the consequences of Maximus' political adventure had been dire for the Romans in Britain.

The attempt to make good the British elite's demand for proper attention to its interests had denuded the island of troops. That was how regional usurpations always worked. They arose from resentment at the centre's neglect. But to defeat the centre, men and material were needed for the challenge. Either way, the centre was a black hole sucking troops out of the periphery. Without enough to go round, a centralised empire was bound to succour the core at the expense of the edges, and regional usurpation was never a long-term solution for elites located on the geographical margins of the system, since sooner or later the centre always sought a settling of accounts. The troops led away by Magnus Maximus never came back, and his deconstruction of the Theodosian system, just half a generation after its inauguration, was therefore permanent. The archaeology of Roman Britain is witness to a sharp downturn between the Valentinianic and Theodosian periods, and the revolt of Magnus Maximus was the hinge on which this transition turned. Many forts in the western Pennines and Wales were evacuated and never reoccupied; the old legionary fortress at Chester was probably now given up. The coin supply to other forts was greatly reduced, which implies smaller garrisons. The importance of this change cannot be exaggerated.

Coins are the clearest archaeological marker we have for the operation of the Roman imperial military-supply economy. Coins mediated the whole revenue-payment cycle on which the Roman state was based. They were issued by the government to pay its soldiers, and, passed on by soldiers, they entered the general economy and facilitated its responses to military demand, keeping Britain locked into an empire-wide system of production and distribution. They then returned to the government through the regular payment of taxes – most of which were again in *specie*, not kind, by the late fourth century. But the coin supply to Britain fell sharply after 378, and even when it recovered somewhat after 388, it never returned to Valentinianic levels. The implications are a reduced Roman army presence, a breakdown in the tax-collection system, a failure of the military-supply network, and a reversion to self-sufficiency and barter-exchange in much of Roman Britain. This is confirmed by archaeological evidence. The period between 375 and 425 (close dating is rarely possible) sees the final collapse of civil settlement in the towns, the abandonment of remaining rural villas, and the decline to nothing of the Romano-British potteries. The fall of Roman Britain was a process, not an event, but the revolt of Magnus Maximus was a key stage in that process, after which further decline was rapid and irreversible. Britain in the 390s already had little about it that was particularly Roman.

THE REVOLT OF CONSTANTINE III, AD 407-11

Theodosius the Great died in 395 – the year after reuniting the Christian Roman Empire at the battle of the River Frigidus – and his inheritance was divided between his two young sons, Arcadius (395-408) in the East, Honorius (395-423) in the West. Both were mere ciphers. The west came to be ruled by Flavius Stilicho, a Vandal barbarian by origin who had risen to the highest rank and married into the imperial family. His policy for the defence of Roman civilisation was the Theodosian one of imperial unity and barbarian alliance. The policy was complicated by the ambition and power of the great Gothic leader Alaric, whose forces repeatedly ravaged Italy itself (capturing Rome in 410), and by the reluctance of Arcadius' government in Constantinople to support the defence of the West. Stilicho was mired in complex diplomatic and military manoeuvres at the heart of the Empire, his attempt to hold the West embroiling him in conflict with the East. His problem, like all great historical problems, was simple enough: 40 per cent of the entire army, including 55 per cent of the more expensive field-army units, was stationed in the western empire (and these, anyway, were not enough to defend it); but fully two-thirds of the tax-revenues necessary to support the army were raised in the East. If Constantinople did not subsidise Ravenna (the new western capital), the West would fall. Stilicho's government failed, and he has been condemned for this, but only by those who do not understand the vice-like contradiction that was now grinding to dust all possibility of reprieve in the West. Constantinople would not pay, for it was looking to its own defence, and Stilicho lacked the power to force it, since he was not even strong enough to hold the West – which was the reason he needed Constantinople's support in the first place. Catch-22: Stilicho's project was doomed. And in the wreckage, hardly noticed in the great centres of civilisation, Roman Britain disappeared.

It was not that Britain was wholly neglected by central government. Stilicho's panegyrical court poet Claudian attributes to his master responsibility for a military intervention in the years 396-9: 'His was the care which ensured [Britain] should not fear the spears of the Scott, nor tremble at the Pict, nor watch all along [her] shore for the arrival of the Saxon with the shifting winds.' But the diocese was retained only as a valuable resource to be consumed when needed. In 401, Alaric mounted the first of several invasions of Italy, and Stilicho rushed troops from Britain and elsewhere to confront him. 'And when our soldiers heard the news ... they assembled with hurrying standards from every region ... The legion came, too, which was set to guard the furthest Britons, which curbs the fierce Scott, and while slaughtering the Pict scans the devices tatooed on his lifeless form.' There would be little opportunity thereafter to put matters right: Stilicho was at war with the Goths in 401-3 and again in 404-5, and in 406 he was busy with a scheme to detach Illyricum from the eastern empire and add it to the western. Archaeological evidence confirms the impression of significant and permanent troop withdrawals at this time. Crucially, there is the testimony of coins. The latest Roman coins to appear in significant numbers in Britain were issues of Arcadius and Honorius down to 402. After this, not only was the Stilicho government not sending money to Britain to pay soldiers, but nor were its local representatives attempting to fill the gap by setting up local mints to produce copies (a practice which had been normal in such circumstances in the past). No coinage, no payments, no revenues: the Romano-British state was facing terminal disintegration. Some interim mechanism for direct provisioning must be assumed, with British officers levying in kind on the countryside around forts for the wherewithal to keep their men supplied with the basics. Such naked parasitism would have been insupportable in the long term. Without the state fiscal cycle, surpluses could not be redistributed in a remotely rational – and thus sustainable – way. Massive burdens would descend on those within striking distance of army units reduced to, as it were, 'living off the land'. The local peasantry would quickly succumb: settlements would empty, fields return to nature, and the soldiers be left to starve. At a hundred windy outposts, the standards of imperial Rome were still held aloft, and knots of armed men huddled about them. But the arteries which supplied these men had clogged up, and what was left of the Roman army in Britain was now on borrowed time.

We cannot be precise about when Britain ceased to be Roman, for the argument about dates is circular. The abandonment of most remaining forts is usually dated around 400, but that is because the coin supply ceased at this time, coins providing our main dating evidence. The events of 407, on the other hand, show that there must have been significant numbers of soldiers in Britain still, and if so, they must have been quartered somewhere. The semi-invisibility of the late Roman army must be remembered. Units of some sort might, in the way suggested above, hold together for a time even without regular payment. But as an army they would be disintegrating – acting more and more like bandits, shedding irreplaceable men through defeat, disease and desertion, merging imperceptibly, bit by bit, back into the primeval countryside. The Roman army in Britain had, though, one last act to perform. However degraded, it remained all that stood between the Romano-British ruling class and the deluge – and the latter came on 31 December 406, when the river Rhine was frozen solid, and across the ice there poured a vast horde of Alans, Suebi and Vandals. The Frankish federate forces opposing them were swept away, and the horde passed into and through Roman Gaul, and on into Roman Spain. Britain was cut off.

Officers of the Roman army in Britain voted to establish a new government, electing a man called Marcus as their emperor. Shortly afterwards, Marcus was killed in a second coup, and Gratian was elected to succeed him; the latter was awarded a bodyguard force, but this did him little good, for he too was promptly murdered after a reign of just four months. The poisoned chalice was passed to Constantine, whose elevation apparently owed much to his illustrious name, and he henceforward styled himself 'Constantine III' in honour of Constantine the Great and his short-lived son and successor Constantine II. The inexorable and contradictory logic of regional usurpation now began to operate. Leaving two men in command of the forces remaining in Britain, Constantine assembled an army and crossed to the continent. His aim was to win over and rally the remnants of the Roman army there, to retake Gaul and Spain from the barbarians, and to challenge Honorius for supreme power in the West. The invading barbarian horde had broken up into numerous raiding parties, and the recovery of Roman territory was easier than might have been anticipated. Moreover, the pro-Theodosian forces were weak, scattered and demoralised, and Constantine's new empire was rapidly consolidated against legitimist opposition. This success was short-lived. New barbarian assaults, divisions within his own ranks, and an effective legitimist counterattack eventually brought Constantine III to defeat and death in 411. Carausius, Constantine I, Constantine II, Magnentius, Julian, Magnus Maximus, Constantine III: in one form or another, Britain had been central to a series of north-west regional revolts against the centre and its politico-military priorities. Most revolts had followed a more or less similar trajectory: a strong local base of support became the launch-pad for a wider imperial challenge, so that men and material were siphoned towards the centre and consumed in civil strife. Now though, in 408-10, the pattern was to be broken.

Constantine III must have taken with him across the Channel virtually all the sound regular troops still left in Britain in 407. What then remained behind? Some forts and walled towns were probably still defended by regular frontier-army detachments, but these are likely to have been under-strength, poorly supplied and increasingly demoralised. They may have been supported by various irregular units, which could have been recruited on the continent, or possibly from the very Scotti, Picts and Saxons who were otherwise attacking the island. Or there may have been federates in Britain, especially in the far west, where all regular units seem to have been pulled out in the 380s, but also perhaps in the north, and maybe even along parts of the south-east coastline. The evidence is patchy and doubtful in the extreme. Some medieval Welsh king-lists claim Magnus Maximus as a founder, and this may represent a distorted genealogical memory of events in the 380s designed to create federate settlements to assist the defence of the west. On the other hand, Scottish settlements are also apparent at the end of the fourth century – on the Lleyn peninsula in the north-west, and on the Gower in the south-west – and these could well be Roman inventions to create a defensive buffer-zone. Elsewhere, there are occasional scraps of archaeological evidence that hint at federate soldiers in late Roman Britain. These include possible barbarian warrior-burials in extramural cemeteries at Winchester (Hants) and Dorchester-on-Thames (Oxon). But nothing is conclusive. Anyway, what seems certain is that whatever was left, it was too little to have any major impact on subsequent events. The remnants of the Roman army in Britain were either absorbed into new warlord retinues, deserted and became bandits, or simply soaked away into the native peasantry.

According to the early-sixth-century Byzantine historian Zosimus, in the year following the departure of Constantine III in 407, Britain came under renewed Saxon attack. 'So the Britons took up arms and, facing danger for their own security, they freed their towns from the barbarians who threatened them ...' Moreover, 'the inhabitants of Britain and some of the Celtic tribes ... threw off Roman rule and lived independently without further submission to Roman laws.' And this policy was popular enough, it seems, to be copied elsewhere, for 'all Armorica [Brittany] and the other provinces of Gaul followed the British example and freed themselves in the same way, expelling their Roman governors and setting up their own administrations as best they could'. When, two years later, the emperor Honorius communicated with his former British subjects – apparently in response to an appeal for assistance – it was 'to tell them to look after their own defence'. Procopius, also a sixth-century Byzantine historian, when describing the fall of Constantine III in 411, commented, '... the Romans were no longer able to recover Britain, which from that time continued to be ruled by those who had seized power'.

But who exactly had seized power? By whom, how and for what reasons had Roman rule in Britain been destroyed?

8

FROM COMMUNE
TO KINGDOM

The cultural collapse of *c.*375-425 was perhaps the most abrupt and complete in the entire British archaeological sequence. Determined attempts have been made to read the evidence otherwise: to detect a residual continuity of Romano-British civilisation after the termination of Roman imperial authority. Particular attention has focused on Verulamium. Towards the end of the fifth century, the Gallic cleric Constantius of Lyon wrote a biography of St Germanus, bishop of Auxerre, in which he described a visit to a Roman-style town near the shrine of the British martyr St Alban. The town referred to is almost certainly Verulamium, and Germanus, who had come to defeat an outbreak of the Pelagian heresy, encountered many inhabitants who were 'showily dressed' (veste fulgentes) and the daughter of 'a man invested with tribunician authority' (vir tribuniciae potestatis). The literary source seems to chime with the archaeological evidence of Sheppard Frere's famous building sequence in insula XXVII: it comprised a grand house built around 380, later alterations and new mosaics, a hypocaust or corn-drier then inserted in one room and subsequently repaired, a barn constructed on the site after the house was demolished, and finally a water-pipe laid across the area once the barn in its turn had been knocked down. Despite a lack of artefacts for dating, dead-reckoning suggested to the excavator a sequence of activity continuing at least until the time of Germanus' visit in 429, and perhaps well beyond. Frere found two other late buildings at Verulamium, and other excavators have reported comparable evidence from other Romano-British urban sites, such as Beeches Road in Cirencester. Largely on the basis of the evidence from Verulamium and other late Roman towns, Frere developed the view in the 1960s that Britain remained broadly Roman in the fifth century.

Four other classes of evidence have been cited since then in support of this view. First, some villas appear to have long sequences like those in the towns, with occupation into and well beyond the early fifth century. Frocester in the West Country is a good example: the main building may have remained in use for much of the fifth century, and after it was burnt down and abandoned, other buildings associated with grass-tempered pottery were constructed. Secondly, some former Roman sites either continued in use or were reused at an early date as Dark Age high-status centres. Two quite different examples will suffice to illustrate the point. The St Paul-in-the-Bail excavations within the Roman forum at Lincoln seem to have revealed a continuous sequence of structures and burials which probably date back to the late Roman period, including two successive early buildings likely to have been timber churches. At Wroxeter, the famous Baths Basilica sequence revealed apparently unbroken activity from the late Roman period onwards, culminating in a 'Great Rebuilding' to construct a high-status timber complex to 'Roman' specifications in perhaps the late sixth century. The third category of evidence is artefactual: the continued use of some Romanised material, whether surviving from an earlier period (including occasional examples of fineware pottery repaired with lead rivets, and occasional finds of Roman coins in Anglo-Saxon graves), or imported into western Britain from the Continent (such as Phocaean Red Slip Ware, African Red

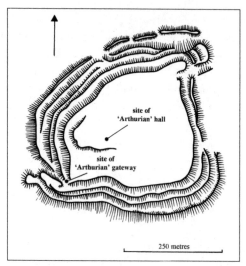

36 A new world order emerges: South Cadbury hillfort, site of an early Dark Age stronghold

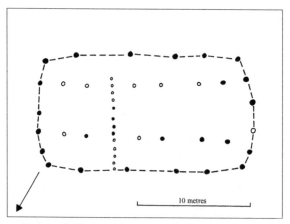

37 The great hall of an early Dark Age lord, South Cadbury hillfort. The black circles are postholes found in excavation, the open ones are inferred postholes, and the dotted lines represent presumed walls. After Alcock

Slip Ware, B-Ware *amphorae*, D- and E-Ware ceramics, and Frankish glassware). Finally, some territorial divisions, political authorities, ecclesiastical institutions, and cultural practices appear to have survived from the fourth to the seventh centuries. The early sixth-century monk Gildas describes one Constantine as 'tyrant of Dumnonia', for example, and another called Vortipor as 'tyrant of the Demetae' – in both cases, the territories named had been Romano-British tribal states. The early medieval inscribed stones of western Britain use the Latin language and occasional Roman titles – as in *MEMORIA VOTEPORIGIS PROTIC-TORIS* ('In memory of Vortipor the Protector') – and here, too, we seem to have evidence of Roman political and cultural continuity.

Or do we? The problem is that all of this evidence, even in aggregate, still amounts to scattered fragments and nothing more. Indeed, viewed in aggregate and alongside all other evidence for the period, we see a radically different archaeological imprint from that of the early fourth century. Instead of whole towns of grand monuments and town-houses, we have occasional buildings still occupied, most of them scruffy, set in townscapes dominated by ruins and refuse. Rather than Romano-British villas being extended with new wings full of mosaics, frescoes and hypocausts, we see most abandoned and a handful turned into farmyards. And where once there had been millions of wheel-thrown pots, coins and other artefacts, we see Romanised material culture shrinking to the tiniest fraction of what it had once been. Any fifth-century evidence we encounter which registers 'Roman' turns out to be exceptional. Let us turn a critical gaze upon some of it. That 'Life of Germanus', over which so much debate has raged in relation to fifth-century *Verulamium*, is a hagiographical fable written two generations after the event in a foreign country. Medieval saints' lives are not history; they are a literary genre with specific didactic purposes that have little to do with recording historical – as opposed to religious – truths. And the most striking thing about

Frere's *insula* XXVII sequence, it must be stressed, is precisely its exceptional character. It is not representative of any large category of evidence and cannot be taken to signal the continuity of town life, whether at *Verulamium* or anywhere else; most likely it was an early fifth-century estate centre. The huge weight of interpretation attached to fragments of evidence like this amounts to argument by anecdote. The correct method is to look at all the evidence and seek broad trends. When that is done, we see an abrupt and near-total collapse of Romano-British civilisation. Most forts and frontier defences were abandoned by the army and left to be plundered by stone-robbers. The towns were virtually deserted, town life came to an end, and almost every Roman urban building eventually fell down or was demolished to salvage its building materials. Whatever happened to estates and landownership, most villas were closed up for the last time and slowly decayed into rubble and scrub. The mines and quarries stopped work. The mass-production pottery kilns shut down. The urban craft-workshops – making iron farm-tools, wooden furniture, bronze figurines, gilt jewellery, bone pins, and a hundred other things – all these disappeared. No stone buildings were erected, no mosaics laid, no frescoes painted. No coins were supplied, minted or used in Britain. There was, in short, an almost complete collapse of the material culture of the preceding three and a half centuries.

What had happened? Was there massive fifth-century depopulation? At first, it might seem so, for almost all Roman sites – not just elite ones – show a cessation of activity in the late fourth or early fifth century at the latest. Roman sites simply stop: there is no post-Roman build-up of deposits with timber postholes, rubbish pits and handmade potsherds to indicate continuing low-grade occupation; usually there is nothing at all. Clearly, this means that the Romano-British settlement pattern as a whole was destroyed by the collapse of the military-supply economy that had fostered it. But this need not mean that the British landscape was emptied of people. If the fifth-century settlement pattern is far less visible –

as it may be if post-Roman Britain was a society of subsistence farmers dispersed across the landscape and wholly dependent on local resources – then the shadowy outlines that are all we can presently see of it in the archaeological record may represent a land still fat and full. Without large settlements, stone buildings and mass-produced artefacts, stratigraphic accumulation would be limited and hard to detect. The problem may be lack of evidence, not lack of people. We can draw no conclusions from our present paucity of fifth-century sites about the size of population in Britain at the time, nor about that population's state of wellbeing. Crucially, there is no positive evidence for large-scale woodland regeneration, and we should therefore assume that most land continued to be worked, and most areas still had their communities of farmers.

The establishment – the Roman imperial state and the Romano-British ruling class – is a different matter. Most Roman material evidence represents not peasant settlement and farming, but the superstructure of army, administration, grandees, gentry, and 'the world of taste'. The disappearance from the archaeological record of forts, towns, villas, mass production, and long-distance trade testify to the liquidation of this superstructure. We are witness to 'the end of civilisation'. The farmers remained, but the officers and landowners had gone. Some had no doubt left with Magnus Maximus and Constantine III. But the majority of the Romano-British elite were local landowners, their wealth and power rooted in the native soil, and there can have been few opportunities in these years of terminal decline for them to sell up, realise their assets, and flee with loaded money-bags. A number of precious-metal hoards containing some plate and much gold and silver coinage were buried (and never recovered) around this time – more than 60 are known in all – and these are clues to the insecurity of upper-class life in Britain at the beginning of the fifth century. But the land itself, and fixed assets built upon it, could not be moved, buried or hidden. This property, I have little doubt, was now the subject of open class warfare, and it is the unsuccessful outcome of this contest for the ruling class that explains the virtual extinction of Romanised material culture in early fifth-century Britain.

Among the ancient peasantry, banditry was endemic. There are countless references in ancient written sources covering all periods and parts of the Empire. Eric Hobsbawm has argued that rural 'social banditry' is, in fact, a normal state of affairs in pre-capitalist class societies where those who work the land are exploited by landlords and governments. Most of the time it would exist only as a nagging, chronic irritant in the background of events, for the bandits would rarely amount to more than one in a thousand of the rural population, the typical robber band numbering no more than 10 or 20, the outlaws flourishing 'in remote and inaccessible areas such as mountains, trackless plains, fenland, forest or estuaries with their labyrinth of creeks and waterways'. Recruited largely from the rural underclass of escaped slaves and serfs, army deserters and fugitives from the law, and impoverished crofters unable to make a living, the bandits still remained part of peasant society, enjoying a measure of protection and support – even sometimes being lionised as champions of the poor – since they made their living by preying on the property of the rich. 'Feed your slaves, if you would stop them becoming brigands' were the words addressed to Roman landlords in the early third century by the famous bandit-chief Bulla. Such 'normal' low-intensity banditry in the ancient countryside was important both as a safety-valve, an escape route for the most desperate, and as a catalyst and kindling for the resentments of the majority who remained oppressed within the law. As such, if conditions in the countryside worsened considerably, and if the state's repressive power weakened, social banditry might flare into peasant revolt:

> Banditry tended to become epidemic in times of pauperisation
> and economic crisis ... In so far as bandits have a 'programme', it

is defence or restoration of the traditional order of things 'as it should be' ... Two things may, however, turn this modest, if violent, social objective of bandits – and the peasantry to whom they belong – into genuine revolutionary movements. The first is, when it becomes the symbol, even the spearhead, of resistance by the whole traditional order against the forces which disrupt and destroy it ... The second ... is inherent in peasant society. Even those who accept exploitation, oppression and subjection as the norm of human life dream of a world without them: a world of equality, brotherhood and freedom, a totally new world without evil. Rarely is this more than a dream ... Yet there are moments when the apocalypse seems imminent: when the entire structure of existing society whose total end the apocalypse symbolises and predicts, actually looks about to collapse in ruins, and a tiny light of hope turns into the light of a possible sunrise. (Hobsbawm)

Did such a peasant war break out in Britain in the early fifth century? It would certainly explain the sudden disappearance of the Romano-British landowning class and its Romanised culture. If the peasants refused to pay rents, or taxes, or perform labour-services; if they kept their family 'hands' at home to work only their own land; if they retained for their own use all that they produced; if, helped by the bandits, they organised collective resistance to armed men sent against them from the outside; if they did all this, then elite surplus-accumulation, and the entire superstructure based upon it, would quickly have collapsed. There is nothing unusual about powerful explosions of peasant revolt from below in periods of crisis for agricultural societies – England 1381, Germany 1525, France 1789, Mexico 1911, Russia 1917, Spain 1937, and many others. But is there any contemporary written evidence that something like this happened in Britain after 407?

Perhaps a little. Zosimus, in his account of the end, does not describe a typical usurpation, where a 'good' and local emperor is elevated in preference to a 'bad' and distant one. The Britons, facing Saxon attack, did not raise a new emperor to replace the departed Constantine III. On the contrary, events proceeded in a distinctly *un*-Roman way. Roman rule was overthrown, Roman laws were no longer obeyed, and the rebels set up their own alternative, independent administration 'as best they could'. The Britons were copied by the Armoricans (in what is now Brittany) and by other Gauls. We happen to know, from other sources, that north-western Gaul was a major centre of peasant revolt from the late third to the mid-fifth century – and that the period 407-17 was one when large areas were under the control of peasant rebels known as *bagaudae*. The Romano-Gallic senator Rutilius Namatianus referred in a poem to a relative's efforts in suppressing bagaudic revolt: 'He has restored the laws and brought back liberty, and he does not allow the Armoricans to be slaves to their own servants.' A second reference to these events, this time in a contemporary comedy written by an unknown author, speaks of life 'beside the Loire', where the inhabitants lived according to 'popular' or 'woodland' law, simple farmers would make political speeches, and court cases would be heard under an oak tree and recorded on bones; it was, in short, a place where 'anything went'. This sounds very like a primitive rural communism, the result of successful peasant revolt to destroy the landlord class and the state infrastructure that sustained it.

In assessing the relevance of the evidence from early fifth-century Gaul to Britain, I would make three comments. First, to repeat, our main source explicitly states that the rebellion began in Britain and was copied in Gaul. Second, because the rebellion was defeated in Gaul, the Romano-Gallic elite survived and was able to comment; had the rebels won, and the elite (including prospective authors) been swept away, our sources might well have been silent about events – as they are for Britain. Third, the archaeological evidence for Britain – in contrast to that for Gaul – might be taken to imply victory for the rebellion and elite collapse.

I want to pursue this a little further by reference to some of the other written sources we have for post-Roman Britain. The focus of these is, of course, the Church – we deal with saints' lives, ecclesiastical histories, and religious polemics. But this is not in itself a problem; on the contrary, religion provided the language in which men and women discussed politics. My contention is that the period *c.*375-450 was, for Britain, one of popular revolt, revolutionary change, and radical politics. My starting point is the archaeological testimony to the *results* of this hypothetical upheaval (as explained above). But I am led then to the early Christian sources, for the Church, the principal ideological apparatus of the age, must have been split asunder by class conflict on this scale. And so it seems. Missionaries and monks were building a popular Christian movement in north-western Europe at the time, and it is interesting to note that Orosius tells us that Constantine III rose from the ranks, had a son who was a monk, and, once on the Continent, chose to promote militant monks to Gallic bishoprics. Was there a radical Christian current already running strongly through British politics? Things we hear about the Pelagian heresy – popular in Britain – certainly suggest this. Pelagius was a British-born monk who argued that people had free will, could choose to act righteously, and in this way accumulate enough heavenly credit to ensure salvation. In contrast to those like St Augustine, who believed that 'sin' was inevitable and God's 'grace' could be earned by 'faith' and 'obedience' alone, Pelagius maintained that people were responsible for their own actions and it was deeds not words that counted; a much harder road for the rich to tread, since it required them not merely to profess to be Christian, but to act in a positively Christian way towards others. Pelagius' message, in short, had potentially radical practical implications. Then there is St Patrick, whose writings testify to a real tension between the orthodox grandees of the Church and the rural priests of popular Christianity. He describes himself as uneducated, expresses scorn for 'priestly intellectuals', and tells us with bitterness that some elements in the hierarchy had attempted to prevent his

Irish mission. It seems possible, on the evidence of Pelagius and Patrick, that the later 'conservatism' of the Celtic Church in the British Isles was rooted in a tradition of popular asceticism and radicalism going back to the years *c.*375-425.

The supreme surviving representative of this tradition – if I am right about it – would then be Gildas. He is the red monk of early Dark Age Britain. Writing in a monastery somewhere in western Britain in the early sixth century, his main work, *The Ruin of Britain*, is a blistering attack on the ruling class of his age for corruption, injustice and oppression. Most commentaries attempt to downplay Gildas' radicalism, either on the grounds that his text is a religious, not a political, polemic, or on the grounds that his target is a specific group of 'tyrannical' rulers, not the ruling class in general. Both arguments are naïve in the extreme. Christopher Hill's analyses of political ideology in seventeenth-century England have shown conclusively that religion remained the principal language of politics until comparatively recent times. As for 'the five tyrants', political polemic is *always* personal: it is bound to attack those who currently rule, since they personify the policies one opposes, and the corollary is almost invariably the implicit belief that other rulers would be better. In contrast, however, to the ghastly power-worshipping panegyrics composed by late Roman courtiers, where political opponents were attacked only as a foil to the supposed virtues of the glorious leader, Gildas was not in the pay of a ruling class faction. He does not advance the cause of an alternative candidate. He hated *all* the rulers known to him. 'Britain has kings, but they are tyrants,' he declares:

> she has judges, but they are wicked. They often plunder and terrorise – the innocent; they defend and protect – the guilty and thieving; they have many wives – whores and adulteresses; they constantly swear – false oaths; they make vows – but almost at once tell lies; they wage wars – civil and unjust; they chase thieves energetically all over the country – but love and even

reward the thieves who sit with them at table; they distribute alms profusely – but pile up an immense mountain of crime for all to see; they take their seats as judges – but rarely seek out the rules of right judgement; they despise the harmless and humble, but exalt to the stars, so far as they can, their military companions, bloody, proud and murderous men, adulterers and enemies of God – if chance, as they say, so allows: men who should have been rooted out vigorously, name and all; they keep many prisoners in their jails, who are more often loaded with chafing chains because of intrigue than because they deserve punishment. They hang around the altars swearing oaths – then shortly afterwards scorn them as though they were dirty stones.

Equally impressive is his contempt for the clerical toadies who attached themselves to royal courts, the spin-doctors of their age:

Britain has priests, but they are fools; very many ministers, but they are shameless; clerics, but they are treacherous grabbers. They are called shepherds, but they are wolves all ready to slaughter souls. They do not look to the good of the people, but to the filling of their own bellies. They have church buildings, but go to them for the sake of base profit. They teach the people – but by giving them the worst of examples, vice and bad character. Rarely do they sacrifice and never do they stand with pure heart amid the altars. They do not reprimand the people for their sins; indeed, they do the same things themselves. They make mock of the precepts of Christ, and all their prayers are directed to the fulfilment of their lustful desires. They usurp with unclean feet the seat of the apostle Peter, yet thanks to their greed they fall into the pestilential chair of the traitor Judas. They hate truth as an enemy, and love lies like favourite brothers. They look askance at the just poor as though they were dreadful snakes; and, showing no regard for shame, the respect the wicked rich as though they were angels from heaven.

The tone of these (quite typical) extracts places *The Ruin of Britain* firmly in the tradition of Judaeo-Christian apocalyptic literature. This tradition begins with the Jewish Prophets of the Old Testament, ascetic holy men who railed against the corruption of Israel's rulers and predicted a divinely-ordained catastrophe that would sweep them away and elevate the humble. Reworked in later ages, these same ideas inspired Jewish national resistance to Hellenistic and Roman imperialism. The followers of Christ were merely one among many apocalyptic sects of the first century AD. The Pauline transformation of Christianity into a universal religion allowed the nexus of ideas represented by the Apocalypse – the rich as corrupt, the poor as God's chosen, the class struggle as a holy war – to enter the Roman Empire and become a rooted feature of Mediterranean and European culture. Norman Cohn has charted the survival of millenarian radicalism as a permanent undercurrent in medieval Europe. It seems likely that its existence, at some level and in certain places, had been continuous since the time of Christ.

Our problem is that ancient and medieval sources have little to say about popular ideology except in moments of mass revolt. We do hear, however, that Christianity spawned a radical wing in fourth-century North Africa, the *circumcelliones*, who waged open warfare on the Catholic Church and big landowners; we are told, amongst other things, that they threatened to punish moneylenders who exacted payment from peasants, and forced landlords to dismount from their carriages and run before them while slaves rode. Closer to home – and interesting in the context of local revolts by *bagaudae* – there is the work of Salvian, a priest writing in Gaul in the mid-fifth century. 'What cities are there,' he asks, 'and not only cities but even towns and villages, in which the councillors are not so many tyrants?' In his work *Concerning God's Government*, Salvian catalogues contemporary popular woes: imperial taxes falling heavily on the poor but lightly on the rich; great lords offering protection to gain control of land and then allowing exploitation to continue unabated; and so-called Christians who were sexually lax, addicted to the games, and cared nothing for the poor. The disasters of the Empire were, therefore, divine retribution for sin, and, in true apocalyptic manner, it was the rich who suffered, for the poor found refuge under barbarian kings who were 'chaste, austere and righteous'. We catch glimpses, then, of an ongoing tradition of Christian radicalism, and Gildas should be seen in this context. What is curious, though, is that, whereas in other periods the radical tradition ('heresy') is usually submerged beneath a mountain of orthodoxy, the voice of Gildas is almost the only one we hear in three centuries of British history. And when another voice does speak out clearly in the early eighth century, it is that of Bede, a conservative historian of Church and state, who, as Gildas might have put it, 'respects the wicked rich as though they were angels from heaven'. The survival of *The Ruin of Britain* – alone among British ecclesiastical texts of the early Dark Ages – argues for the strength of Christian radicalism at the time. Perhaps Gildas represents a popular tradition rooted in the upheavals of *c.*375-425, and his anger reflects the emergence of a new e`lite, a return of class oppression, and therefore, in his terms, like those of so many other ancient, medieval and early-modern radicals, a descent from godliness into the abyss.

THE RISE OF THE TYRANTS

Roman Britain, already much decayed, finally broke up in the fifty-year period from *c.*375 to 425. The better and more mobile Roman army units were successively withdrawn, and when the pay stopped coming to those that remained, though they may have shifted for themselves for a while, they must soon have fallen apart, for they vanish from the archaeological record. We are left to guess that the men who formed them drifted back into the countryside from which they had been recruited. Popular resistance – perhaps organised by bandits and roused to action by 'liberation theologians' – was then easily able to defeat municipal tax-collectors and landlords' bailiffs unsupported by soldiers. Thus, their control over land and labour broken, their sources of expropriated surplus cut off, the Romano-British ruling class disintegrated, its former members presumably reduced to the level of working farmers. The land was now controlled by the people who worked it. The state had ceased to exist. Britain had become a region of largely self-sufficient, independent peasant farms, with only localised networks, and balanced exchanges of goods and services. Something like this, at any rate, seems to be implied by both the literary and the archaeological evidence that we have. Though there is a widespread prejudice against the idea that popular action can be a primary agent of historical change, no other interpretation, in fact, fits the evidence so well.

But the golden age did not last long. From *c.*450 or 475 onwards, new archaeological imprints appear across the landscape. In the east, few Anglo-Saxon cemeteries or settlements can be dated as early as the first half of the fifth century, but thereafter the growing density and westward extent of Anglo-Saxon cemeteries is a dominant feature of the archaeological record, with some 1,500 sites wholly or partially excavated, yielding evidence for no fewer than 30,000 burials. From these it is clear that Anglo-Saxon society was stratified from the outset – contrary to much folk myth – and, as time went on, became more so. While a few men were buried with swords, for example, far more had only spears, and many others had no weapons at all – a grading, perhaps, of clan-chiefs, free warriors, and bondsmen not entitled to bear arms. Though social stratification is less evident in the handful of settlements thus far excavated, the common pattern of rectangular timber 'halls' associated with smaller 'sunken-featured buildings' may represent the residences of free warriors with their dependants and bondsmen. By the late sixth century, the quality of grave-goods in the richest burials indicates a more extended social hierarchy, a process culminating in the early seventh with the first unequivocally royal burials. The Mound 1 ship-burial at Sutton Hoo in Suffolk – the richest grave ever excavated in Britain – is widely believed to be that of Raedwald, King of East Anglia, supposedly the great-grandson of Wehha, 'the first to rule over the East Angles in Britain'. At Yeavering, seat of the kings of Northumbria, the great hall, which was 80 foot long, 40 foot wide, and built of planks 5 inches thick, also dates to the early seventh century. The Anglo-Saxons, then, represent a new, militaristic, class-based order, one in which considerable social division existed as early as *c.*450, and in which royal states were being forged from *c.*550 onwards. The later historical accounts – principally Bede and *The Anglo-Saxon Chronicle* – may often be unreliable about the details of early Anglo-Saxon history, but the broad outline of settlement, expansion, the growth of kingship, and state-imposed Christian conversion gains support from the archaeological record.

What of western or 'Celtic' Britain? It is here especially that some scholars have claimed a continuity of Roman civilisation. I have stressed the weakness of the evidence for this above. Not only do claims of continuity ignore the general collapse of Roman material culture; they also fail to engage seriously with the very different corpus of evidence we have for the fifth and sixth centuries. Sound interpretation must build on the archaeological material, so a quick summary will be useful here. As in the east, there is very little in western Britain that can be confidently dated to the first half of the fifth century, but a new archaeological imprint emerges from *c.*450 onwards. The secular elite established fortified residences on hilltops, on coastal promontories, and in former Roman walled settlements (*36*). The ecclesiastical authorities maintained churches, monasteries and cemeteries, most of them new foundations, but some dating from the Roman period. Traders frequented small coastal sites, either promontory forts with harbours or beaches, or one of the so-called 'sand-dune' sites, which were occasionally visited but not permanently occupied.

Dotted across the landscape were many small farms, often enclosed, some dating back to the Roman period, some reusing former Roman towns or villas, others established on fresh ground. The vernacular architecture was simple: small stone round-houses; small rectangular halls in stone or timber; and, on some elite sites, large timber halls with aisles and partitions – there is nothing distinctively 'Anglo-Saxon' about timber halls (37). Such artefacts as survive are usually few and modest: domestic pottery, brooches, knives, bracelets, combs, and pins. A small amount of residual Roman material was still in use – such as the fineware pots repaired with lead rivets, or the coins pierced for use as pendants. Occasional high-status artefacts included penannular brooches with decorated terminals, hanging-bowls with decorated escutcheons (attachments for the chain-loops), and luxury goods (wine, ceramics, glassware) from the Byzantine Empire or Frankish Gaul. Elite burials were marked by tombstones inscribed with short and crudely-cut Latin texts.

This archaeological imprint could not be more different from that of Roman Britain. Whatever measure we take – settlement hierarchies, the layout of sites, artefact assemblages, distribution patterns – we find ourselves witness to a transformation in the archaeological record. And, as with the Anglo-Saxon material from eastern Britain, we see evidence for an extending hierarchy of wealth and power as time goes on. A large number of small elite sites was replaced by a smaller number of large ones: presumably, great lords were amassing resources by absorbing the territories and retinues of lesser ones. It is not difficult to guess why this might have been happening. The historical sources imply that warfare was endemic in the early Dark Ages, and that Britain was formed of an ever-changing mosaic of small and loosely structured polities. The sources specifically imply two major phases of warfare between 'Britons' and 'Anglo-Saxons', the first in c.AD 450-500 (the 'Age of Arthur'), the second in c.550-600. Archaeology certainly attests a westward expansion of Anglo-Saxon culture. But war *within* each zone, among the 'Britons' or 'Celts' of the west, and the 'Anglo-Saxons' or 'Germans' of the east, was also rife. And it is here, surely, in the chronic insecurity of warband politics, that we find an explanation for the rise of that new system of exploitation and violence that filled Gildas with fury. Let us retrace our steps to that short golden age without landlords or tax-collectors in the early fifth century; let us pull together the threads of evidence for what happened subsequently; and let us see if we can understand the process of change that took us from peasant commune to Dark Age kingdom in two centuries.

Peasant revolution is always limited. The peasant is an individualist whose ambition is restricted to his own farm. He wants to see off the landlord, the tax-collector, and the press-gang; he then wants to be left alone to work his land with his own people; he has no vision of a wider social transformation involving the collective action of peasants in general. There is no such thing, therefore, as a peasant state. When the peasants destroy the state that oppresses them – something they have done surprisingly often in history – they do not build a new state in its place; they just go home. For a time, early in the fifth century, parts of Britain must have been anarchic and lawless, with banditry and raiding rife. Remnants of the old officer and landlord class perhaps gathered together to plot and organise. Or maybe the lead was taken by new 'strongmen' who could offer a measure of protection and security. Bands of retainers and mercenaries were perhaps formed to impose a certain rough-and-ready 'order', allowing farmers to till their fields in peace, and in return for this some 'contribution' might have been demanded. In this way, out of the chaos of troubled times, and in the power vacuum left by successful peasant revolt, 'great men' may have emerged to take charge and re-establish 'authority', embryonic mini-states have acquired shape and substance, and new class divisions thus begun to crystallise out. The process was slow and messy. The warlords were starting from scratch, building up small surpluses, using them to increase their retinues, and then going back with the power to demand a little more. Perhaps Vortigern was such a man, the British leader who, in *c.*440-455, is supposed to have hired Saxon mercenaries to defend his territory against other barbarians, mercenaries who subsequently rebelled against their paymaster and fought to carve out territories for themselves. Or Ambrosius Aurelianus, who, in *c.*475-500, is supposed to have organised a great British confederation to challenge the growing power of the Saxon settlers and hem them into the south-east. In these struggles, the size of a war-chief's armed retinue would have been decisive. Military success would have ensured control over territory and access to the tribute and manpower on which the chiefdom depended. Military failure, by contrast, would have broken the bond between chief and retainer, and opened the way to a successful challenge. This competition between and within war-bands must have compelled chiefs to attempt to increase exploitation and accumulate larger surpluses.

Competition favours the strong. War favours big armies. So the military instability of the age will have ensured that small polities were absorbed by larger ones, that the territories united under each single power became more extensive, and that overall the social hierarchy was extended and the wealth and power of those at the top grew greater. Enlarged resources enabled rulers to construct increasingly sophisticated mechanisms of social control, surplus accumulation, and political legitimation. Royal henchmen became *ealdormen* ('earls') and were granted great estates. Their *thegns*, the armed knights of their retinues, became the lords of nascent manors. A bureaucracy of officials compiled tax registers and militia lists. Traditions, lineages and identities were invented to justify power. Chiefs became kings and claimed descent from gods. They took Roman titles and paraded their 'civilisation'. They converted to Christianity and became champions of the Church. A struggle that had begun as a conflict between local war-chiefs and their retinues was transformed into a conflict between powerful royal states ruled by kings, nobles and bishops. And, so far from representing 'Roman' continuity, this social order of the seventh and eighth centuries – the beginnings of medieval England – was a new system of exploitation and power based on the return to sub-jugation of a peasantry that had briefly broken free.

CONCLUSION

What, then, was the 'legacy' of Roman Britain? What, if you will, did the Romans do for us?

The Roman Empire had attacked and conquered Britain because it was a predatory, expansionist system of military imperialism, and a weak and insecure emperor had needed to prove that he could lead the army to victory and defend the national territory. To facilitate orderly government and efficient tax-collection, the conquerors had recruited the services of native aristocrats in the administration of the new province, and to encourage identification with, and loyalty to, the new order, they had supported their efforts to adopt Roman culture and become 'civilised'. But Rome was already reaching her limits when she conquered Britain, and the island itself had drawn across it the line separating the ploughed from the unploughed which marked these limits. Ancient empires were based on intensive arable agriculture and the large surpluses it generated to fund armies, war-making and defence-works. The wilderness beyond, the haunt of nomads, pastoralists and upland crofters, could not sustain the infrastructure of civilisation and merely drained resources from areas that could. But without new conquests – without the subsidy of plundered wealth – the costs of imperial defence fell wholly on the peoples of the provinces. Taxes, labour-services and extraordinary levies increased, and, with that, so too did resentment and resistance. The fabric of Roman imperial society gradually rotted, as the towns emptied, the gentry retired from public life, and the countryside became an alien continent. The barbarians on the frontiers, now better organised and equipped, repeatedly broke through depleted, over-stretched defences. Troops were shifted from one front to another, mainly from periphery to centre, from expendable places like Britain to the Mediterranean heartlands. The tensions of imperial decline exploded periodically in palace coups, secessionist revolts and civil wars. And as the Roman state pulled back from its north-west frontier, as the government revenue-payment cycle ceased to operate and the military-supply economy it sustained seized up, the whole edifice of Romanised Britain – its forts, towns and villas, its mosaics, frescoes and hypocausts, its stone-quarries, potteries and markets – all collapsed in the space of a generation or two. Rome had arisen through violence and robbery. At the end, it perished in the same way. The mass of British people could then enjoy a short golden age free from landlords and tax-collectors.

The new elite that emerged shortly after had to begin again. At first they were no more than warrior chieftains leading small bands of retainers and mercenaries, with only a fraction of the wealth and power of the 'men of honourable rank' who had ruled Roman Britain a century before. They belonged to, and were in the process of building, a very different world. From it, the Anglo-Saxon and British kingdoms of the seventh century would eventually arise. But a great cultural chasm separated the Dark Age warlords of the late fifth century, with their tin badges and inflated titles, from the Roman gentleman-bureaucrats who had run towns like *Verulamium* in the early fourth. Roman Britain had, by this time, long since ceased to exist.

A CHRONOLOGY FOR ROMAN BRITAIN

Emperors and events
(major ones only)

Events in Britain
(many dates are approximate)

First Triumvirate (60-53 BC)
Caesar's Gallic Wars (59-1 BC)   Caesar's two expeditions to Britain
                                        (55-4 BC)

Civil War (49-5 BC)
Caesar (45-4 BC)
Second Triumvirate (43-36 BC)
Julio-Claudians (30 BC-AD 68)
Augustus (30 BC-AD 14)
Tiberius (14-37)
Caligula (37-41)   Caligula's abortive invasion of Britain (40)
Military coup in Rome (41)
Claudius (41-54)   Invasion of Britain; defeat of Catuvellauni;
                                        capture of Colchester (43)
                                    Advances north, north-west and south-west;
                                        Vespasian's defeat of Durotriges (44-7)
                                    Possible Fosse Way frontier established;
                                        early campaigns in Wales; defeat and capture
                                        of Caratacus (47-51)
                                    Continuing campaigns against Silures and
                                        other Welsh tribes (51-61)

	Client kingdoms of Regni (Togidubnus), Iceni (Prasutagus) and Brigantes (Cartimandua); first towns founded
Nero (54-68)	Boudiccan Revolt (61); suspension of major campaigns (61-71)
Civil war (69)	
Flavians (69-96)	
Vespasian (69-79)	New offensives: invasions of the north (69, 71-4); conquest of Wales (74-8)
Titus (79-81)	Governorship of Agricola (78-84); conquest of northern England and southern and central Scotland (79-84)
Domitian (81-96)	Many new towns founded
Dacian War (85-9)	Inchtuthil line held in far north (mid 80s)
	Withdrawal to Gask Ridge line in far north (late 80s)
	Withdrawal to Newstead line in far north (90s)
Nerva (96-8)	
Trajan (98-117)	
Dacian Wars (101-2, 105-6)	Withdrawal to Stanegate line in north (early 2nd century)
Persian War (114-7)	
Hadrian (117-38)	Hadrian's tour of Britain (121-2)
	Construction of Hadrian's Wall (122-39)
Antonines (138-92)	
Antoninus Pius (138-61)	Antonine I: invasion of far north; first abandonment of Hadrian's Wall; construction and first occupation of Antonine Wall (139-55)
	Revolt in north?; first withdrawal from Antonine Wall; reoccupation of Hadrian's Wall (155-8)
	Antonine II: new advance in far north; second abandonment of Hadrian's Wall; second occupation of Antonine Wall (158-63)
Marcus Aurelius (161-80)	Second withdrawal from Antonine Wall; reoccupation of Hadrian's Wall (163)

Parthian War (161-6)
Great Plague (166)
German Wars (167-75, 177-80)
Commodus (180-92)   War in north Britain (181-4)
                                  Mutinies in Roman army in Britain (185-7)
Civil war (193-7)   Clodius Albinus, governor of Britain, hailed
                                      emperor (193); defeated and killed after
                                      invasion of continent (197)
                                  Many towns acquire earth-and-timber
                                      defences.

House of Severus (193-235)
Severus (193-211)   War in north Britain (197-205)
                                  Extensive building work on northern frontier
                                      defences
                                  Invasion of Scotland by Severus and Caracalla
                                      (208-10); death of Severus and withdrawal
                                      from Scotland by Caracalla (211)
                                  Britain reorganised into two provinces,
                                      Britannia Prima and *Britannia Secunda*

Caracalla (211-7)
Elagabalus (218-22)
Severus Alexander (222-35)   First Saxon Shore forts constructed
Third century crisis (235-84)
Maximinus (235-8)
Gordian III (238-44)
Philip (244-9)
Decius (249-51)
Gallus (251-3)
Valerian (253-60)
Gallienus (253-68)
Gallic Empire (259-73)   Successful secessionist revolt in north-west
                                      provinces (259-73)

Postumus (259-69)
Victorinus (269-71)
Tetricus (271-3)
Claudius Gothicus (268-70)   Many towns acquire masonry defences
Aurelian (270-5)   More Saxon Shore forts constructed

Probus (276-82)	Abortive revolt by Bonosus in north-west provinces (281-2)
Carus (282-3)	
Carinus (282-5)	
Diocletian (284-305)	
Maximian (286-305)	
The Tetrarchy (293-305)	
Constantius I (293-306)	
Galerius (293-311)	
British Empire (286-96)	
Carausius (286-93)	Secessionist revolt of Carausius and establishment of Allectus (293-6) rival empire in north-west provinces (286); Carausius' loss of northern Gaul, assassination and replacement by Allectus (293); Constantius' invasion of Britain and Allectus' defeat (296)
	Extensive building work on frontier defences
	Reorganisation of Britain into diocese of four provinces with two major military commands
House of Constantine (306-63)	
Constantine I (306-37)	War in north Britain (305); death of Constantius at York; Constantine hailed emperor (306)
Maxentius (307-12)	
Licinius (308-24)	Constantine campaigning in Britain (312-4)
Constantine II (337-40)	
Constans (337-50)	Visit to Britain by Constans (winter 342-3)
Constantius II (337-61)	
Magnentius (350-3)	Revolt by Magnentius with British support defeated (350-3); purge and reprisals by Paul 'the Chain' (354)
Julian (355-63)	Troops sent to Britain to fight Picts and Irish (360)
House of Valentinian (364-92)	
Valentinian I (364-75)	Raids by Picts, Irish and Saxons (364)

Valens (364-78)

'Barbarian conspiracy' of Picts, Irish, Attacotti and Saxons; large parts of Britain overrun and plundered (367); campaigns of recovery by Count Theodosius (368-9); extensive reconstruction of British defences initiated (369)

Gratian (375-83)
Valentinian II (375-92)
Battle of Adrianople (378)
Magnus Maximus (383-8)

Revolt of Magnus Maximus; troops withdrawn from Britain for invasion of continent; many frontier forts now abandoned (383); defeat and death of Magnus Maximus (388)

House of Theodosius (379-450)
Theodosius I (379-95)
Arcadius (395-408)
Honorius (395-423)
Supremacy of Stilicho (395-408)
Gothic Wars (401-3, 404-5)

Rhine frontier overrun (406)

Constantine III (407-11)

War in Britain (395-9)

Troop withdrawals from Britain for defence of Italy (401)

Revolt in Britain: elevation of Marcus, Gratian and then Constantine (406-7); Constantine withdraws troops from Britain for invasion of continent (407)

Saxon attacks on Britain; overthrow of Roman administration by British rebels (408)

British appeal for help from Honorius fails (410)

Peasant war in countryside?

Successful revolt of Saxon mercenaries against Vortigern and other British leaders (440-55)

Successful defence of British-controlled territory against Saxon inroads by Ambrosius Aurelianus (475-500)

SELECT BIBLIOGRAPHY

Referencing is every academic author's nightmare. Current practice is often laborious and pedantic; the text is sometimes left peeping out from behind a jungle of parentheses. This cannot be right: it is certainly highly distracting for the reader, and I doubt whether it is of much use to anyone. It is a particular problem in a book like mine, since this is a short work of general synthesis, and, as such, it would probably be true to say that most sentences embody evidence and ideas from several places. To cite all possible sources would be absurd, and to cite only some, arbitrary. In any case, the evidence quoted usually consists of examples well known to specialists and therefore easily checked. The interpretation offered is a consistent one – the book sets out to offer a 'grand narrative' rather than an exhaustive critique of alternative theories and secondary sources – and I have felt no particular need to reference other people's theories in a text which does not discuss them in any detail. The book, after all, is not a catalogue of evidence and alternatives; it is an attempt to provide a single explanatory framework to make sense of Roman Britain as a whole. I have therefore taken the radical decision not to include any references in the text, and to rely solely on the select bibliography below. It is intended both as an aid to specialist readers who are curious about my sources of evidence and ideological leanings, and to general readers seeking ideas on further reading and study.

Alcock, L., 1971, *Arthur's Britain, history and archaeology,* AD *367-634* (Allen Lane, London).

Alcock, L., 1972, *'By South Cadbury is that Camelot ...', the excavation of Cadbury Castle 1966-1970* (Thames & Hudson, London).

Applebaum, S., 1975, 'Some observations on the economy of the Roman villa at Bignor, Sussex', in *Britannia* 6, 118-32.

Barrett, A.A., 1989, *Caligula, the corruption of power* (Batsford, London).

Birley, A.R., 1988 (2nd ed), *Septimius Severus, the African emperor* (Batsford, London).

Branigan, K., 1987, *The Catuvellauni* (Alan Sutton, Gloucester).

Breeze, D.J., 1982, *The Northern Frontier of Britain* (Batsford, London).

Breeze, D.J. & Dobson, B., 1987 (3rd ed), *Hadrian's Wall* (Penguin, Harmondsworth).

Brown, P., 1991, *The World of Late Antiquity* (Thames & Hudson, London).

Burnham, B.C. & Wacher, J., 1990, *The 'Small Towns' of Roman Britain* (Batsford, London).

Cameron, A., 1993, *The Later Roman Empire, AD 284-430* (Fontana, London).

Campbell, J. (ed.), 1991, *The Anglo-Saxons* (Penguin, London).

Cary, M., 1935, *A History of Rome down to the Reign of Constantine* (Macmillan, London).

Christie, P.M.L., 1987, *Chysauster Ancient Village* (English Heritage, London).

Cohn, N., 1970, *The Pursuit of the Millennium, Revolutionary Millenarians and the Mystical Anarchists of the Middle Ages* (Paladin, London)

Collingwood, R.G. & Myres, J.N.L., 1937, *Roman Britain and the English Settlements* (Clarendon, Oxford).

Collingwood, R.G., 1961, *The Idea of History* (OUP, Oxford).

Collingwood, R.G. & Richmond, I.A., 1969 (2nd ed), *The Archaeology of Roman Britain* (Methuen, London).

Collingwood, R.G. & Wright, R.P., 1995 (2nd ed amended by Tomlin, R.S.O.), *The Roman Inscriptions of Britain, Volume I, Inscriptions on Stone* (Alan Sutton, Stroud).

Crow, J., 1995, *Housesteads* (Batsford, London).

Crummy, P., 1997, *City of Victory, the story of Colchester – Britain's first Roman town* (Colchester Archaeological Trust, Colchester).

Cunliffe, B., 1991 (3rd ed), *Iron Age Communities in Britain* (Routledge, London).

Dark, K.R., 1994, *Civitas to Kingdom, British political continuity, 300-800* (Leicester University Press, London).

Dark, K.R., 2000, *Britain and the End of the Roman Empire* (Tempus, Stroud).

Dark, K. & Dark, P., 1997, *The Landscape of Roman Britain* (Sutton, Stroud).

Davis Hanson, V., 1989, *The Western Way of War: infantry battle in Classical Greece* (Hodder & Stoughton, London).

de la Bédoyère, G., 1993, *Roman Villas and the Countryside* (Batsford, London).

de la Bédoyère, G., 1999, *The Golden Age of Roman Britain* (Tempus, Stroud).

de Ste Croix, G. E. M., 1981, *The Class Struggle in the Ancient Greek World* (Duckworth, London).

Detsicas, A. (ed), *Current Research in Romano-British Coarse Pottery* (CBA, London).

Down, A., 1988, *Roman Chichester* (Phillimore, Chichester).

Duncan-Jones, R., 1990, *Structure and Scale in the Roman Economy* (CUP, Cambridge).

Esmonde Cleary, A.S., 1989, *The Ending of Roman Britain* (Batsford, London).

Esmonde Cleary, A.S., 1993, 'Late Roman towns and their fate', in Vince, A. (ed), *Pre-Viking Lindsey* (The City of Lincoln Archaeology Unit, Lincoln), 6-13.

Faulkner, N.M., 1996, 'Verulamium: interpreting decline', in *The Archaeological Journal* 153, 79-103.

Faulkner, N.M., 1998, *The Rise and Fall of the Romano-British Towns* (unpublished University of London PhD thesis).

Faulkner, N. & Reece, R., 2002, 'The Debate about the End, a review of evidence and methods', in *The Archaeological Journal* 159, 59-76.

Faulkner, N.M., forthcoming, 'The Case for the Dark Ages', in Collins, R. and Gerrard, J. (eds), *British Archaeological Report*.

Finley, M.I., 1992, *The Ancient Economy* (Penguin, Harmondsworth).

Fox, C., 1959, *The Personality of Britain, its influence on inhabitant and invader in the prehistoric and early historic times* (National Museum of Wales, Cardiff).

Frere, S.S., 1964, 'Verulamium – then and now', in *Institute of Archaeology Bulletin* 4, 61-82.

Frere, S.S., 1964, 'Verulamium: three Roman cities', in *Antiquity* 38, 103-12.

Frere, S.S., 1972, *Verulamium Excavations, Volume I* (The Society of Antiquaries, Oxford).

Frere, S.S., 1982, 'The Bignor Villa', in *Britannia* 13, 135-95.

Frere, S.S., 1983, *Verulamium Excavations, Volume II* (The Society of Antiquaries, Oxford).

Frere, S.S., 1984, *Verulamium Excavations, Volume III* (Oxford University Committee for Archaeology, Oxford).

Frere, S.S., 1987 (3rd ed), *Britannia, a history of Roman Britain* (RKP, London).

Fulford, M.G., 1975, *New Forest Roman Pottery* (British Archaeological Reports, Oxford).

Going, C., 1987, *The Mansio and Other Sites in the South-eastern Sector of Caesaromagus: the Roman pottery* (CBA, London).

Greep, S. (ed), 1993, *Roman Towns: the Wheeler inheritance, a review of 50 years' research* (CBA, York).

Hanson, W.S., 1991 (2nd ed), *Agricola and the Conquest of the North* (Batsford, London).

Harris, A., 2003, *Byzantium, Britain and the West, the archaeology of cultural identity, AD 400-650* (Tempus, Stroud).

Harris, W.V., 1979, *War and Imperialism in Republican Rome, 327-70 BC* (OUP, Oxford).

Henig, M., 1984, *The Art of Roman Britain* (Batsford, London).

Henig, M., 1984, *Religion in Roman Britain* (Batsford, London).

Henig, M., 2002, *The Heirs of King Verica, culture and politics in Roman Britain* (Tempus, Stroud).

Higham, N., 1992, *Rome, Britain and the Anglo-Saxons* (Seaby, London).

Hingley, R., 1989, *Rural Settlement in Roman Britain* (Seaby, London).

Hobsbawm, E.J., 1972, *Bandits* (Harmondsworth, Penguin).

Holbrook, N. (ed), 1998, *Cirencester Excavations V, Cirencester, the Roman Town Defences, Public Buildings and Shops* (Cotswold Archaeological Trust, Cirencester).

Hood, A.B.E. (ed. and trans.), 1978, *St Patrick, his writings and Muirchu's life* (Phillimore, London).

Hopkins, K., 1980, 'Taxes and trade in the Roman empire, 200 BC-AD 400', in *Journal of Roman Studies* 70, 101-25.

Howe, M.D., Perrin, J. R. & Mackreth, D. F., 1980, *Roman Pottery from the Nene Valley: a guide* (Peterborough City Museum, Peterborough).

Ireland, S.,1996 (2nd ed), *Roman Britain: a sourcebook* (Routlege, London).

James, S., 1984, 'Britain and the late Roman army', in Blagg, T.F.C. & King, A.C. (eds), *Military and Civilian in Roman Britain* (British Archaeological Reports, Oxford), 161-86.

James, S., 1999, *The Atlantic Celts: ancient people or modern invention?* (British Museum Press, London).

Johnson, S., 1976, *The Roman Forts of the Saxon Shore* (Elek, London).

Johnson, S., 1982, *Later Roman Britain* (Paladin, London).

Jones, A.H.M., 1959, 'Over-taxation and the decline of the Roman Empire', in *Antiquity* 23. 39-43.

Jones, A.H.M., 1964, *The Later Roman Empire, 284-602, a social, economic and administrative survey* (Blackwell, Oxford).

Jones, B. & Mattingly, D., 1993, *An Atlas of Roman Britain* (Blackwell, Oxford).

Jones, M.E., 1996, *The End of Roman Britain* (Cornell UP, New York).

Keegan, J., 1993, *A History of Warfare* (Pimlico, London).

Kenyon, K., 1935, 'The Roman theatre at *Verulamium*, St Albans', in *Archaeologia* 84, 213-61.

King, A., 1978, 'A comparative survey of bones assemblages from Roman sites in Britain', in *Bulletin of the Institute of Archaeology* 15, 207-32.

Leech, R., 1982, *Excavations at Catsgore, 1970-1973, A Romano-British village* (Western Archaeological Trust, Bristol).

Levick, B., 1990, *Claudius* (Batsford, London).

Lewis, N. & Reinhold, M. (eds), 1966, *Roman Civilization, Sourcebook II: the Empire* (Harper & Row, New York).

Luttwak, E.N., 1979, *The Grand Strategy of the Roman Empire, from the first century* AD *to the third* (John Hopkins University Press, Baltimore).

MacMullan, R., 1988, *Corruption and the Decline of Rome* (Yale UP, New Haven).

Mann, J.C. & Penman, R.G., 1996 (3rd ed), *LACTOR 11: Literary Sources for Roman Britain* (London Association of Classical Teachers).

Marsden, P. & West, B., 1992, 'Population change in Roman London', in *Britannia* 23, 133-40.

Maxfield, V.A. & Dobson, B., 1995 (3rd ed), *LACTOR 4: Inscriptions of Roman Britain* (London Association of Classical Teachers).

McWhirr, A., 1986, *Cirencester III, Houses in Roman Cirencester* (Cirencester Excavation Committee, Cirencester).

Meheux, K.L., 1997, *Space and Time in Roman Britain: a case study of the Severn Valley/Welsh Marches region* (unpublished University of London PhD thesis).

Miles, D. (ed), 1981, *The Romano-British Countryside: studies in rural settlement and economy* (British Archaeological Reports, Oxford).

Millett, M., 1990, *The Romanization of Britain* (CUP, Cambridge).

Millett, M., 1996, *Roman Britain* (Batsford, London).

Milne, G., 1995, *Roman London* (Batsford, London).

Monaghan, J., 1997, *Roman Pottery from York* (CBA, York).

Neal, D.S., Wardle, A. & Hunn, J., 1990, *Excavation of the Iron Age, Roman and medieval settlement at Gorhambury, St Albans* (English Heritage, London).

Orwell, G., 1970, 'Hop-picking', in *The Collected Essays, Journalism and Letters of George Orwell, Volume I, An Age Like This, 1920-1940* (Penguin, Harmondsworth), 75-95.

Parker, H.M.D., 1935, *A History of the Roman World, AD 138-337* (Methuen, London).

Perring, D., 1991, *Roman London* (Seaby, London).

Reece, R., 1980, 'Town and country: the end of Roman Britain', in *World Archaeology* 12, 77-92.

Reece, R., 1987, *Coinage in Roman Britain* (Seaby, London).

Reece, R., 1988, *My Roman Britain* (Cotswold Studies, Cirencester).

Rees, J., 1998, *The Algebra of Revolution, the dialectic and the classical Marxist tradition* (Routledge, London).

Rees, S.E., 1979, *Agricultural Implements in Prehistoric and Roman Britain* (British Archaeological Reports, Oxford).

Rich, J. (ed), 1992, *The City in Late Antiquity* (Routledge, London).

Richmond, I.A. (ed), 1961, *Roman and Native in North Britain* (Nelson, London).

Rodwell, T. & Rowley, T., 1975, *Small Towns of Roman Britain* (British Archaeological Reports, Oxford).

Rostovtzeff, M., 1926, *The Social and Economic History of the Roman Empire* (Clarendon, Oxford).

Salmon, E.T., 1968, *A History of the Roman World* (Routledge, London).

Salway, P., 1993, *The Oxford Illustrated History of Roman Britain* (OUP, Oxford).

Sharples, N.M., 1991, *Maiden Castle* (Batsford, London).

Southern, P. & Dixon, K.R., 1996, *The Late Roman Army* (Batsford, London).

Starr, C.G., 1982, *The Roman Empire, 27 BC-AD 476, a study in survival* (OUP, Oxford).

Swift, E., 2000, *The End of the Western Roman Empire, an archaeological investigation* (Tempus, Stroud).

Thomas, C. (ed), 1966, *Rural Settlement in Roman Britain* (CBA, London).

Thomas, C., 1981, *Christianity in Roman Britain to AD 500* (Batsford, London).

Thompson, E.A., 1952, 'Peasant revolts in Late Roman Gaul and Spain', in *Past and Present 2*, 11-23.

Thompson, E.A., 1977, 'Britain, AD 406-410', in *Britannia 8*, 303-18.

Wacher, J., 1995 (2nd ed), *The Towns of Roman Britain* (Batsford, London).

Wells, C., 1992 (2nd ed), *The Roman Empire* (Fontana, London).

Wheeler, R.E.M. & Wheeler, T.V., 1936, *Verulamium, A Belgic and Two Roman Cities* (The Society of Antiquaries, Oxford).

White, R. & Barker, P., 1998, *Wroxeter, the Life and Death of a Roman City* (Tempus, Stroud).

Wilson, P.R., 1989, *Crambeck Roman Pottery Industry* (The Roman Antiquities Section, Yorkshire Archaeological Society, Leeds).

Winterbottom, M. (ed. and trans.), 1978, *Gildas, the Ruin of Britain and other works* (Phillimore, London).

Young, C.J., 1977, *The Roman Pottery Industry of the Oxford Region* (British Archaeological Reports, Oxford).

Yule, B., 1990, 'The 'dark earth' and late Roman London', in *Antiquity 64*, 620-8.

Ziegler, P., 1969, *The Black Death* (Penguin, Harmondsworth).

INDEX

I have designed the index to guide readers to substantive comments without wasting their time on minor passing references; the latter have generally been omitted. Readers should note in particular the following. Some secondary subjects are listed under more general categories (eg. legions under 'army', governors under 'government, provincial', etc.). Specific events are usually to be found under the name of the ruler (emperor or governor) in whose period of office they fell. Emperors (legitimate and usurper) and ancient writers appear under their usual name in historical discourse (eg. 'Marcus Aurelius', 'Tacitus', etc.), whereas Roman governors appear under their last known name (*nomina* or *cognomina*) (eg. 'Scapula, Publius Ostorius'). Colour plates are referred to specifically, but black and white illustrations are subsumed within the general page references. I must stress that, since this book is not essentially a work of reference but one which offers an interpretative narrative, the index cannot be a comprehensive guide to the contents.

If you are interested in purchasing other books published by Tempus,
or in case you have difficulty finding any Tempus books in your local bookshop,
you can also place orders directly through our website

www.tempus-publishing.com

or from

BOOKPOST, Freepost, PO Box 29, Douglas, Isle of Man IM99 1BQ
Tel 01624 836000   email bookshop@enterprise.net